ADVANCED LANGUAGE CONSTRUCTION

Advanced Language Construction

by Mark Rosenfelder

YONAGU BOOKS

www.yonagu.com • Chicago • 2012

ISBN 978-1478267539

ed. 1.0

Contents

Introduction

Often when I finish an introduction to a new subject, I want to *keep going*. It's possible to read another intro, or dive into specialist subjects, but what I'd really like is Volume Two.

That's what this book is: it's a sequel to the *Language Construction Kit*, and the idea is to learn more about CONLANGING (language creation) and more about languages.

What can you expect?

- I've gone into more detail on the process of **creating a grammar**: how to organize it, what to put in it, how to write glosses, and so on.
- We'll cover **new topics** only barely touched in the first volume: logic, sign language, pidgins and creoles, logographic systems.
- There's a chapter on the **life cycles** of languages: where they come from, how they interact, how they die.
- There's a beefy section on **morphosyntax**, which goes into much more detail on features that only got a few pages in the *LCK*: case, gender, alignment, aspect, valence, modality, polysynthesis. Also included are case studies of Latin, Mandarin, and the Northwest Caucasian languages.
- I'll show what you can do with a fully worked out **conworld**, covering topics such as borrowing, slang, and how much of your conlang you can show off in a novel.
- There's two new **tools** to explore: a vocabulary generation program and an updated Sound Change Applier.

What if I didn't read Vol. 1?

You didn't read the *LCK*? Well, it's not too late! I've tried to make the book readable even if it's your first look at linguistics, but I'm not going to repeat the basics from the first volume.

You can get a lot of the basics from the online *LCK*; see the Web Resources section below.

Typographical conventions

These are the same as in the *LCK*.

I've put technical terms in SMALL CAPS. This tells you two things:

- I didn't make the term up, so you can safely use it in your grammar.
- You can get more information by Googling. (If you get a choice between (say) Linguist List and Wikipedia, look at the former. Wikipedia isn't bad at basic linguistic terms, but it can be wrong or misleading.)

Italics are used when I'm discussing a word or phrase. If it's not in English I'll provide a gloss in 'single quotes'.

For the conventions on **glosses** see p. 32.

Referring to phonetics:

boldface refers to a letter, or informally to a sound

/ / slashes indicate a phonemic representation

[ ] brackets are used for phonetic representations

> **Sidebars**
>
> Sidebars give tips, warnings, or interesting facts, or provide pointers to additional reading.

Greek and Cyrillic

Aspiring linguists should already know the **Greek** alphabet, at least if they were paying attention in math class. For reference, here's the alphabet with the classical (5th century BC) phonetic values as given by W. Sidney Allen in *Vox Graeca*:

Αα	Ββ	Γγ	Δδ	Εε	Ζζ	Ηη	Θθ	Ιι	Κκ	Λλ	Μμ
a	b	g	d	ɛ	zd	ɛ:	t^h	i	k	l	m

Νν	Ξξ	Οο	Ππ	Ρρ	Σσ	Ττ	Υυ	Φφ	Χχ	Ψψ	Ωω
n	ks	ɔ	p	r	s	t	y	p^h	k^h	ps	ɔ:

σ appears as ς at the end of a word.

For the purposes of this book no harm will be done if you pronounce θ φ χ with their post-classical fricative values [θ f x]. But Πλάτων would look at you funny.

And if you know the Greek alphabet, there's little excuse for not reading **Cyrillic**. Here are the basic Russian values:

Аа	Бб	Вв	Гг	Дд	Ее	Жж	Зз	Ии	Йй	Кк
a	b	v	g	d	jɛ	ʒ	z	i	j	k
Лл	Мм	Нн	Оо	Пп	Рр	Сс	Тт	Уу	Фф	Хх
l	m	n	ɔ	p	r	s	t	u	f	x
Цц	Чч	Шш	Щщ	Ъъ	Ыы	Ьь	Ээ	Юю	Яя	
ts	tʃ	ʃ	ʃ:		ɨ		ɛ	ju	ja	

Russian actually has *two* series of consonants, regular ('hard') and palatalized ('soft'), and these are marked not by modifying the consonants but by changing the normal vowels **а э ы о у** to **я е и ё ю**. That is, да is /da/ and дя is /d^{j}a/. The second series is also used for the diphthongs j + V, as in союз 'union'.

These rules sometimes aren't enough, and that's where the unlabelled letters come in. The soft sign ь marks the previous consonant as palatalized when there's no following vowel, as in читать 'to read'. The hard sign ъ similarly marks a consonant as unpalatalized; it's rarely necessary except in foreign words, such as Нъю-Йорк 'New York'.

Thanks to palatalization, transliterations of Russian are either inaccurate or ugly; thus my preference for citing forms in Cyrillic.

> There is of course more to both Greek and Russian pronunciation. These are transliterations, not language courses.

Web resources

There are a lot of great resources on the web. But URLs rot quickly, so instead of listing sites in this book, I'll list a single permanent URL that will be kept up-to-date with a list of links:

http://www.zompist.com/resources/

I mention a number of **books** in the text; these are not only great further reading, but are my major sources.

Acknowledgements

Much appreciation to Steven Foley and Drew Bennett for providing detailed information on polysynthesis; to Alex Fink and Sai for the UNLWS example; to Daniel von Brighoff for lending books and expertise, and to John Cowan for reviewing the logic chapter.

Many thanks to Daniel von Brighoff, Drew Bennett, Hannah Griffith, Anthony Duncan, Phillip Krohn, Jan Strasser, Benjamin Buckley, Matthew Pennington, Quinn Albaugh, Alex Fink, and Sai for reading the whole book, making it better, stronger, faster, but not harder. And thanks to the entire ZBB for support and useful discussions.

Also thanks to Aaron Toivo for suggestions, including a brilliant idea for the title that, perhaps foolishly, I didn't use: *The Language Construction Kaboodle.* And thanks to my wife Lida, for her patience and support, as well as checking over the Spanish bits.

Mark Rosenfelder

August 2012

Abbreviations

Here are the abbreviations I've used in glosses in this book.

>	acts upon (subject > object)
*	(words) reconstructed (sentences) bad syntax
?	(sentences) dubious syntax
Ø	null morpheme, nothing
0	unmarked for person
1p	first person plural
1pi	inclusive we (1p + listener)
1px	exclusive we
1s	first person singular
2p	second person plural
2s	second person singular
3p	third person plural
3s	third person singular
3sf	3s feminine
3sm	3s masculine
3sn	3s neuter
3x	unspecified actor
4	obviative
abl	ablative
abs	absolutive
acc	accusative
adv	adverb
adver	adversative
aff	affirmative
agr	agreement particle
agt	agentive
ant	anterior converb
antip	antipassive
aor	aorist
applic	applicative
art	article
augm	augmentative
ben	benefactive
caus	causative
com	comitative
comp	complementizer
compl	completive
con	connective vowel
cond	conditional
conj	conjunct
cont	continuous
decl	declarative
deduc	deductive
def	definite
dim	diminutive
distrib	distributive
dur	durative
dyn	dynamic
emph	emphatic
erg	ergative
exper	experiential
f	feminine
fin	finite
fut	future
gen	genitive
hab	habitual
hor	horizon of interest
hsy	hearsay
imper	imperative
impfv	imperfective
incep	inceptive
include	inclusive
indic	indicative
inf	infinitive
inst	instrumental
intr	intransitive
irr	irrealis
loc	locative
lparen	left parenthesis
m	masculine
masd	masdar
MW	measure word
n	neuter
neg	negative
nfin	nonfinite
nh	nonhuman
nom	nominative
NP	noun phrase
obl	oblique
opt	optative
part	participle
past	past tense
perf	perfect
pfv	perfective

pind	past indefinite
pl	plural
plu	pluperfect
poss	possessive
pot	potential
PP	prepositional phrase
pred	predicative
prep	prepositional
pres	present tense
pret	preterit
prog	progressive
prosp	prospective
pv	preverb
q	question
real	realis
refl	reflexive
rel	relativizer
retro	retrospective
rparen	right parenthesis
s	singular
sim	simultaneous coverb
stat	stative
sub	subordinator
subj	subjunctive
topic	topic
trans	transitive
voc	vocative
VP	verb phrase

Writing a grammar

Basic outline

Beginning a novel, you have to face the horror of staring at a blank page. It's easier with a conlang: you can start by writing an outline! Then you can stare at a blank outline instead.

Here's the overall outline I start with:

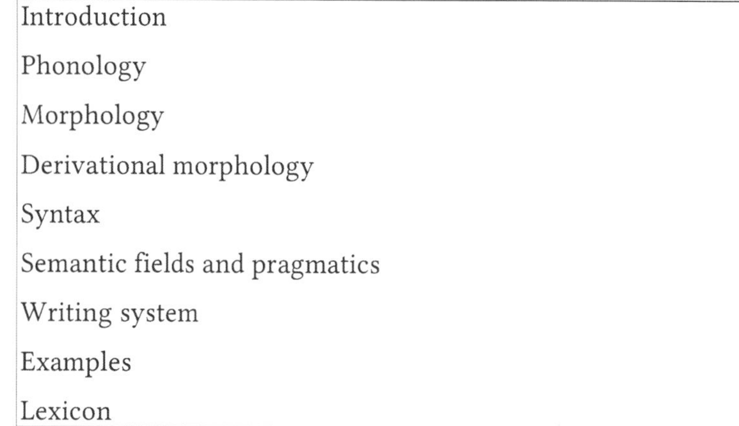

Introduction

Phonology

Morphology

Derivational morphology

Syntax

Semantic fields and pragmatics

Writing system

Examples

Lexicon

If you're not used to outlining, the idea is to state your topics and their order before you actually write anything. You don't write straight ahead from the first sentence of the introduction all the way to the words in Ž. You can work on topics in any order; the outline makes sure they're in the right place and you don't forget anything.

When you think of a new topic, add it to the outline; you don't have to fill it out immediately. Topics can have subtopics, to any level you like.

For instance, you could go add subtopics to Phonology right now:

- Phonology
    - Consonants
    - Vowels
    - Stress
    - Phonotactics

Start adding text to the topics, in any order. You could start with a list of vowels (you can make a nice table later):

> Vowels
>
> i e ɛ ɑ ɔ o u

Any modern word processor, like Word, will have useful facilities to work with outlines. E.g. you can move entire topics around, or view just the titles of the outlines without the text.

You may find it helpful to add a symbol so you know what hasn't been filled in yet. I use STD or $$$. Then I can jump quickly to that section by searching for this text.

Some of the sections may not make sense for a given language, or will logically appear in a different place. E.g. if you have an alphabet, it's convenient to treat that under Phonology; while if you have an isolating language, you may have no morphology at all beyond compounding.

I am simple caveman, not know 'computer'

You can work on paper if you prefer— that's how I did Verdurian. Just expect to go through multiple drafts.

If you use a binder and loose pages, you can easily replace just a section of the grammar. Start new sections on a new page, and keep everything about a language together— avoid having your notes in five different piles or notebooks.

You can keep a dictionary in alphabetical order by using two columns. Put the words you have so far in the left column only:

bau	quiet
beda	sister
bi:	white
bori	island
buku	deer

Now, as you add new words, put them in the right column:

bau	quiet		
beda	sister	**ben**	under
bi:	white		
bori	island	**bo**	one
buku	deer		

When the page starts to get unreadable, it's time to make a new edition: copy out all the words, again only into the left column.

Index cards work too, with less rewriting but also less portability.

Plan of attack

I work on a grammar iteratively, going back and forth between sections. But my overall progress usually looks something like this:

- Put the words you have so far (perhaps from a map, perhaps from the SCA) into the **Lexicon**.
- From those words. create tables of consonants and vowels, under **Phonology**. *Always keep your phonological inventory up to date*; it guides the word creation process.
- Start the **derivational morphology** section. You'll need this even for a naming language[1], as it's very useful to be able to form terms like "of NAME", "NAME person", "NAME speech", "NAME place". Plus it's a good habit to create derived words as you add lexical entries (*war* → *warlike, warrior, make war*).
- Create the basic **morphological paradigms** for verbs, nouns, and pronouns. At the very least you'll want the present tense forms, plurals, and a complete set of pronouns.
- Start listing your **adpositions**, or their equivalent. It's useful to be able to form expressions like "at NAME", "from NAME", "near NAME", and so on. Plus it's likely to greatly multiply your stock of verbs: e.g. *go* gives you *go to, go back, go away, go on behalf of, go with, go near*, etc.
- Start the syntax section by deciding on basic **NP order**. That is, what order do these elements go in?

  articles
  numerals
  demonstratives
  adjectives
  quantifiers

[1] A conlang worked out just enough to provide names for places or characters. See the first chapter of the *LCK*.

prepositional phrases
relative clauses
the noun itself

Create examples and the necessary supporting words for these.

- It's useful to have tables of demonstratives, numbers, quantifiers, and prepositions, both for reference and to help you think of them as a system rather than just imitating English.
- Decide on basic **sentence order**— SOV etc. (However, that should normally *precede* NP order in the Syntax section.) Write some sample sentences, things like *The lawyer read the manuscript* and *The girl gave the book to the duke.*
- Within each section, place the basics first: the simplest forms before the insane compound forms; simple interrogatives before subordinate irrealis clauses. If you have some feature which affects a huge part of the grammar, like Old Skourene's triliteral roots (p. 235) or Elkarîl's oddball case analysis (p. 236), discuss that as early as possible.
- Now comes a long period of *filling out* **details**. You can take two basic approaches— or alternate between them.
    - Go through the sections of the grammar, thinking how you're going to approach each item. Work through the *LCK* and this book for ideas.
    - Work on your examples, and as you come to things you haven't said how to do, fill out the appropriate section of the grammar. E.g. to translate *The king decided to execute the man who slept with his wife*, you might have to work out the past tense, or auxiliary verbs, or relative clauses.
- At any point, you can take some time to just create words. I often use the wordlists at the end of the *LCK* (p. 260), filling out the Swadesh list or the geographical terms.
- What if you need to make **changes**? Well, it happens. Just do it: make the changes, then examine existing words and samples to get them up to date.
- At some point the outline is pretty much filled out. Are you done? The best way to find out is to work on your **sample texts**— these days I make sure I have at least three. You'll almost always run across a few constructions you need to work out. Plus you'll have sample texts!

- Some topics should only be addressed if you need them. If you're going to write a novel in this setting, it'll be very useful to work out the calendar, common expressions, and how names and titles work. If you plan to write much text in the language, think about pragmatic particles, slang, and swearing. If this is your major language, add sections on allophony, dialects, and class variation.
- Once I have a fairly good grammar and three sample texts, the language is beginning to feel done, but I probably only have about 500 words. That's a lot for a naming language, but it means that translating almost any text will require word creation. So create more words, till you have a thousand or so. Work through wordlists, or just translate more texts.

Ultra-modingo-conlangs

What's that? You want a conlang for the ages, which will awe the conlanging boards and allow you to be the one to write Volume Three? All right, take on these tasks:

A language learning textbook and at least an entire short story (as I've done for Verdurian)

Substantial spoken recordings, with more than one speaker

Descriptions of the historical stages of the language, every 200 years or so

Meaty descriptions of the major dialects, with extended texts, and maps of isoglosses (regions where we find particular realizations of phonemes, or particular cognates)

A syntax section covering dozens of constructions, following your favorite syntactic theory

At least three places where the pragmatics differs interestingly from English

A lexicon where at least 75% of the entries are not single-word translations from English, and where every word has an etymology, with semantic changes

The lexicon gives not only meanings but pragmatic complications, register differences, and historical attestations

Creating paradigms

I work out the morphology pretty early, because without it I can't create sample sentences. You can leave gaps, but it's hard to (say) introduce a whole new dimension of verbal conjugation late in the process.

The key moment in creating a paradigm is not deciding on the affixes, but creating the structure of the table. So if you create a blank table

person	*sing.*	*pl.*
1		
2		
3		

you've already decided that your verbs are conjugated by person and number— and already eliminated interesting alternatives like obviative, dual, gender, and politeness forms!

Similarly you can easily create a present tense paradigm, then past and future, and not even realize that you never considered aspect, modals, or irrealis forms.

So, take a moment before filling out the table to think about whether it has the features you really want. (You can add more dimensions later; but if you do, don't forget to check your sample sentences in case they need updating.)

If you look at an actual paradigm, like the present tense of French *finir* 'finish'—

person	*sing.*	*pl.*
1	fin-is	fin-issons
2	fin-is	fin-issez
3	fin-it	fin-issent

you may wonder where all that juicy variation comes from. How do you know how different to make the endings, or how many identical endings speakers will put up with?

- If you have a parent language, run the entire paradigm through the SCA (p. 260). Then try to simplify the output with analogy.
- For a fusional language where you don't have the parent worked out, *simulate* the above process: start with a regular, agglutinative system, then mangle it.
- Fusional paradigms are often *partially* regular. So it may be fusional *except* in two of the forms.

It may be helpful to think about where that beautiful French paradigm actually came from.

- Indo-European originally marked the three persons with final *-m*, *-s*, *-t*. 5000 years of sound change have played havoc with this, but we still see the 3rd person *-t*, as well as the *-s* in the 2s and the *-m-* (changed to *-n-*) in the 1p. (They're all silent in French, but maintained in the orthography.)
- Indo-European however didn't come up with a consistent way to mark the plural; a different method was used in each person (and to boot, in each subfamily). For another example of multiple pluralizers see Quechua, p. 171.
- The *-i* is really part of the root— it appears in every form of *finir*. The equivalent for other conjugations is less stable (e.g. the *-e-* in *parler* 'speak'), so it's convenient to treat it as part of the suffix.
- *-iss* isn't really a plural marker; it's the *-i* from the root plus the Latin inchoative *-sc-* (see p. 135).

I like to keep the Morphology section focused on the paradigms, leaving their usage to the Syntax section. That's for two reasons:

- It keeps the Morphology pages compact, making them a better reference for the paradigms.
- The usage section can then address compound tenses, auxiliaries, and other issues that don't really go under Morphology.

But you can discuss the uses of the paradigms as they come up, if you prefer. In that case, a chart of just the paradigms may be useful (i.e., a few pages containing compact morphological tables, so it's easy to look up forms).

For complicated paradigms, as for Old Skourene (p. 240), I've created Javascript conjugation utilities. If you can code, these can keep you from making mistakes in your own conlang.

Placeholders vs. filling out

If you're aiming at a grammar like mine, it's apt to be 25+ pages of dry linguistic prose. Don't be intimidated by the task of generating all that text. Start with placeholders, like this:

Questions: auxiliary verb **pol**

Assuming you've figured out how auxiliaries actually work, that's all you need to use the language. In the final Munkhâshi grammar, I expanded this as follows:

> Questions use a combination of topicalization and an auxiliary; **pol** 'do' must be used if no other is present. The subject is fronted together with the auxiliary:
>
> **Wowal gotalh threwap tujno?**
> do.A.past ktuvok eat.A.past iliu
> *Did the ktuvok eat the iliu?*
>
> **Gpuki tutujno matâ?**
> can.E-pl pl-iliu swim.E-pl
> *Can iliu swim?*
>
> The question is ***answered*** with appropriate forms of the auxiliary: **Wothôl** 'Yes, B is going'; **Potôrul** 'No, D isn't going.'

It's not just a matter of writing full sentences. Trying to explain the procedure, you'll find you have to work out minor details. In this case: what if there's another auxiliary; how is the question answered; what about negative questions (not shown).

It's work to create sample sentences and glosses, but every sentence you write is another chance to develop the vocabulary and add new points to the language.

Wordcrafting on the go

As you work on the grammar you'll be inventing words; never create one without adding it to the lexicon, in alphabetical order. Not only does this ensure they don't get lost, but it keeps you from accidentally creating homophones. (A few homophones are fine, especially if they're not likely to co-occur often. But it's easy to create too many, especially if you use a vocabulary generator.) Plus, it's a lot of work to generate a lexicon, so every bit you do gets you closer to the finish!

E.g. the Dhekhnami word for *swim* was entered into the lexicon like this:

math	*v*	swim, float [*mat*]

I always use a table format, which looks neater than straight text. If there are morphological peculiarities (such as the out-of-control plurals in Xurnese), I indicate these in a column just after the word itself:

púsaup	pusú	*n*	poor bastard [*poukuvi* 'fallen']
puš	pauč	*n*	stomach, abdomen [*puč*]
puxamu	puxamú	*n*	return [*poudixamou*]
pwes	pwesi	*n*	pebble, stone [*puvik* dim. of 'stone']

(Some languages have a morphology that just spits on alphabetical order— e.g. Old Skourene *agaşti* 'beloved', *eguşeta* 'romance', *gşiutta* 'affair', and *iggşet* 'loving' are all formed from one root. So the lexicon is sorted by roots, and all these words are entered under *gaşt-* 'love'.)

It's a good habit to provide a **part of speech** column. This provides a place for morphological data (e.g. gender of nouns, conjugation class for verbs), it disambiguates glosses (e.g. 'a bear' vs. 'to bear'), and it allows searches— e.g. you can look for all your prepositions.

Another good habit is to provide **multiple glosses**. Fight the tendency to make every word a one-for-one equivalent of one English word. This makes your language more naturalistic, and can save time later when you find you need the other word.

Extra credit if you take the time to work out some quick **derivations**. E.g. *swim* could generate words for *swim (n), swimmer, swimming hole.* Extra extra credit if some of the derivations aren't also derivations in English. E.g. *swim-thing* might be the word for *fish*; *swim + diminutive* might be *bathe.*

I hate to create a word without an **etymology**. Dhekhnami is created mostly from Munkhâshi using the SCA, so to invent *math* I actually created *mat*, added it to the Munkhâshi lexicon, and ran it through the SCA. Often I'll borrow the word instead (p. 220), or derive it as a compound.

Words usually don't retain a single meaning for millennia on end— you should often take the opportunity to modify the meaning of an inherited or borrowed word (p. 226).

How do you **look up a word** when you need it? Well, you're doing this on the computer, right? Use the search function. If it's a common word, you can save time by placing the cursor at the beginning of the lexicon, or just keep your lexicon in a separate file.

An alternative is to include a separate English-to-Conlang lexicon. That's not a bad thing to have, but it's a huge hassle to maintain, and it makes it all too easy to create ciphers of English— e.g. you create a word for *can* and later when you want to translate *ability* you create a different word just because *ability* doesn't yet have an entry. So it's best to create such a lexicon when the language is pretty much done.

Am I done yet?

You read the *LCK*, so you know you should have a *Syntax* section, and it contains the single word "VSO". What else goes there?

Here's a checklist, not at all exhaustive, of things that you should consider putting in the grammar somewhere.

- The basics: sentence and NP order; questions; negatives; relative clauses.
- Can people violate the basic order— for topicalization, for emphasis, for passives, or just as an afterthought?
- How do verb + verb combinations work? This includes auxiliaries (*You may go*) as well as ordinary verbs *(I advise you to go*).
- Where do time and place clauses live? You'll probably have single words (*never*), NPs (*last week*), and clauses (*when Oblivion freezes over*).
- Existentials (*There's a Chinese place near here*) are often a special construction.
- How do you handle sentential arguments? These can be subjects (*[That people still read Nietzsche] offends me*) or objects (*Holmes deduced [that the criminal wore a tartan]*).
- Make sure your relativization scheme clearly handles the four basic combinations of transitivity:

sentence	*subclause*	*example*
subject	subject	*The man [who caught the fish] is here*
subject	object	*The fish [the man caught] is tasty*
object	subject	*I hate the man [who caught the fish]*
object	object	*I ate the fish [the man caught]*

  Pay attention to cases (which case is *who* in?) and to word order (the subclause omits arguments, so it may complicate your basic sentence order).
- How do you translate *if* statements? Are deductions (*If that's Camelot, we're almost home*) handled differently from counterfactuals (*If grandma had wheels, she'd be a wagon*)?[2] Condition-

---

[2] F.R. Palmer calls these REAL and UNREAL conditions. The 'real' conditions are still unknown, but languages often use the REALIS form for them (i.e. the one they use for known events).

als are a playground for seeing how your conlang handles not-quite-real events.

- How do you handle causatives? (*I made her go, I advised her to carry a gun*). These tend to play havoc with case systems as the caused person is the object of the main clause and the subject of the subclause.
- Pronouns may be an exception to word order rules, as in French *Je le lui ai donné (I gave it to him)* vs. *J'ai donné le livre à mon ami (I gave the book to my friend).*
- You worked out the numbers from 1 to 10, great! How do you form larger numbers, ordinals, fractions? How about basic mathematics?
- Are there restrictions on relativization? Think about questions like these:

  Where is the hat [I believe [the cat wears __]]?

  When was the day [the cat bought the hat on __]?

  Who did [John said ["I'll kill __!"]]?

  I remember the summer [we visited Rio last __].

  The man [my sister dated the brother of __] was a crook.
- How do you form comparatives? (See the next section.)
- How do NP + NP combinations work? You'll need these for titles (*King Alric*), geographic names (*Lake Van*), and brands (*Yonagu Books*), and there are alternatives to English's concatenation method.
- Are there ways to indicate that a referent, or a relative clause, refers to something known to exist? Compare *I met a queen* vs. *I met the queen.* In English *I'm looking for a man with one arm* is ambiguous as to whether I have a specific man in mind, but other languages differ.
- You can nominalize a verb (*know → knowledge);* how do you nominalize a VP? Note the combination of cases and prepositions in *John's knowledge of Linux.*

Is it complicated enough?

You may be trying for a simplified language— or you're just in a hurry to get done. But a hallmark of natural languages is their almost fractal complexity. There's always another exception or complication, and linguists can write entire dissertations on a single word.

Complexities may occur to you if you just think hard about a feature. Say you're thinking about comparatives: you work out how to say *bigger than a mammoth.* Revolve the concept of comparison around in your head— does your method work on these cases?

- superlatives *(biggest of all)*; note that speakers may turn absolutes into intensives (*fortissimo* 'strongest' often means just 'very strong')
- degrees of comparison (e.g. mathematics uses >> for *is very much greater than*)
- equalities *(as big as a mammoth*; note the difference from the morphological comparative *bigger*)
- negatives *(no bigger than a fly)*
- examples with and without a comparison class *(a better mousetrap; a mousetrap better than Roger's*— hey, the word order changed!)
- comparisons of adverbs *(more slowly)* or verbs *(he cried more than he laughed)*

You can't always think of such complexities just staring at the computer. Alternatives include looking at other people's grammars, and waiting till interesting cases come up in sample texts.

Sometimes an idea that didn't make it into the morphology may pop up elsewhere. E.g. French doesn't have evidentials, but it can use the conditional as one: *il aurait allé* can be used for 'he supposedly went'. English doesn't have a topic particle, but clefting is a substitute: *what I'm looking for is a cheap bicycle.*

Another source of complication is to think about variations of dialect or register. Come up with three ways to solve the problem and assign one to the yokels from Nowheresville and another to colloquial speech. If you've derived your language from a parent, the newer language may have innovated a new method but kept the parent's method in formal written language.

Ten quirky constructions

Languages are full of minor constructions with their own odd syntax; here's a sampling. You don't have to address these in particular; the point is that once you start looking you'll find more and more.

(The asterisk indicates sentences that aren't acceptable.[3])

Let alone

I wouldn't live in Vyat, let alone Verduria.
She won't pet the dragons, let alone clean up their dung.

This may seem straightforward, but what type of constituent is the 'let alone' phrase? And where did it come from? We have *let (NP) alone* in other contexts, but can't move the NP:

Let the boy alone!
**Let alone the boy!*

What, dative + VP

What, me worry?
What, him get elected?

It looks like something got left out, but what? And if it's a deletion, why is it allowed only after *What*?

**How, me worry?*

Damn them!

Fuck you.
Damn those robots.

Yes, you can do syntax on profanity. The oddity here is that the object isn't reflexive, as in *Hit yourself!* Maybe it's not an imperative but a wish, perhaps an abbreviation for *If only someone would fuck you.* But then why can't we make a similar abbreviation for *If only someone would kill you*?

Do so

Itep cheated on the test, and Deru did so too.

---

[3] Don't get upset if you disagree with some of my asterisks. Idiolects vary. It happens in every syntax class.

Do so is interesting because it's a verbal ANAPHOR— just as a pronoun stands for an NP, *do so* stands for a VP.

In Verdurian I created a demonstrative verbal anaphor: *fassec* means *do that:*

> **Vulre dy žusru soa carđä er faššao.**
>
> want-past-3s that sell-past-1s the.f.acc sword.f.acc and do.that.past-1s
>
> *He wanted me to sell the sword and I did it.*

Quechua has the verbal anaphor *nay* which stands for a verb you can't think of the moment— cf. *whatchamacallit* for nouns:

> **Wallpata narankichu?**
>
> chicken-acc whatsit-past-2s-q
>
> *Did you do that thing to the chicken?*

Hard to like

> *My grandmother is hard to like.*
> *It's hard to like my grandmother.*

These have been derived transformationally from

> *[(For someone) to like my grandmother] is hard*

though note that not all adjectives work:

> *[(For someone) to like my grandmother] is outrageous*
> → **My grandmother is outrageous to like.*

The surface form is identical to *The elf is eager to please*, but the semantics differ: my grandmother is the underlying object; the elf is the underlying subject. Noam Chomsky used such sentences to show that the surface structure of sentences isn't enough to determine their meanings.

While we're at it, this construction is an example of an ADJECTIVAL PHRASE, something you might not expect to see if you thought of adjectives as nothing but modifiers. Compare also *afraid to go, capable of flight, important to know, lucky to be alive, glad you came, new to the city.*

As well as

> *John put books as well as records in the closet.*
> *Chris played Deus Ex on the PC as well as on Xbox.*
> *We've had pizza yesterday as well as today.*

As well as (and similar expressions: *in addition to, rather than, instead of*) look like conjunctions. But curiously, they don't play well with VPs or entire sentences:

> *?It rained as well as snowed.*
> **John looks like Justin Bieber as well as owns a bank.*
> **We had pizza as well as Julie did a dance.*

Each other

> *The angels sang to each other.*
> *Give each other a kiss.*

Compare to the older construction *They sang one to another*, which seems more intuitive. How did *X prep Y* (also used in Russian, below) get reanalyzed as *prep X Y*?

> **Они не могут жить друг без друга.**
>
> 3p not can-3p.indic live-inf. friend without friend-gen.
>
> *They can't live without each other.*

Another oddity is the construction seen in *a whole 'nother story*, which you can hear every day but looks strange in print.

Center embedding

> *The girl the boy seduced is pregnant.*

That's an example of CENTER EMBEDDING, which just means that one sentence is inserted in the middle of another: *The girl [the boy seduced her] is pregnant.* It isn't very difficult, but look what happens when we extend it:

> *The man the girl the boy seduced trusted hid her.*

For some reason such sentences are very difficult to parse. (If you're baffled, the boy seduced the girl, she trusted the man, the man hid her!) One more step sounds like word salad:

> *The cabinet the man the girl the boy seduced trusted hid her in fell open.*

And yet you can right-embed all day long:

> *We repaired the cabinet that the man used to hide the girl who was seduced by the boy who ignored the teachings of his rabbi who raised him following the death of his mother who disappeared in the war that, like this sentence, never seemed to end.*

If you've concluded that two center embeddings are the maximum, Anne de Roeck has this reflection for you:

> *But don't you find that sentences that people you know produce are easier to understand?*

Modified pronouns

Here's an example from a Latin comedy by Plautus:

Tū sussultas, egō miser vix asto prae formīdine.

2s spring.up-2s.pres 1s wretched barely stand-1s.pres before dread-abl

You spring up, and wretched I barely stand, from dread.

You might blow past this without a pause, but note that the pronoun *egō* is modified by an adjective (and yet fulfills its ordinary role in the sentence). This isn't supposed to happen, according to some accounts of pronouns, which are said to replace entire NPs.

The English gloss is awkward, but we can do this in some constructions:

I thought I could read this book in a day. Foolish me!

Prepositional pronouns

So you're learning French, and you understand case in pronouns, you understand the preverbal clitics, you understand prepositions. But you're likely to still stumble on *y* and *en.*

If most pronouns are really pro-NPs— they stand for a noun phrase— these are pro-PPs, standing for a prepositional phrase. *Y* stands for *à + NP*, and *en* for *de + NP*:

Je vais à la ville. 1s go.1s to the.f city *I'm going to the city.*	**J'y vais.** 1s to.NP go.1s *I'm going there.*
Tu veux des grenouilles? 2s want.2s of-pl frog-pl *You want some frogs?*	**Tu en veux?** 2s of.NP want.2s *You want some of them?*

There's also a relativizer, *dont*, that incorporates *de*:

les choses [tu as besoin des choses]

→ les choses dont tu as besoin

the.pl thing-pl sub.of 2s have.2s need

the things you need (lit., the things of which you have need)

Is it simple enough?

Maybe you're making an auxlang, or a pidgin, or an interlanguage for talking to AIs, or something else where simplicity is a virtue. In that case the thing to watch for is borrowing complexities from English (or other natlangs) that you don't really need.

- Check your verb conjugations... do you really need each dimension of inflection? Do you need tense *and* aspect?
- Do you need cases *and* adpositions?
- Do your pronouns need different roots in the plural? Do you need the third person at all? (You can use deictics instead: *this, that.*)
- Do your nouns need plurals?
- Can you bag the adjectives, by making them nouns or verbs? Lots of languages get by without articles, too.
- Instead of *adding* roots, take the time to *remove* some: find ways to make the word out of other roots (*like = love a little; ice = solid water; show = cause to see; uncle = parent-sib; six = twice three*), or double up (one word could serve for *road, route, street, path, way, passage*).
- Subclauses add complexity— why not prohibit them? Pronouns are one approach:

  I met the man. He caught the fish.
  "It was easy." He said that.

- If something is signaled on every word, consider not doing that. E.g. this Esperanto sentence marks the plural five times, and almost every word shows part of speech.

  La birdoj estas konstruontaj— eĉ jam konstruantaj—siajn nestojn.

  the bird-noun-pl be-pres-fin.verb construct-fut-part-adj-pl even already construct-pres-part-adj-pl own-adj-pl-acc nest-noun-pl-acc

  The birds are about to construct, or are already constructing, their nests.

The defining characteristic of human languages, in some tellings, is the ability to talk about *anything*. But maybe you can give up on that. Maybe you just can't use the language to talk about computers, or crafts, or agriculture— think of all the terms you'd save!

Less radically, you can ruthlessly combine categories, in the manner of the Australian AVOIDANCE LANGUAGES. These are languages that were required for all conversation with taboo relatives, such as mothers-in-law. One word in the avoidance language often corresponded with half a dozen in ordinary language— e.g. in Jalnguy, the avoidance language of Guwal, *nyirrindan* stood in for seven Guwal words used for different kinds of spearing or poking. You might have only one word for all sorts of small omnivores, or all older relatives, or all ways to hurt someone. It's less precise, but it works and it sure cuts down on words.

While I've got the book open, here's a cool word from Guwal: *banyin* means 'get a stone tomahawk and bring it down on a rotten log so the blade is embedded in the log, then pick up both tomahawk and log by the handle of the tomahawk and bash the log against a tree so that the log splits open and the ripe grubs inside it can be extracted and eaten.'

Is it weird enough?

Conlanging isn't a weirdathon. You could copy a natlang in every respect and, after all, it would be naturalistic. And contrariwise, putting in every feature you've ever heard of— a KITCHEN SINK CONLANG— is a classic noob move.

But yeah, it's generally less interesting to just redo English or do a neo-Romance language. How close is your language to the following?

Standard Fantasy Phonology (i.e. English plus kh)

Pronouns: one for each person and number, plus object forms, and separate words for 'he' and 'she'

Nouns have singular and plural only, and maybe case

Adjectives are a separate class, which either don't decline, or decline like nouns

Verbs conjugate by person and number

Verbs have three tenses: past, present, future, plus maybe a conditional

Modality is expressed with a conjugated auxiliary

Definite and indefinite articles

No gender

SVO

Nominative-accusative alignment

Prepositions

Questions and negatives formed by adding a particle

Decimal number system

If it's pretty close— again, it's no sin, but you're not taking advantage of the breadth and strangeness of natural languages. Review the Grammar chapter in the *LCK,* or the *Morphosyntax* chapter (p. 108), to see what some of your options are.

I'm generally satisfied if I can point out four or five **'interesting features'** of a language... these can be unusual features, or just things I want to play with. For instance, for Old Skourene:

- Verbs have triconsonantal roots with vowel changes for conjugation
- Most nouns, including everyday words, are derived from verbs
- The case structure is ergative/absolutive
- There is no subordination per se, but a wide array of conjunctions
- There are four genders: masculine, feminine, animate, inanimate
- The phonology is highly tolerant of clusters, and features a retroflex series

Don't feel that if half a dozen non-English features are good, two dozen are even better. You can always put that really neat feature you just ran across in your *next* conlang.

If you're creating an auxlang, you don't want weirdness per se, but if your idea can be described as "Esperanto done right", be aware that Esperanto is blandly European and that its creator would have done well to learn a lot more about Amerindian or East Asian languages.

Sample texts

Writing texts in your language is like exercise: it's work, but it's good for you. Every sentence you write is an opportunity to develop the lexicon, confront syntactic oddities, and show off the culture.

For the last reason, I don't advocate translating standard texts (like the Babel story). Instead, showcase something from your culture. Some ideas:

A conversation with a visitor (a chance to work out greetings and other mechanics of conversation)

A religious text: a prayer, a myth, an argument against the unbelievers

Part of the novel you're writing

A native's description of his capital city, or his marriage, or a dungeon, or a spaceship

A complaint about a foreign nation, or another intelligent species

A scene from a play (e.g., a daughter contests the marriage arranged by her father; a courtier wants the king to arrest an enemy; a girl passes herself off as a boy)

Common proverbs

The most notable quotations from a culture hero (think Buddha, or Oscar Wilde, or Merlin, or Chuck Norris)

Instructions for casting a magic spell

A comic story (a drunkard gets in trouble; a cheating couple is found out; a robot malfunctions)

An intercepted letter from a spy

If your conculture differs spectacularly from modern earthly models, focus on that. E.g. the Lé are female-dominant, so one of my Lé sample texts is a pious letter from a mother instructing her son on how to fit into the matriarchal clan he's marrying into.

Glosses

Your glosses should look like this:

В России все работают на заводе.

V Rossii vse rabotajut na zavode.

[vɾɔs ˈsʲi i fsʲɛ ɾə ˈbɔ ta jut na zə ˈvɔ dʲɛ]

in Russia-s.gen everyone-pl.nom work-3p.pres.impfv on factory-s.loc

In Russia, everyone works at the factory.

Ha, I'm just winding you up. You don't need all of that— though it's all useful. In order, the lines are:

1 Native writing system

2 Transliteration

3 Phonetic representation

4 Gloss

5 Free translation

You won't be able to provide the native writing system unless you have a font for it[4], and if your Phonology section is good enough the phonetic representation is just a convenience. So that leaves us with the transliteration, gloss, and translation.

When I was starting out I'd often skip the gloss, but now I think it's essential. It allows the reader to follow the grammatical descriptions without learning the language. (And it's a big help even if they're learning it.)

Glosses are chunky to read. You could try expanding them—

> in Russia-singular.genitive everyone-plural.nominative work-third.person.plural.present.imperfective on factory-singular.locative

but that's not really more readable, is it?

The convention is that - separates morphemes, while . separates words required to explain the morpheme. So work-3p.pres.impfv above means that работают is divided into two morphemes:

работа	work
ют	third person plural present imperfective

That is, the dots tell us that 3p.pres.impfv describes a single, indivisible morpheme. We can use the same convention for words that require more than one word in the English gloss; e.g. we could gloss French *sortir* as go.out.

Compare Quechua *llamka-n-ku* which means the same as работают but whose gloss is work-3-pl. That is, *-n-ku* can be divided into *-n* = 3rd person, *-ku* = plural.

Some people like the neatness of a tabular format, though I think it's overkill and makes the transliteration hard to read:

---

[4] Even if you do have a font, displaying it on the Web is a problem. However, fonts will embed into a PDF, so that's an alternative if you want to use your writing system extensively.

V	**Ross-**	**ii**	**vse**	**rabota-**	**jut**	**na**	**zavod-**	**e**
in	Russia	s.gen	everyone .pl.nom	work	3p .pres	on	factory	s.loc

You can separate the morphemes in the transliteration:

V Ross-ii vse rabota-jut na zavod-e.

That's useful but again hard to read. A useful compromise is to do this contextually: e.g. if we're talking about verbs divide up *rabota-jut* but don't bother with the nouns.

An alternative is the approach J. Randolph Valentine takes in his *Nishnaabemwin Reference Grammar*:

Gii-gshkitoon wii-nsaaknang Maanii shkwaandem.

Mary was able to get the door open.

Gii-gshkitoon *vti ind 3sProx»0s 'ANsg was able to do IN';* ***wii-nsaaknang*** *vti conj 3sProx»0 'CONJ ANsg open IN';* ***Maanii*** *na 3sProx 'Mary';* ***shkwaandem*** *ni 0s 'door'*

Although this takes a lot of space, it fits the language since (as the glosses suggest) there's a lot of grammatical information to get across.

Valentine's » marks polypersonal agreement (p. 170), more generally represented >. Thus a morpheme 3s>1s agrees with a 3s subject and 1s object.

The translation should be unforced English, not an attempt to capture the feel of the original— that's what the glosses are for. For instance, if you're translating Quechua

Gringuqa hamukunsi kaballupi.

gringo-topic go-to.speaker-3-hsy horse-loc

don't try to use the nuances or syntax of the original:

As for the gringo, he came, I hear, by horse.

Rather, supply the sentence as we'd say it:

A gringo was coming along by horse.

The reader can look at the glosses to see the differences from English.

You can force it a bit if you are contrasting two constructions— e.g. if you had a variation with *hamukunmi*, which uses the direct knowledge evidential *-mi*, you can write contrasting glosses:

(I know) a gringo was coming along by horse.
(I hear) a gringo was coming along by horse.

You can use whatever **abbreviations** are appropriate for your language; the list at the beginning of the book is a good start.

For pronouns I like to write e.g. 1s.nom. You could write 'I', but then you quickly run into complications in the 2nd person (where 'you' doesn't distinguish number or case) and the 3rd (where the pronoun structure is usually different from English's).

You can capitalize grammatical morphemes (go-TO.SPKR-3-EV), though I think this is over-fussy; the distinction is usually obvious.

Sometimes it's useful to treat a word as if it had a null morpheme, written Ø:

> **Академи-я Наук-Ø**
>
> academy-s.nom science-pl.gen
>
> *Academy of Sciences*

The alternative would be to gloss наук as science.pl.gen, which would be misleading— it's just the stem of the word, not a suppletive form.

The Leipzig Glossing Rules (see the URL on the web resources page) cover more advanced cases like infixes and bipartite stems. You won't go wrong following them, though they're a bit more work (e.g. they require the tabular format and capitalizing grammatical morphemes).

A taste of logic

This chapter is a whirlwind tour of logic. There's two reasons to embark:

- Logical notation is often the quickest and most precise way to explain some linguistic feature.
- Logic can inspire logical conlangs or LOGLANGS, of which the best known is Lojban, created by theLogical Language Group.

I'm not going to teach logical argument here; if you want more, from a linguistic perspective, try James McCawley's *Everything that Linguists have Always Wanted to Know about Logic (but were ashamed to ask).*

To a linguist, logic is something like an intensive (but useful) semantic analysis of half a dozen words— the conjunctions and quantifiers, and *not.* And even there, as we'll see, logicians and ordinary speakers don't always use these words the same way.

Propositional logic

Propositional or BOOLEAN logic deals with the connections between entire propositions. If you've studied some programming, you'll find the notation familiar.

Propositions are represented by single letters like p, which are considered to be either true (T) or false (F). That's a major difference from natural language, which deals with various degrees and kinds of reliability; see Modality, p 146.

Negation is indicated by ¬, so $\neg p$ is *not p.* If p is true then $\neg p$ is false, and if p is false then $\neg p$ is true.

CONJUNCTION (***and***) is expressed $p \wedge q$ (the operator is reminiscent of A), and DISJUNCTION (***or***) as $p \vee q$. However, there are other notations:

Here	McCawley	C, C#, Java
$\neg p$	$\sim p$	!p
$p \wedge q$	$\wedge pq$	p && q
$p \vee q$	$\vee pq$	p || q

These operators can be defined by a TRUTH TABLE which gives their value for all the possible truth values of their arguments:

p	q	$p \wedge q$	$p \vee q$
T	T	T	T
T	F	F	T
F	T	F	T
F	F	F	F

This accords with our intuitions about *and*, but note that ∨ is always INCLUSIVE OR— $p \vee q$ is true if **either one** of p or q is true. If you want an EXCLUSIVE OR, where **only one** of p or q is true, we define another symbol, using another truth table:

p	q	$p \oplus q$
T	T	F
T	F	T
F	T	T
F	F	F

Latin distinguishes exclusive *aut* and inclusive *vel*.[5] English *or* is ambiguous, but there are heuristics— e.g. bureaucratic language is usually ∨ (*You may take this deduction if you are blind or over 65*), while offers are usually ⊕ (*Entrées come with soup or salad*). The construction 'either p or q' narrows the meaning to ⊕; 'p and/or q' to ∨.

We might also say that *or* means ∨ but implicates ⊕. If we know that Big Jim is both fat and loud, it'd be odd to say that he's 'fat or loud'. We'd say 'fat *and* loud'. But 'fat or loud' wouldn't actually be a contradiction. (For more on implicature see p. 44, or the *LCK* p. 131.)

Logicians define the relation → or ⊃ as IMPLICATION, or ***if***.

p	q	$p \rightarrow q$
T	T	T
T	F	F
F	T	T
F	F	T

Is this really what *if* means? Consider *If it's Tuesday, this must be Belgium.* Consider what the table is telling us:

- It's Tuesday and we're in Belgium: that checks out, so $p \rightarrow q$ is true.
- It's Tuesday and we're not in Belgium: that certainly contradicts the English statement, so $p \rightarrow q$ is false.

[5] To be more precise, *vel* implies that the choice doesn't matter. It may or may not be compatible with being able to take both choices.

- It's not Tuesday, so *whether or not we're in Belgium*, we declare that $p \rightarrow q$ is true. Huh?

Now, it can be shown (McCawley has a proof) that there's no other truth table that works *better* for *if*. But it certainly doesn't fit our intuitions. At the least we'd like to say that if it's not Tuesday, we *just don't know* whether $p \rightarrow q$ is true. Or we could say that *if* statements have to be semantically coherent: there's *something about it being Tuesday* (like a tour schedule) that makes it relevant to concluding that we're in Belgium.

But Boolean logic doesn't allow indefinite truth values, and doesn't let us 'look inside' a proposition. So take → as 'logicians' implication', or an abbreviation for $(\neg p) \vee q$, and let's move on.

If you have a systematic mind, you may be wondering if there are names and operators for **every possible truth table**. There are, though frankly most of them are not very interesting for logic *or* linguistics.

But a loglang might want to have ways to express them all, so here's the whole set, with English paraphrases. The order is the same as in the above tables (*p* and *q* true; *p* true *q* false; *p* false *q* true; *p* and *q* false).

	Notation	*Truth condition*
FFFF	F	always false
FFFT	$\neg(p \vee q)$	**nor**: both must be false
FFTF	$\neg(q \rightarrow p)$	not if ($q \rightarrow p$ is false)
FFTT	$\neg p$	*p* is false (*q* irrelevant)
FTFF	$\neg(p \rightarrow q)$	not if ($p \rightarrow q$ is false)
FTFT	$\neg q$	*q* is false (*p* irrelevant)
FTTF	$p \oplus q$	exclusive or: only one can be true
FTTT	$\neg(p \wedge q)$	**nand**: can't have both true
TFFF	$p \wedge q$	**and**: both must be true
TFFT	$p = q$	both have the same truth value
TFTF	q	*q* is true (*p* irrelevant)
TFTT	$p \rightarrow q$	**if**: when *p* is true, *q* must be too
TTFF	p	*p* is true (q irrelevant)
TTFT	$q \rightarrow p$	when *q* is true, *p* must be too
TTTF	$p \vee q$	**or**: one is true, or both are
TTTT	T	always true

As the *Notation* column suggests, many rows can be defined in terms of other rows. There are other possible subsets; in fact, you can define all the rows using just one operator, **nand** ↑. I don't know of any natlang where *nand* is primary, but this might be a good approach for an alien language!

How does that work? Here are the basics; can you work out the rest? (If you find it hard to follow the formulas, use truth tables: evaluate for the four possible values of p and q.)

$\neg p$	$p \uparrow p$
$p \vee q$	$(p \uparrow p) \uparrow (q \uparrow q)$
$p \wedge q$	$(p \uparrow q) \uparrow (p \uparrow q)$
$p \rightarrow q$	$p \uparrow (q \uparrow q)$

Rules of inference

What logic is *for* is making **proofs**; ironically, this is where linguists may tune out, as proofs are not really needed to describe languages. Still, the RULES OF INFERENCE for propositional logic are easily listed.

Here's McCawley's set.[6] The right-hand column shows the form of a proof using each rule: first the premise(s), then the allowable conclusion, marked by ∴ 'therefore'.

∧-introduction	p q $\therefore p \wedge q$
∧-exploitation	$p \wedge q$ $\therefore p$
∨-introduction	p $\therefore p \vee$ (anything)
∨-exploitation	$p \vee q$ subproof that assumes p and proves r subproof that assumes q and proves r $\therefore r$
¬-introduction (reductio ad absurdum)	suppose p subproof that q and $\neg q$ follow $\therefore \neg p$
¬-exploitation	$\neg\neg p$ $\therefore p$
→-introduction	p proof that q follows $\therefore p \rightarrow q$
→-exploitation (modus ponens)	$p \rightarrow q$ p $\therefore q$

[6] This is a form of NATURAL DEDUCTION, worked out by Gerhard Gentzen to avoid axioms and to approximate mathematical practice.

Language does use logic— e.g. people use negation, conjunctions, *if* statements. But it's worth asking whether they use the same rules as logicians. Pretty clearly they don't.

Some rules which people actually seem to use:

- ABDUCTION: $p \rightarrow q$, and q, therefore p:

  Communists cause strikes, and there are strikes, so Communists are involved.

  A clearer example should demonstrate the wrongness:

  Echidnas are mammals; you're a mammal; therefore you're an echidna.

- INDUCTION: p has always been true, so it will continue to be true. (In arguments, often expressed "We've always done it this way" or "Everybody knows...")
- Correlation is causation: the Great Vowel Shift happened at the same time as the discovery of America, so one caused the other.
- Argument by pattern: *Gaijin* looks like *goyim*, so they must be related.
- Argument by prototype: to see if a proposition is true of a member of a class, apply it to a typical example. (*Birds can fly, so penguins must be able to fly.*)
- BEGGING THE QUESTION: 'proving' a point by assuming it: *How do I know atheism is true? Because there aren't any gods!*
- CHERRYPICKING: assuring yourself of a point by looking for only positive evidence. Some people can spend years at this.
- Argument by authority: I believe p because Zompist said so. Or the opposite, AD HOMINEM: Zompist says p, so it can't possibly be true.

These are all FALLACIES, that is, false arguments. At least some of these deserve a bit of respect, though: they're not bad *heuristics*— for primates. We often have to make decisions in a hurry, or based on inadequate or merely probabilistic data. Even a rational person may have no better support for most of her beliefs than induction, authority, and prototyping.

Predicate calculus

The name may be terrifying, but PREDICATE CALCULUS isn't hard. Instead of propositions, we deal with PREDICATES, which you can think of as verbs and adjectives, and ARGUMENTS, which are NPs. For instance, *Sappho is a woman* can be represented as

WOMAN(Sappho)

Multiple arguments as well as Boolean operators can be used; e.g. *This road leads from Verduria to Zeirdan* could be

ROAD(r) ∧ CONNECTS(r, Verduria, Zeirdan)

See if you can express the following in English:

EGGMAN(you) ∧ WALRUS(me)

¬NUMBER(me) ∧ FREE(me)

¬RAINS(weather) ∨ POURS(weather)

A predicate still has a truth value, true or false, so we're still limited in how much of natural language we can represent.

The use of English words may obscure the fact that the predicate and argument names are arbitrary. WALRUS(me) doesn't inherently mean anything different than POOMBLAT(xiff); proofs in predicate calculus look only at the form of the statements, not at the labels.

Quantifiers

QUANTIFIERS are used to tell how much of a set a predicate applies to. Logicians can go far with just two.

The EXISTENTIAL QUANTIFIER ∃ asserts that something **exists** with the given properties. For instance,

∃x: WALRUS(x)

says that some *x* exists for which WALRUS(x) is true. This might be translated *There is a walrus* or *Some walruses exist.*

∃x: WOMAN(x) ∧ LOVES(x, me)

This can be read *There is a woman who loves me*, or *Some woman loves me.*

The UNIVERSAL QUANTIFIER ∀ asserts that something is true for **all** instances of its variable. E.g.

$\forall$x: WALRUS(x)

means that for all *x*, WALRUS(x) is true— that is, *Everything is a walrus* or *All things are walruses.*

Universal claims are rarely useful, but universal implications are:

$\forall$x: WALRUS(x) $\rightarrow$ FAT(x)

This can be read *For all x, if x is a walrus then x is fat*, or just *All walruses are fat.*

Now we can state classic syllogisms:

$\forall$x: WOMAN(x) $\rightarrow$ MORTAL(x)

WOMAN(Sappho)

$\therefore$ MORTAL(Sappho)

All women are mortal.

Sappho is a woman.

Therefore Sappho is mortal.

The rule of inference here is $\forall$-exploitation, which tells us that if $\forall$ *x: Fx* $\rightarrow$ *Gx* and *Fn*, then *Gn*.

Quantifiers and negation

Quantifiers make negation tricky. Now, $p \wedge \neg p$ is a contradiction, right? So why can we say this?

Some zombies are fast and some zombies aren't fast.

The formulation for existentials explains this— they are actually compound statements, so we have to be clear what exactly is negated.

$\neg\exists$x: ZOMBIE(x) $\wedge$ FAST(x)

The $\neg$ symbol always applies to what's just to its right, in this case the $\exists$ symbol. So this should be read *There doesn't exist any x such that it's a zombie and fast,* or more naturally, *No zombies are fast.*

Now these two statements do contradict:

$\exists$x: ZOMBIE(x) $\wedge$ FAST(x)

$\neg\exists$x: ZOMBIE(x) $\wedge$ FAST(x)

but the obvious interpretation of *Some zombies aren't fast* is different:

$$\exists x\text{: ZOMBIE}(x) \wedge \neg\text{FAST}(x)$$

So does English negation apply to the predicate rather than the existential? Not really; it's hard to interpret *All zombies aren't slow* as anything but

$$\neg\forall x\text{: ZOMBIE}(x) \rightarrow \text{SLOW}(x)$$

e.g. *All zombies aren't slow— I just saw one sprinting along!*

We could also say *Not all zombies are slow*. But for some reason English doesn't let us say **Not some zombies are slow.*

How would you express this?

$$\forall x\text{: ZOMBIE}(x) \rightarrow \neg\text{SLOW}(x)$$

To be precise we need a fussy statement like *Zombies are all not slow. Zombies are not slow* works, but pragmatically I think we expect exceptions to such non-quantified claims— they're really statements about prototypes.

If you have a systematic mind you may wonder about

$$\exists x\text{: }\neg\text{ZOMBIE}(x) \wedge \text{FAST}(x)$$

but in natural language this isn't a quantification on zombies at all— we'd have to state this as *There are fast things that aren't zombies* or *Some non-zombies are fast.*

Are **both quantifiers necessary**? No; using negation, you can express each quantifier in terms of the other:

$$\forall x\text{: WALRUS}(x) \quad = \quad \neg\exists x\text{: }\neg\text{WALRUS}(x)$$

That is, *everything is a walrus* is equivalent to *there is nothing that isn't a walrus.* Likewise

$$\exists y\text{: KING}(y) \quad = \quad \neg\forall y\text{: }\neg\text{KING}(y)$$

So *someone is a king* is equivalent to *'Nothing is a king' is false.*

English quantifiers

Can actual English quantifiers really be equated to logical quantifiers? Compare

$\forall x$: MAN(x) $\rightarrow$ LOSER(x) *All men are losers.*

$\exists x$: MAN(x) $\wedge$ LOSER(x) *Some men are losers.*

Logically the first statement implies the second. In ordinary language, if we say *Some men are losers,* we would probably deny *All men are losers*— that is, if *Some men are losers,* then *some men are not losers.*

But this isn't ironclad— it's fine to say *Some men are losers, in fact all of them are.* Deniability without contradiction is the mark of an IMPLICATURE, which can be explained by the Gricean maxim of quantity (*Be informative*). Speakers should choose the most accurate quantifier: if we know that all men are losers, we should say so.

Along the same lines *some* may be said to implicate *more than one,* on the grounds that if we meant *one* we'd say so.

Now consider $\forall$, which corresponds to *every* and *any.*

$\forall x$: MAN(x) $\rightarrow$ LOVE(x, Faye)

Every man will love Faye.

Any man will love Faye.

Or does it? The first statement is a broad but straightforward claim about all men— at one time or another, they'll all love Faye. But the second is more of a hypothesis: take any man, put him together with Faye, and he'll love her. It's compatible with most men never meeting her and thus never loving her.

It's been claimed that *every,* but not *any,* implicates existence.

Everyone who conlangs will end up crazy.

Anyone who conlangs will end up crazy.

The first of these seems to implicate that there are people who conlang, while the second doesn't.

Each can be equated with $\forall$ too, though *each* often has an iterative, individual sense:

Lore wrote to each of his supporters.

Lore wrote to all of his supporters.

The first sentence implies that each supporter got an individual note; the second is compatible with a mass mailing.

No or *none,* as suggested in some of the examples, can be equated to $\neg\exists$. But our other quantifiers— *several, few, many, most*— all comment on the **size** of the specified group. We could express these using sets:

Many conlangers are crazy.

$\exists\mathbf{M}$: LARGE($\mathbf{M}$) $\wedge$ $\forall y \in \mathbf{M}$ CONLANG(y) $\wedge$ CRAZY(y)

That is, there is a set **M** such that for each member *y, y* conlangs and *y* is crazy, and **M** is large. ($\in$ means 'member of'.) Complicated as this is, it's still not very satisfactory, as LARGE is both vague and highly context-dependent. No wonder logicians largely stick with their two quantifiers.

Deep structure

If these expressions scare you, that's fine, you can quietly turn to the next chapter. But for some of you, gears are turning. *This could handle almost anything in language! In fact, this would be a great way to represent meaning!*

Similar thoughts occurred to linguists back in the '60s, and the school of GENERATIVE SEMANTICS posited deep structures that were pretty much predicate calculus. I mentioned some of the problems with this in the *LCK* (p. 108), but the general lesson is that predicate calculus is a simplified abstraction, and can't represent everything that's going on in language. A few striking gaps:

- Context— how we handle utterances rather than statements of eternal verities; includes things like deixis and topicalization, and indeed the whole Pragmatics chapter of the *LCK*.
- Fuzzy truth values— humans are quite comfortable with shades of reliability. As McCawley says, while for logicians contradictions make all hell break loose, for ordinary humans contradictions make only some hell break loose.
- Tense, modality, and aspect— at the least these become cumbersome, and can be entirely baffling (what's the logical form of a perfective?).
- Speech acts besides assertion— very little of what we say is an assertion of truth.

The general lesson is not to overextend any representational structure, whether it's predicate calculus or syntactic trees or translations into LISP. Use the notation for what it's good at, and if it starts to be cumbersome, be prepared to change notations or metaphors.

McCawley offers the warning story of Bertrand Russell, who analyzed *the* as a matter of logic:

$\exists$x: KINGF(x) $\wedge$ ($\forall$y: $\neg$(y=x) $\rightarrow$ $\neg$KINGF(y)) $\wedge$ BALD(x)

The king of France is bald.

That is, there's some dude *x* for which these three things are true:

- *x* is the king of France
- for all *y*, if *y* isn't *x*, *y* isn't the king of France— in other words, *x* is the *only* king of France
- *x* is bald

One problem is that Russell's formulation asserts that *The king of France is bald* is false when there is no king of France. Peter Strawson argued that in that case the statement is undetermined, not false.

But something is more seriously wrong with the second bullet point, as *the* is not restricted to unique referents. If we say *The man is bald* we don't mean that there's only one man in the world.

One suggestion is that *the* still implies uniqueness in the universe of discourse— we've made it clear (somehow) that we're talking about some set, and in that set there's only one man, and he's bald. But this won't work either, as we can say things that make it clear that the universe of discourse includes other men:

The man hates all other men.

The man criticized another man on his blog.

Pragmatics comes to the rescue, telling us that *the* merely tells us that a given speaker and listener, at the time of utterance. can agree on which referent is meant. Prototypically we first introduce the referent, with an indefinite, extended reference; subsequent references can use the simple noun with *the*:

A man entered the room. The man was bald.

The logical parallel is thus not a uniqueness claim; it's the use of bound variables. E.g. in this representation

$\exists$m: ENTERED(m, room) $\wedge$ BALD(m)

what corresponds to *the* is the use of the already defined variable *m*.

Setting a scene can be said to drag in a set of SCRIPTS or FRAMES (*LCK* p. 151), and these implicitly define referents without our having to mention them.

In Paris in 1789, the king was bald.

Here the time and place adverbials, plus our knowledge that a country has only one king at a time, allow us to interpret which king was meant even though he wasn't referred to earlier.

Propositional arguments

One of the most powerful features of language is that sentences can be nested. This can be represented in predicate calculus by allowing arguments to themselves be predicates:

KNOW(me, LISTEN(you, me))

I know you're listening.

∀x: PERSON(x) → WANT(x, ∃y: LOVE(y, x))

Everybody wants someone to love them.

As we'll see below (p. 143), languages are very concerned with VALENCE, the number of arguments of a verb. This could be expressed by adding arguments:

DIE(Abel)	*Abel died.*
KILL(Cain, Abel)	*Cain killed Abel.*

But it's clearer to express the relationship between these by using a causative, which treats an entire situation as an argument:

CAUSE(Cain, DIE(Abel))

Cain caused Abel to die (i.e., he killed Abel).

Again, be aware that the things predicate logic leaves out, such as topicalization and tense, are important parts of language— e.g. the causing and dying can occur at different times, while the killing only has one slot tense; and *Abel died* is a statement about Abel, while *Cain killed Abel* is a statement about Cain.

Loglangs

If you attempt to give your conlang some of the attractive properties of logic, you're probably creating a loglang.

You can take a soft approach— you want to **facilitate logic**— or a hard line— you want to **prevent illogic**.

Facilitating logic

A loglang will probably make it easy to express logical statements, much as the notation we've been using does. Lojban, for instance, has a direct existential quantifier:

> **Da zo'u da viska mi.**
>
> a such.that a sees 1s
>
> ∃a: SEES(a, me)
>
> *There's something that sees me.*

Da is actually a variable; you can use *de* and *di* as well, and there are ways of creating more variables.

Adding *ro* turns it into a universal quantifier:

> **Ro da zo'u da prami mi.**
>
> for.all a such.that a loves 1s
>
> ∀a: LOVES(a, me)
>
> *Everything loves me.*

You can specify a set with **poi**:

> **Ro da poi gerku zo'u da vasxu.**
>
> for.all a which is.dog such.that a breathes
>
> ∀a∈**DOG**: BREATHES(a)
>
> *All dogs breathe.*

(There is a presupposition that the set named by *poi* isn't empty— in the example, at least one **DOG** must exist.)

A loglang can also be expected to be careful about negation, avoiding things like NEG HOPPING (p. 151). Note that the negative placement of Lojban matches the logical notation:

Ro da poi prenu zo'u mi <u>naku</u> prami da.

for.all a which is.person such.that 1s not loves a

$\forall a \in$ **PERSON**: $\neg$LOVES(me, a)

I don't love anyone.

<u>Naku</u> ro da poi prenu zo'u mi prami da.

not for.all a which is.person such.that 1s loves a

$\neg\forall a \in$ **PERSON**: LOVES(me, a)

I don't love everyone. (Or: 'I love everyone' is false.)

Lojban's logical operators cover four of the sixteen possible truth tables; the ones shown here are used for connecting NPs.

	Notation	*Lojban*
TFFF	$p \wedge q$	**e**
TFFT	$p = q$	**o**
TTFF	p	**u**
TTTF	$p \vee q$	**a**

Then there's the special vocabulary referring to sets, special determiners referring to typical (*lo'e*) or stereotypical (*le'e*) things, ways to represent mathematical equations... Lojban is full of things that will appeal to the geek mindset; for a full description see John Cowan's *The Complete Lojban Language.*

Regularity

Probably every auxiliary language (AUXLANG) ever has prided itself on reducing the irregularity of natural languages, especially the messy fusions, irritating variations, and confusing orthographies of Indo-European.

Though I mostly try to steer students in the other direction— into the glorious chaos of naturalism— if this is your goal, let me suggest possible regularities many auxlangers miss:

- The plural pronouns could be derived from the singulars, as in Quechua and Chinese.
- Do you have an animate/inanimate distinction for interrogatives (*who/what*) but not for pronouns (*he/it*)?
- Probably you've made it easy to change parts of speech, but is the base form (noun, verb, adjective) predictable?

- Be consistent about whether the base form of a verb is transitive or intransitive.
- If you've borrowed vocabulary, have you brought along multiple derived forms— e.g. Esperanto's *meti* 'put' / *permesi* 'permit', or *ĉambro* 'room' / *kamero* 'chamber'?
- Are semantic roles consistently mapped to syntactic roles? E.g. the beneficiary in English may be marked with *to,* or *for,* or nothing.
- A subtle snare is to use the same nominalizer with multiple meanings. Consider separate suffixes for person / tool / place / abstract process / art / physical product / material.

A loglang may also seek to have **precise, unambiguous definitions**. Loglangers feel horror at the dozens of senses of 'run', even more at words with contradictory senses: *cleave* can mean 'stick together' or 'cut apart'. *Bertie's left* may mean that Bertie's gone or that he's still here!

Precision is laudable, but lists of such 'contradictions' sometimes give the impression that the compiler doesn't understand how language works. E.g. *cool* has positive and negative senses— cf. *a cool dude, a cool reception.* But these are just two chains of metaphors:

> *cool temperature → not affected by heat*
> *→ unruffled, calm → desirable, neat*
>
> *not (warm in temperature) → not (warm in emotion)*
> *→ unfriendly*

You can't guarantee that such conflicting senses won't develop without prohibiting metaphor.

Bertie's left is short for either *Bertie has left* (only an active meaning possible— he's gone) or *Bertie is left* (by the others who went away— only the passive meaning is possible). Here you'd have to prohibit contraction. And *cleave* has two meanings because etymologically it's two different words.

Classificatory lexicons

Ferdinand de Saussure maintained that the relationship between sign and symbol is arbitrary, but early auxlangers begged to differ. Many created systems where the form of the word was itself a classification.

The Verdurian scholar Osör Ružeon created such a scheme, the *Řon Lebië Kestië* (Language of the New Categories).[7] He began with 21 categories, corresponding to the 21 consonants of the Verdurian alphabet, in order:

k *ked̂esa* production, in the sense of creation or art
ř *řon* language
p *poča* the land, including physical features
c *celdoni* trade
b *bežia* motion
g *gaiec* form
d *dascoi* animals
s *syel* sky (astronomy and the weather)
š *šalea* the spirit
z *zëi* the sea
č *čistë* purity, virtue
t *travët* crime
d̂ *d̂itelát* engineering, including crafts and tools
r *razum* reason
h *hicet* numbers and mathematics
l *leria* perception
m *mör* custom, law, and government
f *ftaconî* elements
n *nëronát* holiness, religion
v *veži* plants
ž *žes* home

Each of these was further subdivided:

- *du* named mammals
- *dug* named large herbivores
- *dugu* were those that were domesticated but not eaten
- *duguk* was the word for horse

The vowels were also used in Verdurian alphabetical order; so **u** referred to the first category of a given level. Thus the categories could also be used as a numerical classification: *duguk* could be written 7.1.6.1.1.

[7] Verduria is part of my conworld Almea, but this sort of classification/language has earthly counterparts, such as the Philosophical Language of John Wilkins.

Such schemes have gone out of favor, perhaps because science has advanced so quickly that it's hard to maintain confidence in any one classificatory system. (Where should Ružeon put bacteria? What happens when the scientists combine light and magnetism? Did he leave a letter open for subatomic particles?)

I doubt anyone has actually tried to speak in such languages; if they did they'd be plagued by misunderstandings. E.g. Ružeon's word for 'cow' was *dugak*— the *a* was for large domesticated herbivores that *are* eaten. Any description of the animals of a farm is going to be a tongue-twister...

Preventing illogic

A more ambitious goal is to make it hard or impossible to say illogical things.

Perhaps the ultimate expression of this goal is **Newspeak**, the language George Orwell describes in *1984.* Newspeak is partly a parody of Esperanto and other highly regularized conlangs (as in such expressions as *ungood, goodwise,* and *thinked*), partly of Soviet neologisms (compare *Ingsoc* to terms like *Comintern*), and partly of half-brain-dead political propaganda (which Orwell calls *duckspeak*). But its chief feature is the attempt to make unorthodoxy impossible to express.

The chief method is impoverishment of vocabulary; what we don't have names for, it's hard to think about. Oldspeak terms like *honor, justice, morality, democracy, science, religion,* Orwell tells us, could only be expressed in the single despective *crimethink.* All unusual sexuality fell under the single word *sexcrime.* The word *free* had no political meaning at all, though it was still allowed in the sense of 'lacking'.

This is a rather Whorfian view[8]; Orwell was reacting to the brutalities of totalitarian propaganda, but propaganda couldn't prevent the fall of totalitarian states. Newspeak might make it difficult to talk about oppression, but it was the surveillance and the secret police, not the language, that preserved the state. People can invent new terms for new concepts.

Can a language make sloppy thought more difficult? One idea is to eliminate the slipperiest constructions. David Bourland proposed **E-prime**, which is simply English without 'to be'; the idea is that statements of identity and predication lead to error and emotion. So we should rewrite

---

[8] Benjamin Lee Whorf maintained that the structures of language affect how we think; see the *LCK* p. 153.

The electron is a wave.

Alfred is brilliant.

Aristotle is a menace.

The computer is on.

How are you?

as

The electron appears as a wave in such-and-such an experiment.

Alfred seems brilliant to me.

Robert says that Aristotle behaves as a menace.

I can see light from the computer monitor.

How goes it?

Now, any language game can teach you something— Georges Perec wrote an entire novel, *La Disparition*, without the letter **e**, and that certainly required enormous creativity.[9] You'd probably be a better writer if you tried E-prime for a month. But it seems crankish to simply demonize a common and useful aspect of language— why focus on *is* if the problem is subjectivity or dogmatism?

Besides, such paraphrases would very likely simply end up being a new form of the copula, just as euphemisms introduced in place of insults end up being used as insults themselves.

John Cowan cites Lewis Carroll's White King, who takes statements like *Nobody walks slower than you* as referring to a person named Nobody. He points out that this confusion couldn't occur in Lojban, because names are phonologically marked (with a glottal stop or pause) and thus can't be mistaken for a pronoun. But Carroll, a logician, was making a joke. (Has any conlanger attempted to make a language where *more* jokes are possible? Perhaps only DiLingo, the guttural utteral.)

More seriously, Lojban can be **unambiguously parsed.** There are no syntactic ambiguities; this is checked with a computer parser. Natlangs are relatively hopeless in this regard; e.g. if a parser is reading

I have met John and...

---

[9] He couldn't do anything about his name, which appears on the cover in red, as a regrettable exception. Fortunately he found a publisher (Gallimard) and a commendatory blurb that followed the rules.

it can't guess what syntactic constituent will come next:

auxiliary	*...can vouch for him.*
participle	*...drunk his absinthe.*
main verb	*...think he's brilliant.*
argument	*...Ivan.*
sentence	*...he's a character.*

This particular problem is solved in Lojban by having different types of conjunctions for different constituents.

So Lojban should disallow GARDEN PATH sentences, which lead the reader down one branch of syntactic interpretation, only to yank it away:

Amateur plumbers like rivers end up wet.

I stopped believing in college.

If you want to get rid of such problems, first analyze carefully to see exactly what they are. E.g. the first is due to homonymy between verbal and prepositional *like*; one solution is to make sure none of your grammatical words can be mistaken for a verb form.[10]

The second example, like the *and* problem, is a matter of bracketing. That is, the ambiguity would disappear if we spoke brackets out loud, as Victor Borge once proposed— then we could hear the difference between

I stopped [believing in college].

[I stopped believing] in college.

or

little [girls' school]

[little girls] school

You can do just that in Lojban, with *ke / ke'e*:

---

[10] E.g. in Esperanto parts of speech each have distinctive forms. This good work is undone by its generous word-building rules, which allow confusions (or puns) like *persono* = 'person' or 'a sounding out'; *dieto* = 'a diet' or 'a minor deity'; *avaro* = 'avarice' or 'a collection of grandfathers'.

Ta ke melbi cmalu ke'e nixli ckule.

that lparen beautiful little rparen girl school

That's a [beautiful little] girl school.

i.e., That's a school for girls who are beautifully small.

Ta melbi ke cmalu nixli ke'e ckule.

that beautiful lparen little girl rparen school

That's a beautiful [little girl] school.

i.e., That's a school for small girls who are beautiful.

I emphasize that I've only scratched the surface of Lojban; it's a very deeply worked out system for expressing statements with great precision.

Logographic writing

LOGOGRAPHIC writing systems were covered in the *LCK* (p. 202-4), but let's look at how to create them in more detail. I'll use mostly examples from Chinese and one of my conlangs, Uyseʔ.

I use logographic to emphasize that these writing systems represent words, not ideas. Even more narrowly, the symbols of Maya, Chinese, and Sumerian writing largely represent single syllables that are also MORPHEMES (units of meaning). But SYLLABOMORPHIC is awkward, and doesn't quite cover Egyptian, where some glyphs represent multi-syllabic roots.

A full logography would require creating many thousands of glyphs. Naturally you don't have to actually complete it! For purposes of writing a grammar, or even filling out a map, a few dozen symbols will suffice, but you'll still have to understand how such systems work.

These systems are complex and arguably rather cumbersome. Historically, Sumerian, Egyptian, and Japanese all moved in the direction of turning them into SYLLABARIES (a much smaller inventory of signs representing the language's possible syllables). However, don't assume that the users of a logography view the difficulty of the script as a fault. After all, mastering the system is a mark of education and keeps the scribes in business. (It's like the difficulties of English spelling: if you're used to it, more phonetic schemes can look barbaric.)

Logographic systems have the advantage that they're relatively unaffected by sound change and dialect diversity. E.g. Chinese 你 'you' (Old Chinese **nə*) serves for all of these:

Mandarin	ni^{3}	Jīxī	n^{3}
Zhèróng	ny^{3}	Guǎngzhōu	nei^{4}
Yángzhōu	liɪ^{3}	Táishān	ni^{1}
Shànghǎi	noŋ^{2}	Méixiàn	ɲi^{2}
Dānyáng	ŋ^{3}	Jiànyáng	noi^{9}
Línchuān	li^{3}		

The Chinese languages are not mutually intelligible, and the unity of the writing system is one of the factors that have kept China, unlike say the Romance languages, together as a cultural and political unit.

Note that when I use *Chinese* in this book, I'm referring to the writing system or the whole family; *Mandarin* is one dialect, which the standard language (*pǔtōnghuà*) is based on.

Ideas

For centuries people have been enchanted by the idea of an IDEOGRAPHIC system, and often mistakenly think Chinese is one. It's not; every Chinese character represents a particular word.

That's not to say an ideographic language is impossible. Mathematics provides one— if you write

$$\int_0^1 \sqrt{x}\,dx$$

it can be pronounced in many ways— e.g.

the integral from 0 to 1 of the square root of x times dx

integration over the range 0, 1 of square x dx

l'intégrale de zéro à un de la racine carrée d'x multiplié par dx

Of course, once you start thinking in these terms, almost any graphical display of information can be considered ideographic— maps, charts, Ikea instruction sheets.

An ideographic system

Many conlangers have tried to work out graphical representations that have the breadth of language. One very well done example is UNLWS (Unker Non-Linear Writing System), by Alex Fink and Sai. Here's a sample:

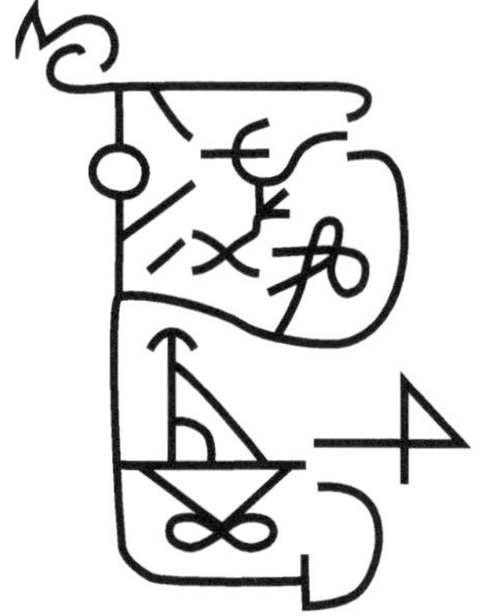

I understood from my parents, as they did from their parents etc., that they became happier as they more fully grokked and were grokked by their cat.

As with the mathematical example above, this is just one way of verbalizing the UNLWS expression; the diagram represents the ideas, not the English words (*unlike* a logographic system). And it really is nonlinear; there is no defined traversal order.

Glyphs correspond to predicates, and have BINDING POINTS for their arguments. For instance, here's the glyph for *groks*; it has binding points for the grokker and the grokkee.

X Y

Here's *A cat groks me*, with the binding points labeled. (They aren't actually drawn except in explanations like this.)

MYSELF(m)
CAT(c)
GROKS(c, m)

I include the predicate calculus equivalent to make it clear that the glyphs for *myself* and *cat* are predicates, not arguments.

You may be able to work out most of the sample sentence with the following lexicon of glyphs:

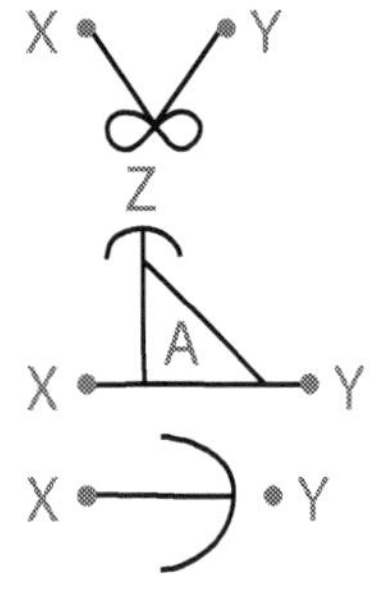

X is the parent of Y

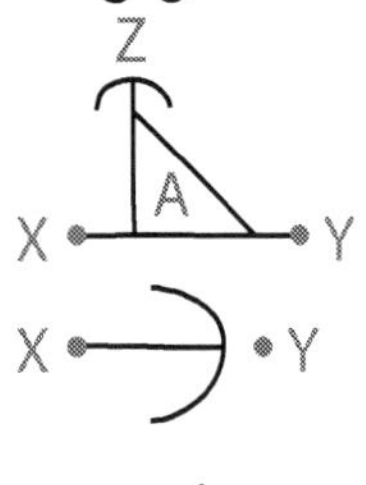

X shows Y that Z with modality A (vision, hearing, etc; an arc means a gestalt)

Quotative, seen in the previous glyph— in the sample, the perceived item is the entire top of the diagram

G is a homogenous group of members M

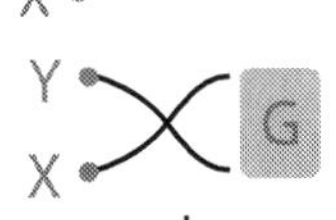

X is happy about Y

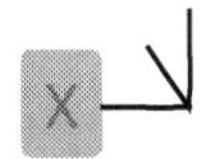

G is a graph expressing the X/Y relationship. / for G indicates that X increases as Y does

X

an aspect marker on X: the event goes to its natural completion

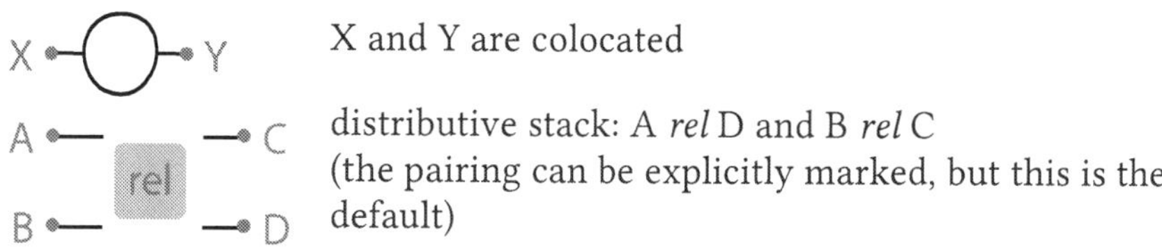

X and Y are colocated

distributive stack: A *rel* D and B *rel* C (the pairing can be explicitly marked, but this is the default)

Stacks are used to make the recursion happen. Conceptually, the stack repeats the relation:

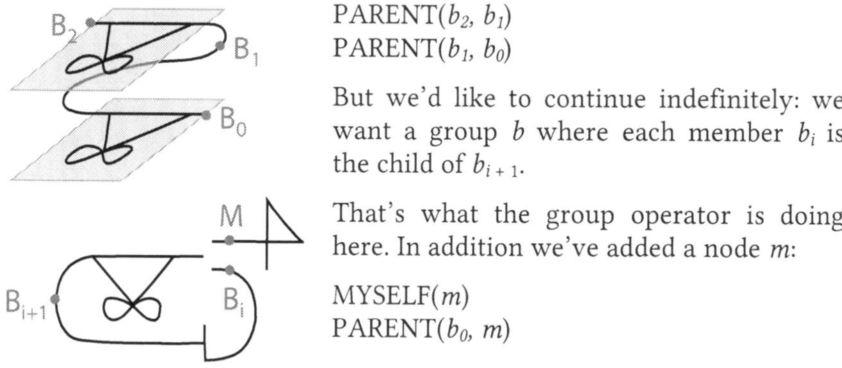

PARENT(b_2, b_1)
PARENT(b_1, b_0)

But we'd like to continue indefinitely: we want a group b where each member b_i is the child of b_{i+1}.

That's what the group operator is doing here. In addition we've added a node *m*:

MYSELF(*m*)
PARENT(b_0, *m*)

So this is 'me and my parents and their parents and so on'.

In the original sentence the group is defined not only by parenthood but by communicating something (the truth about cats) from parent to child.

It's also worth looking closer at the top of the diagram. For convenience I use labeled binding points here.

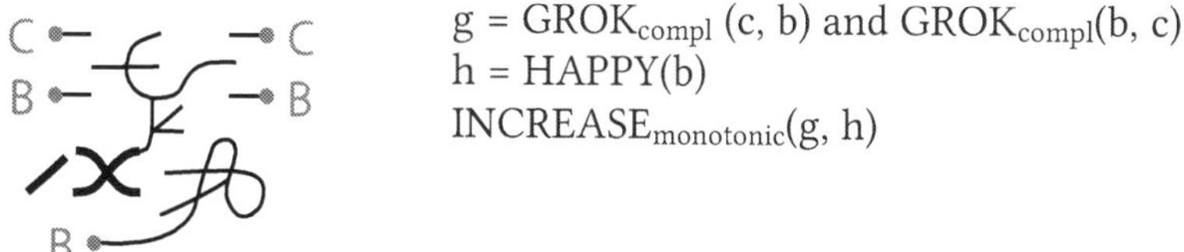

g = $\text{GROK}_{\text{compl}}$ (c, b) and $\text{GROK}_{\text{compl}}$(b, c)
h = HAPPY(b)
$\text{INCREASE}_{\text{monotonic}}$(g, h)

The heart of this diagram is the reflexive grokking between *c* and *b*. An aspect marker is attached: the grokking proceeds to its natural completion. Plus, *b* is happy.

The bolded section is the glyph representing the relationship over time of two functions *g*, *h*; the slash is the graph itself, and represents a simple increase[11]: the more *g*, the more *h*.

---

[11] If you look at the lexicon the glyph is upside-down— but the slash rotated 180° looks the same!

But what are *g* and *h*? They're the relationships we just defined: *g* is the grokking, *h* is the happiness. So as *c* and *b* grok each other more, *b* gets happier.

See the resources page for a link to more about UNLWS.

Origins

How do logographic systems originate? We don't know for sure, and you can devise one without knowing. But it may be useful to review some of the possibilities, as they may affect the form of the glyphs or which ones you start with.

In the Middle East, writing seems to have originated in **accounting**. Intriguingly, archeologists have found a large number of small clay objects— spheres, cones, tetrahedra, animal heads, and more— some of them marked with patterns. Many were placed inside hollow clay balls (bullae), some of which were impressed on the outside with representations of the tokens inside.

The bullae may have accompanied goods as a record of what was shipped. Eventually it was realized that the actual clay tokens were unnecessary— the impressions into the surface were enough. Another advance was to record (say) three sheep not as ⊕⊕⊕— a system that didn't scale up easily to 30 or 300 sheep— but the more language-like 𒐈⊕.

The **quipu** of the Incas was also primarily an accounting system; numbers were represented as knots along a string, in a decimal notation. Some strings represented the totals of another set of strings, as in a spreadsheet. (There are some knot combinations that can't be interpreted as numbers, but not enough that the quipu could have been a full writing system.)

Another motivation for writing is **fortunetelling**; many of our earliest examples of Chinese writing are oracle bones, messages inscribed onto bones, which were then heated till they cracked, and omens divined from the cracks.

The writing system of Uyseʔ was derived from three separate sources:

- Accounting systems—including the numerals and glyphs for common goods
- Astronomical records— which gave the names of astronomical bodies and events such as eclipses, and thus a calendar

- Chronicles, starting with heraldic symbols for places and lineages; once symbols for common events were added ('accede, conquer, marry'), lists of kings became lists of events, and these could be read as sentences ("Mwatwor conquered Thestyet in the 14th year of his reign")

These branches each contributed early glyphs, as well as the motivation to write more and more complex messages.

Pictures

The first stage of creating a logographic system is to draw little pictures. These will be the graphemes of your system, and you can hardly have too many. Chinese for instance has about a thousand basic graphemes. Here's a sampling of the pictures I drew for Uyse?:

har man	*nyen* bed
hey flower	*hrin* long yam
fyer piebird chick	*se?* speak
hai shell	*fril* comet
 *hlim* boat	*kroy* sword

Don't worry about artistic ability— you *want* cartoony glyphs. We're going to stylize them later anyway.

One warning though: even tiny little drawings involve conworlding. A stick figure in a skirt for 'woman' implies that skirts are female attire. A crowned face for 'king' implies that the crown is a symbol of authority. *Kroy* above implies that Uytainese swords were straight rather than curved, *hlim* that boats had sails.

Obviously, the easy bits will be people, animals, everyday objects, and geometric relationships (*left, right, over, behind...*). Some concepts can be captured with a little cleverness... this is a chance to indulge your creativity and even humor. Here's some quirkier examples from Uyse?:

 *fwuy* wind	trees in the wind
 *fyat* year	seed, plant, harvest, snow
 *mwat* great	equally divided circle
 *pyey* I	person abasing himself
son count	face marked with soot as counted

thrum conquer	lord over enemy ancestors, army, fields
tur return	man turning back at a barrier
uy ancestor	ancestors' skulls were retained and venerated

Think about script direction— Uyseʔ is written right to left, so the man pictured for *tur* is turning back, not moving forward.

You'll run into concepts where you can't think of a picture— *green, mistake, myth, proverb, classical, font*. That's fine, we'll talk about how to represent these below.

On the other hand, don't worry if the association is obscure or very culture-specific. All we want are word → picture mappings; we don't need picture → word. It really doesn't matter if a neutral observer can guess what the picture represents.

Graphic variants

Some words that are hard to picture can be represented with tricks such as these:

- Rather than drawing a body part, mark the area on a schematic of the body or face.
- METONYMY: represent something with an associated item that's easier to draw, e.g. a scepter for 'king', an altar for 'god', a stick figure with a big head for 'baby'.
- Associated objects make good representations of verbs: a stylus or quill for 'write', a foot for 'go', a bed for 'sleep'.
- Double a symbol. Uyseʔ *ram* 'people' doubles the glyph for *har* 'man'. Chinese 林 *lín* 'forest' doubles 木 *mù* 'tree'.
- Combine two pictures. Uyseʔ is a picture of a man and a woman, originally used for *wimhwai* 'marriage'.[12] Chinese 東 *dōng* 'east' is a picture of the sun behind a tree.

[12] As the writing system matured glyphs were restricted to one syllable, so this glyph is now used only for *wim* 'acquire'.

The rebus principle

All known logographic scripts have eventually resorted to the rebus principle: using similar sounding words to represent things that are hard to picture. In English, we could imagine usages like the following:

word for...	borrowed for...
bear (animal)	*bear (put up with)*
half	*have*
peas	*peace*
bee	*be*
arrow	*error*
eye	*I*
shark	*shock*
nun	*none*
mirror	*mere*
field	*feel*
three	*free*

Chinese makes extensive use of the rebus principle— for instance, 辟 **piek* 'prince' was used for **piek* 'walk lamely', **biek* 'open', **biek* 'beat the breast', and half a dozen more. Often the principle has been obscured by two thousand years of sound change. E.g. 可 **khâiʔ* 'can' was used for **gâi* 'Yellow River', but the relationship is not so close in modern Mandarin *kě, hé*. Similarly 我 **ŋâiʔ* 'I' was used for **ŋâi* 'slanting', and these two words look quite different as Mandarin *wǒ, é*.

In my English examples I allowed several different kinds of phonetic substitution; you may want to make this narrower. Chinese, for instance, seems to have required that the syllables rhymed and that the initials were HOMORGANIC (pronounced at the same place of articulation, like *k, g*).

In Uyseʔ I followed the rule that the syllables must rhyme and the initials must be similar (either homorganic or acoustically similar, like *f* and *h*).

glyph	*word*	*borrowed for...*
	hre 'flow'	**he** 'be'
	phau 'jar'	**phrau** 'heavy'
	khet 'small bowl'	**khyet** 'if'

If you develop a syllabary from your system (p. 69), these 'sounds-like' decisions imply a phonological analysis, which may be important for later developments of the system. E.g. an Uyse? syllabary would probably ignore liquids and semivowels after an initial, as in the above table.

Grammatical endings

What if the language you're representing has extensive affixation, or is fusional? There are several approaches.

- Ignore the endings, as in early Sumerian. It's scandalous if you're used to an alphabet, but writing systems don't have to record everything.
- Use other glyphs for their phonetic value. E.g. for English *-ing* we might use the glyph for *ink*.
- Use glyphs for their meaning. E.g. the Akkadian dual affix could be represented by the numeral 2.
- As we'll see below, Japanese uses a syllabary for its grammatical endings.

Mandarin Chinese has one subsyllabic morpheme, the diminutive *-r*. Etymologically it derives from 儿 *ér* 'child', so it's written that way—e.g. 花儿 *huār* 'flower'.

Determiners

The principles above are likely to leave you with symbols that have a multitude of readings and meanings, making text a challenge to read. The usual solution is to add DETERMINERS, graphemes which disambiguate readings. These can be specially devised symbols, or simply other glyphs.

- A **semantic** determiner or SIGNIFIC, called a RADICAL in Chinese, gives a hint about the meaning. E.g. 河 *hé* '(Yellow) River', which we met above, is distinguished from 可 *kě* 'can' by the addition of the 'water' radical. Uyse?  *kroy* 'sword' was used for  *khwoy* 'trash' with the addition of the signific  *tri?* 'discard'.
- A **phonetic** determiner, or simply a PHONETIC, gives a hint about the sound. E.g. Sumerian  *an* 'sky' was also used for *dingir* 'god'. To indicate which was meant, glyphs reading *ra* or *na* would be appended, giving the final consonant.

A writing system can use one or both types of determiners. Chinese makes such extensive use of determiners that 95% of characters can be analyzed as a binary combination of radical + phonetic.

Determiners may simply be written next to the glyph they apply to, as in cuneiform. In Uyseʔ, significs are written in a smaller form beneath the phonetic. Chinese writes every syllable in a square, whether it's one stroke like 一 *yī* 'one' or a monster like 魔 *mó* 'devil'.

Same word or not?

Suppose we have two forms that sound the same (HOMONYMS). The English convention is that they're different words if they have different etymologies (e.g. *ear* of the head vs. *ear* of corn); otherwise they're just different senses of one word (e.g. a linguistic vs. a judicial *sentence*).

The people devising a script, however, have no dictionaries to consult; they can only guess at this. Consider Chinese 眉 *méi* 'eyebrow' and 楣 *méi* 'lintel'. The fact that the 'wood' radical was added to the latter suggests that the scribes thought of it as a homonym; but probably it was just a metaphorical extension of 'eyebrow'.

Chinese words can have multiple senses, of course— indeed, they have so many that word-for-word translation from Chinese usually ends in tears. E.g. 点 *diǎn* has the senses 'drop, drip', 'dot, point', 'a bit', 'aspect, feature', 'touch, skim', 'check over', 'select, order', 'hint', 'light, kindle', 'o'clock', plus idiosyncratic senses used in compounds, as in 点头 *diǎn-tóu* 'nod one's head', 点心 *diǎnxīn* 'dim sum'.

Stylization

Once you've drawn all those beautiful little pictures, it's time to wreck them. Glyphs simplify over the centuries, and soon enough the pictures aren't recognizable. (Egyptian hieroglyphics retained their complexity in inscriptions, but for everyday purposes people used a cursive called HIERATIC.)

Chinese characters have gone through many stages:

- The earliest Chinese characters, from the Shāng period in the second millennium BC, were clearly pictorial.
- Under the Qín dynasty (after 221 BC) forms were simplified and standardized as the seal script (*zhuànshū*), still used today as a decorative archaism.

- The bureaucracy developed a faster version named *lìshū* 'clerical script' characterized by its square forms; this is the basis for the traditional printed characters.
- Scribes later developed a cursive known as *cǎoshū* 'grass script', often allowing a complex character to be drawn as one stroke. These turn calligraphy into an art form, but are a chore to read.
- Finally the PRC simplified thousands of characters in the last century.

Here's a single character, *sī* 'silk', over the centuries:

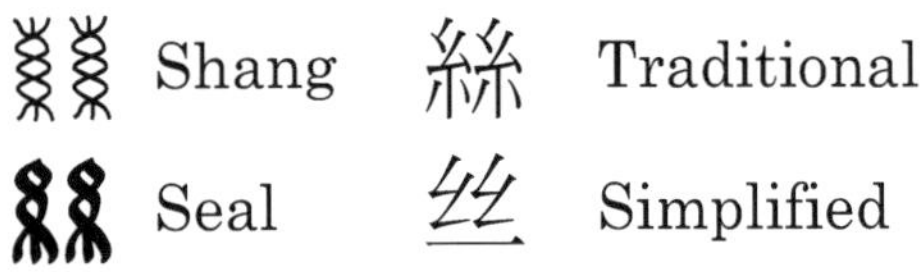
Shang
絲 Traditional
Seal
丝 Simplified

For Almea, I created a logographic system for Wede:i, which is clearly pictorial– e.g. *do:n* 'horse', *lu:* 'water'. The Axunemi adapted it to write their own language, and came to write all the glyphs as a combination of dots and straight lines; these two characters became . Finally, their descendants the Xurnese wrote them in a connected cursive: .

Here's an even more complicated example, showing a single character *hwai* 'woman' from Uyse? and its development over time and space. First, here are the ancient forms (~ Z.E. 1200) from three different regions:

Uykhrai
Krwŋ
Phetai

Then, historical developments within Uytai over the centuries:

1900
2100
2600
3000

Variants in the modern countries (Z.E. 3480):

Uytai
Hlüim
Nyandai

Finally, some historical and regional variations in the Bé languages which borrowed the writing system for their own use:

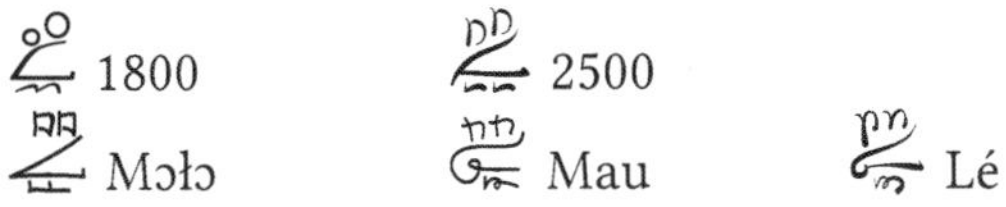
1800
2500
Mɔłɔ
Mau
Lé

I emphasize that I didn't create these variations for every character, only this one! But you should be aware how scripts change over time, and that the forms in everyday use are likely to be quite different from the pictorial origins of the script.

How exactly do you create such variations?

- Draw the character as fast as you can, multiple times—your hand will suggest simplifications.
- Abstract the shapes (as in above).
- Impose a change in medium, e.g. from painting (hieroglyphics) to pens (hieratic), or from pens (Roman alphabet) to carving in wood (runes), or from pen and ink to typography.
- Efficiency: in early cuneiform the stylus could be impressed at any angle, but in later cuneiform the range of angles was much reduced, requiring less effort.
- A change in orientation, as happened in Sumer: at some point all the characters were rotated 90° to the left.
- A change in aesthetic style— e.g. as you can see, the Bé preferred square rather than circular shapes.

Cross-language adaptations

Writing systems are rarely developed from scratch. Why go to all that work when you can adapt someone else's system?

The easiest approach is simply to write in the other guy's language. Assyrians learned to write Sumerian; 7th century Japanese wrote in Chinese; even today, literacy for Latin American Indians often means learning to write Spanish.

The rebus principle can be use to write a different language. It's like the 17th century joke that Latin *Ah, mihi beate Martine* 'Oh bless me, Martin' was overheard by an Englishman as "All my eye and Betty Martin." Japanese was once written using *manyōgana*, that is, Chinese characters used only for their sounds. A poem in the *Manyōshū* renders *fukushi* 'trowel' as 布久思, Middle Chinese **puo kjəu sɨ* (Mandarin *bù jiǔ sī*).[13]

---

[13] The bottom half of 思 is 心 'heart' which we met a few pages ago in 点心 'dim sum'. Learning to write Chinese is all about making these connections; what looks like a horrific mess of strokes is often a simple combination once you've mastered the commonest characters.

The phonologies of the languages will be different, complicating the process. For instance, Uyseʔ writing was borrowed for Lé, which had voicing and vowel distinctions Uyseʔ doesn't have, as well as tone. So *theʔ* 'hand' had to do for Lé syllables including *te, tes, de, des, tɛ, tɛs, dɛ, dɛs....* times five tones each. Unsurprisingly, the Lé needed to devise their own set of phonetic determiners to make the system work.

Another approach is to borrow by meaning. For instance, *advanced language construction* could be wrangled into Chinese script as 前进的语言建造 *qiánjìnde yǔyán jiànzhù.* This is *not* a translation, though you'd have to know some Chinese to know that— the syntax is all wrong for Chinese.

The problem with borrowing by meaning is that meanings don't line up neatly between languages. Grammatical words (pronouns, articles, demonstratives, adpositions) may work very differently, and even content words are a morass. E.g. *construction* should be handled differently depending on whether you mean 'something built' or 'a turn of phrase'.

As it happens, Japanese has a mixed system: content words are written in *kanji* (Chinese characters), while grammatical words and endings are written in *hiragana*, a syllabary ultimately derived from a standardized (and very stylized) set of *manyōgana.*

An example from *Ranma ½*:

> あたしはおねーちゃんと違って男なんか、大っ嫌いなの。
>
> **Atashi wa onēchan to chigatte otoko nanka, daik-kirai na no.**
>
> 1s topic elder.sister with differing boy and.so.on / big distasteful is
>
> *I don't share big sister's opinions about boys and such; I* ***hate*** *them.*

Four *kanji* are used (corresponding to the underlined bits of the transliteration); the rest of the characters are *hiragana.* Rather neatly, the simplicity of the *hiragana* makes it evident which words are *kanji.* Note that a Chinese reader could make almost nothing of the sentence!

Two other complications of Japanese writing are worth noting:

- Some content words don't have *kanji*, either because of script reform or because they're borrowed from English. Rather than use *hiragana*, these are written in yet another syllabary, *katakana*. E.g. *anime* is written アニメ.

- *Kanji* are used both for native Japanese words and for the mass of Chinese borrowings— e.g. 山 (Mandarin *shān*) is used both for native *yama* and borrowed *san*. Nothing about the glyph tells you which reading is meant! And to make it even worse, Chinese words were borrowed at different periods *with their contemporary pronunciations*, giving even more readings.

On to syllabaries

Once you have a logography, you're in a good place to develop a syllabary. Indeed, if you've followed my advice and liberally used the rebus principle, you probably already have one hiding in the logographic system.

All you need to do is inventory the possible syllables in your language and choose one symbol for each. Here, for instance, is the syllabary for one of my languages, Axunašin. Each glyph derives from a Wede:i logograph.

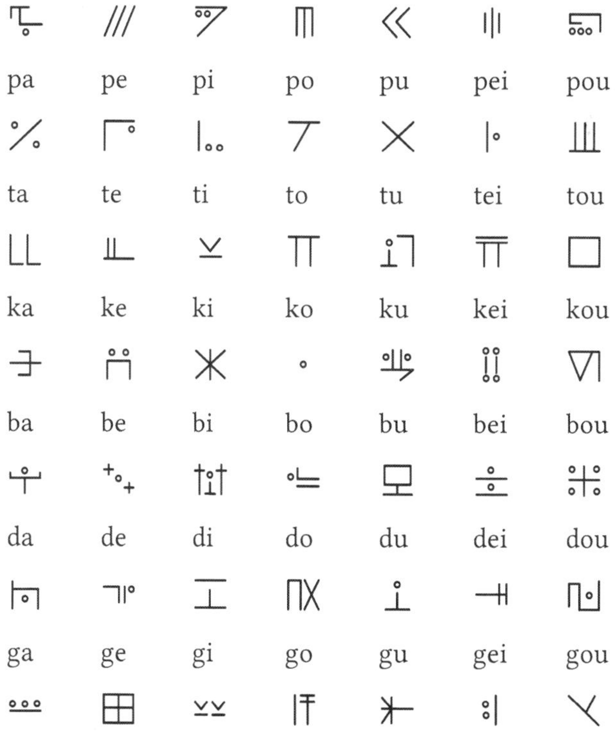
pa pe pi po pu pei pou
ta te ti to tu tei tou
ka ke ki ko ku kei kou
ba be bi bo bu bei bou
da de di do du dei dou
ga ge gi go gu gei gou

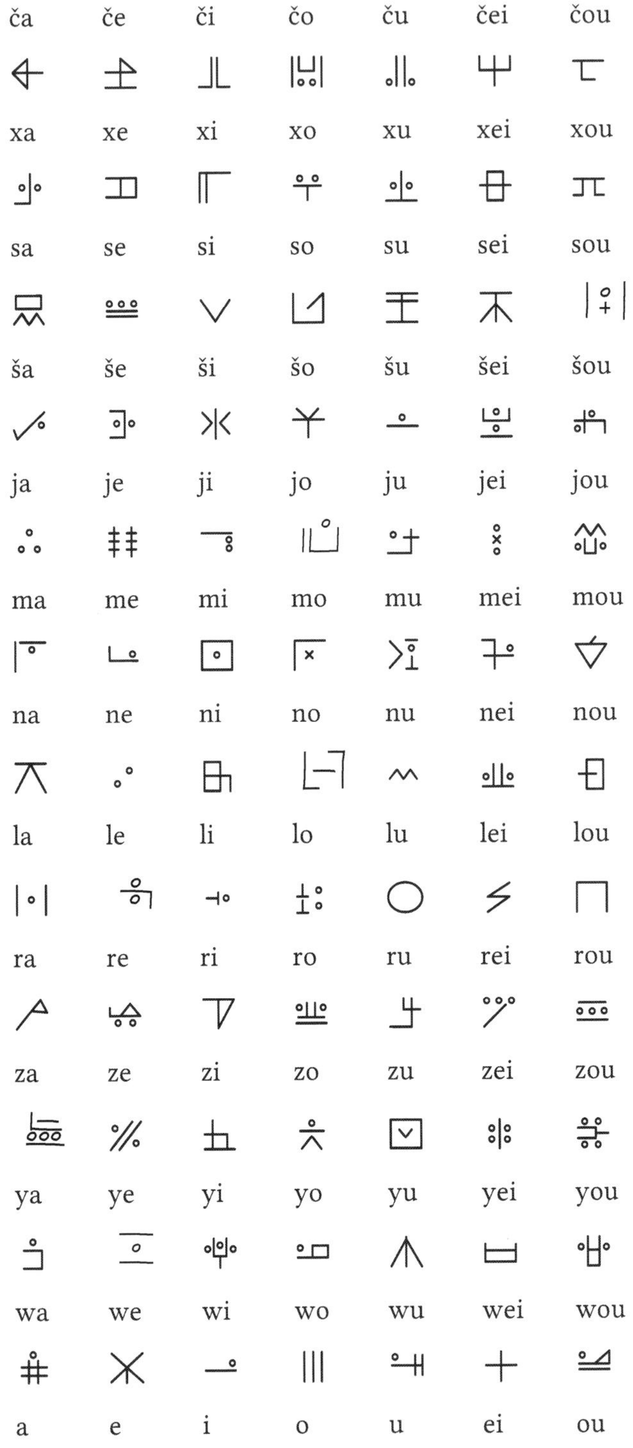

ča če či čo ču čei čou

xa xe xi xo xu xei xou

sa se si so su sei sou

ša še ši šo šu šei šou

ja je ji jo ju jei jou

ma me mi mo mu mei mou

na ne ni no nu nei nou

la le li lo lu lei lou

ra re ri ro ru rei rou

za ze zi zo zu zei zou

ya ye yi yo yu yei you

wa we wi wo wu wei wou

a e i o u ei ou

The syllabary need not be very phonemic— Linear B, for instance, used for writing Greek, merged voiced and voiceless consonants and largely ignored consonants at the end of a syllable.

If the syllabary continues in use for centuries, it will be affected by sound change. For instance, the row marked *ta te ti to tu tei tou* would be read in modern Xurnese as *ta te ci to cu ti te*, where *c* is [ts].

There are several options for dealing with consonant clusters:

- Provide glyphs for all the possibilities; this will be attractive only if your phonotactics are quite simple
- Ignore them— e.g. treat *pra, pya, pwa* as if they were *pa*
- Add diacritics; e.g. *pra* might be *pa* plus a special mark
- Treat extra consonants as if they were another syllable: e.g. *pra* could be spelled as if it were *pa-ra*
- A diacritic could cancel the vowel, turning *pa* into *p-*

The same techniques can handle syllable-final consonants— e.g. *pan* could be written *pan, pa, pã, pa-na, pa-n~~a~~*.

A syllabary need not displace a logography— the Axunemi, like the Japanese, continued to used hundreds of logographs.

Dictionaries

How do you sort a set of several thousand logographs so people can look up an unknown word? Chinese uses several methods (often more than one):

- Number of strokes. One of my dictionaries has a list running from 一 *yī* 'one' to the 27-stroke 纜 *lǎn* 'grasp'. There is a convention on how to count strokes— e.g. 口 *kǒu* 'mouth' is three strokes, not four.
- Angle of initial stroke (used as a sub-sort): horizontal stroke, vertical stroke, upward slash, downward slash.
- Group characters by radical. There were 214 traditional radicals, themselves sorted by stroke order from 一 *yī* 'one' to 龠 *yuè* 'flute'. (That's just a radical; it can be used as the basis for further characters such as 鑰 *yuè* 'lock'.)

- Group characters by rhyme and tone. This was the method used in dictionaries like the *Qièyùn* of AD 601, still important as a source of information on what rhymed in Middle Chinese.
- Sort by alphabetization; modern dictionaries often include a *pīnyīn* index.
- The four-corner method, where a digit is assigned based on what's in each corner of a character.[14] E.g. 法 *fǎ* 'law' is encoded as 3413:
    - 3 for downward slash (*diǎn* 'dot') in upper left
    - 4 for cross in upper right
    - 1 for horizontal stroke in lower left
    - 3 for downward slash in lower right

The dots and bars of Axunašin, a couple pages back, lend themselves to a systematic ordering.

- The top-level sort is by number of lines, ignoring the dots.
- Glyphs of *n* lines are organized by how the last line was added to a glyph of *n − 1* lines: underline, added vertical line, bisection, adjacent line, completion of a triangle, or oblique line. E.g.:

  ∘≐ *do* is an underline added to └ *te*

  ⋀ *wu* is a bisection of └ *te*

  ⊿ *šo* is an adjacent line added to ⊓ *rou*
- Next, glyphs are ordered by number of dots: e.g. after — *vume* 'two' comes ∸ *ju*, ¬ *mi*, °°° *ča*.
- Finally, rotations, mirror images, and differences in stroke length are listed after the base character; e.g. ⊥ is listed as a variant of 十, °⊥° after ⸫丅.

You need not go to the trouble of producing a dictionary in native order, but understanding the principles on which it works can be useful, as they may be applied to other things— consider how we number points in an document by letter of the alphabet, or have schoolchildren sit in alphabetical order.

[14] To be precise: if there are multiple strokes (as there usually are), you look at the one that's written first. (You're taught to write the strokes of a character in a particular, conventional order.)

Further reading

See "Writing English Chinese-style" on zompist.com for a detailed look at how English might be written in a system modeled on Chinese. DeFrancis's book below includes a chapter on how the Chinese system could be directly adapted to English.

The grammars of Uyse? and Wede:i on zompist.com include more details on their logographic systems.

The first of the books below is an excellent overview of writing systems in general; the second is the standard but expensive reference on *all* natlang writing systems. I've added some good books on specific writing systems.

Geoffrey **Sampson**, *Writing Systems* (1985)

Peter T. **Daniels** and William **Bright**, eds., *The World's Writing Systems* (1996)

Michael D. **Coe**, *Breaking the Maya Code* (1999)

John **DeFrancis**, *The Chinese Language: Fact and Fantasy* (1984)

Bernhard **Karlgren**, *Analytic Dictionary of Chinese and Sino-Japanese* (1923)

Pidgins and creoles

Pidgins and creoles are languages people devise in language contact situations where it's not practical to learn each other's language— trade, conquest, slavery— and could appear in your conworld in similar contexts. They should also be of interest to auxlangers, since pidgins are simplified, designed for quick learning.

Why don't people just learn the languages? Well, because learning languages takes years, and it requires sustained access to native speakers. Where pidgins develop, model speakers may be few, or come by only rarely.

Pidgins still require mastering hundreds of words and a fair amount of syntax, and creoles take even more effort. But speakers of the source languages often react to them with disdain. Keep this in mind if you're writing a narrative— the audience may assume certain things about a character when they hear "Mesa day startin pretty okee-day with a brisky morning munchy, then BOOM!"

Pidgins

A PIDGIN is a language that speakers of different languages work out for basic communication. It differs in two major ways from other languages:

- It's highly simplified compared to its source language(s).
- It isn't learned by children from native speakers, but by adult speakers who are inventing it as they go along.

Pidgins are an age-old phenomenon, and can develop whenever there's contact between people without a language in common. We can see the process beginning in interactions between a tourist and a shopkeeper, between a nanny and her employers, between traders. If such contact is prolonged and involves many people, a pidgin will develop.

There are several dozen pidgins that developed in the colonial era based on English, Spanish, French, and Portuguese. However, there are non-Indo-European pidgins and creoles too:

Pidgin/creole	*Based on*
Naga Pidgin	Assamese
Fanagalo	Xhosa
Kituba	Kikongo
Sango	Ngbandi
Juba	Arabic
Hiri Motu	Motu
Chinook Jargon	Chinook
Mobile Trade Language	Muskogean family

Many pidgins have one main source language, but they may also draw lexicon from several languages.

It's not uncommon for a group to teach outsiders a pidgin, keeping their actual language for themselves. In 1628 a Dutch minister, Michaëlius, complained that the Delaware Indians "rather design to conceal their language from us than to properly communicate it... and then they speak only half sentences, shortened words...; and all things which have only a rude resemblance to each other, they frequently call by the same name." There are similar stories from other centuries and other continents.

When pidgins acquire native speakers they become creoles; one confusing corollary is that most of the examples you may have heard of, such as Tok Pisin, are really not pidgins at all.

A pidgin can persist for generations, in which case its grammatical rules and lexicon will be stabilized; it can then be called a STABLE PIDGIN.

The word 'pidgin' may have originated as the Chinese Pidgin English word for *business.* This pidgin gave us a few expressions, such as *long time no see, chop chop, no go, look-see, chow [food], lose face.*

How do you create one?

Let's say that a pidgin develops between the Mounians and the Eruveros.

The source language depends on the details of the contact situation. Mounia is an advanced nation and the Eruveros are nomads, but it could still go either way. A few isolated Mounian traders might well use a simplified Eruvero. But let's say they're coming in numbers and founding settlements. In that case the pidgin is likely to be based on Mounian.

You should already have Mounian worked out. The more you know about Eruvero the better— at the least, work out the phonology.

- For the **phonology**, take the Mounian phonetic inventory and eliminate any sound not easily pronounced by the Eruveros. This may cause some mergers, and simplification of clusters.
- For **morphology**, the simplest thing is to throw it all out: all words appear in a single form. Tense and aspect can be expressed by particles.
- Keep the **syntax** simple. All those interesting exceptions I told you to put in— word order changes for pronominal objects, variant question formation, etc.— throw 'em out.
- Add some oddities from Eruvero. E.g. the way to form possessives, or the structure of the pronoun system, may look more like Eruvero than Mounian. The Eruveros might insist on evidentials, or dual pronouns, or measure words.
- Simplify the prepositions (if any)— you may be able to get along with three rather than thirty.
- Throw out most of the educated vocabulary. Replace some of it with paraphrases based on simpler words.
- Sprinkle in a light or heavy sampling of Eruvero words.

In all areas, remember that the Mounians who supply the vocabulary are traders, settlers, soldiers— people who will speak a very colloquial and sometimes vulgar register. (Cf. Tok Pisin *bagarap* 'break', from 'bugger up'.) Some of these people may trade in other areas too, so words from other contact situations might end up in the pidgin.

For extra credit, borrow some of the pidgin expressions back into standard Mounian.

If your pidgin is based on languages in the same family, it needn't be quite so simplified. Kituba, for instance, developed as a pidgin between Bantu speakers. It simplifies but retains the Bantu gender system, has nine tense/aspect particles (cf. the 17 in Kikongo), and its phonology includes tone.

A people may develop multiple pidgins, and carry over features in unusual ways. For instance, Russians used Russenorsk to talk to Norwegian fisherman, and developed Russo-Chinese Pidgin in Manchuria; both use SOV order— which is strange, as it isn't found in Russian, Norwegian, or Chinese! The explanation seems to be that earlier Russians had developed pidgins with speakers of SOV Turkic and Altaic languages. It evidently became an expectation of Russians that "foreigners use SOV", so this was extended to pidgins developed later, even though the generalization was wrong.

Creoles

A pidgin becomes a CREOLE once it has native speakers. Creoles are characterized by an expanded vocabulary and a more flexible, more complicated syntax.

Often the source language is a model, which leads to a process of DECREOLIZATION. This was common in colonial environments: educated natives learned the colonial language, dragging the creole closer and closer to its origins. The end result would be a version of the source with some local flavor.

The source language or ACROLECT is obviously prestigious, and high-status speakers may even deny that they speak the creole at all; however, the creole, as the language of the people, may be considered the language of solidarity and sincerity. In Haiti *palé français* means both "speak French" and "offer a bribe". In Jamaica, schoolboys actually moved away from standard English as they got older; apparently creole was perceived as more manly.

The creole/standard distinction isn't binary; there may be intermediate forms, as in these found in Jamaica:

English	*I didn't eat any*
	Ai didn it non
	A in nyam non
	Mi inn nyam non
Creole	*Mi na bin nyam non*

If you want to develop a creole conlang, the obvious method is to create a pidgin first, then restore some of the complexities from the source language. How far the process goes should be determined by your sociolinguistic situation, and may vary by class— often, the poor simply don't have the educational resources to learn the standard. The degree of contact with the colonial power may also be important; independent countries are more likely to make use of creoles in education and public information.

Origins

Pidgins the world over have some intriguing similarities of syntax; e.g. compare a French-based creole from the Caribbean with an English-based one from Cameroon, as well as to their source languages:

Haitian Creole	*li*	*pa*	*te*	*konẽ*
Kamtok	*i*	*no*	*bin*	*sabi*
French	*il n'a pas connu*			
English	*he didn't know*			

There are various explanations for this; the most intriguing is that both European-based creoles are in fact related— that they all derive from the Italian-based Lingua Franca, which was the lingua franca of the Mediterranean in the Middle Ages. The Portuguese would have spread a Portuguesized version to the coast of Africa, then to Brazil and China; and the local versions were RELEXIFIED as different colonial overlords took over. A tantalizing clue to this process is the existence of some Iberian vocabulary even in English-based pidgins and creoles, e.g. *sabi* 'know' ('savvy', from *saber*) and *pikanini* 'child' (from *pequeninho* 'little one').

This is an idea you can adapt to your world. E.g. in my conworld Almea the great navigators of southern Ereláe were the Jei, and undoubtedly Jei-based pidgins sprang up. These might have been relexified under the influence of later peoples— Gurdagor, Xurnese, Skourenes, Tžuro. In the north the first traders were Meŝaiun, and Meŝaiun-based pidgins would have been relexified by the Verdurians and Kebreni.

Another explanation is that the language contact situation brings out the default syntax of the language organ. However, this looks less reasonable when we look at other creoles:

- Hiri Motu places the negative at the end (*Lau mai [lasi]* 'I'm [not] coming'),
- Tok Pisin adds an agreement particle: 'He didn't know' would be *Em i no bin save.*
- The Russo-Chinese pidgin of Kjaxta is SOV, has postpositions, and puts negatives after the verb (all Altaic features).
- Chinese Pidgin includes an obligatory measure word (*piece*) after numerals, and requires the copula with predicate nouns but not predicate adjectives.

If creators of pidgins are following universal grammar, why couldn't they agree on these details?

Tok Pisin

To get a favor of what pidgins and creoles look like, let's take a deeper (but still superficial) look at Tok Pisin.

Tok Pisin is an English-based creole that's one of the official languages of Papua New Guinea, a region with hundreds of mutually unintelligible languages. It has at least two million speakers, and tens of thousands of native speakers.

Its phonological inventory can be described as English Lite. It's lost the ð and θ sounds, and merged [ʃ tʃ dʒ] as *j* [dʒ]— which however many speakers merge with *s*. English *f* becomes *p*. English's rich array of vowels is reduced to *a e i o u*, plus the diphthongs *ai au oi*.

Here's a sample sentence:

> **Em i lukim mi.**
>
> 3s 3.agr look-trans 1s
>
> *He looks at me.*

All the words derive from English: "Him, he look-'im me." Your first reaction to seeing a swatch of Tok Pisin may be that it's "just bad English". Try to get past this and notice some of the interesting things going on here— things that are not mere simplifications.

- In the third person, sentences require an AGREEMENT PARTICLE *i*, even if the subject is an NP: *Bill i luk-im mi.* Compare colloquial French *Lui i me r'garde moi.*
- Transitive verbs are explicitly marked with the *-im* suffix. This can be used derivationally: cf. *wok* 'work' → *wokim* 'make, build'.

Word order is SVO; negatives are formed with *no (Em i no karim ruksak* 'He's not carrying a bag'); and yes-no questions by intonation (*Yu get plet?* 'Do you have a plate?).

The pronoun system, like the language itself, looks like a steely-eyed accountant was told that words cost money and eliminated everything he could.

1s	mi	*1pi*	yumi
		1px	mipela
2s	yu	*2p*	yupela
3s	em	*3p*	ol

But note the differences from English: 'he, she, it' have collapsed down to *em*, and inclusive and exclusive 'we' are distinguished. In some areas we find dual pronouns like *mitupela* 'two of us (excl.)' and *yumitupela* 'two of us (incl.)', and in areas where the local languages have TRIAL forms, there are trial pronouns like *yumitripela.*

The suffix *-pela* (from 'fellow') is here used as a plural; it's also suffixed to demonstratives, numbers and adjectives (*dispela* 'this', *tripela* 'three', *bikpela* 'big'). Nouns can be pluralized with *ol (ol man* 'the men'), but this isn't necessary if a number is given.

Verbs don't conjugate for number and person— but since the source language is English, this is a fancy way of saying that our 3s ending *-s* isn't used.

It isn't necessary to mark tense, but the particles *bin / bai* may be used to mark past and future: *Ol kakaruk i bin ranawe* 'the chickens ran away'; *Bai mi go long taun* 'I'm going into town'.[15]

Perfective aspect can be marked with the particle *pinis*: *Mi ritim nius-pepa pinis* 'I finished reading the newspaper.' There are also ways of expressing ongoing and habitual actions:

> **Em raun i stap bilong pain-im wok.**
>
> 3s go.round 3.agr cont of find-trans work
>
> *He's walking around looking for work.*
>
> **Em i save kaikai ol man.**
>
> 3s 3.agr hab eat pl. person
>
> *It used to eat people.*

There's only two prepositions: *bilong* for possessives (*haus bilong mi* 'my house'), *long* for everything else.

There are several ways to form relative clauses. One of the simplest is simple concatenation, without a relativizer.

> **Dispela man i kam asde em i papa bilong mi.**
>
> this man 3.agr come yesterday 3s 3.agr father of 1s
>
> *This man who came yesterday is my father.*

---

[15] It's no surprise that *bin* comes from 'been', but *bai* is less obvious; it's from 'by and by'.

An alternative is to bracket the expression with a pair of markers *ya.* (We use such bracketing in written language, and in computer languages, but it seems to be rare in natlangs.)

> **Dispela man ya em i stap long bus ya em i redi na em i kisim bonara.**
>
> this man sub 3s 3.agr stay loc bush sub 3s 3.agr ready and 3s 3.agr get-trans bow.and.arrows
>
> *This man who lived in the bush was ready to get his bow and arrows.*

There's yet another alternative— using relative pronouns such as *husat* 'who' and *we* 'where'.

Mixed languages

Thomason & Kaufman describe a rare phenomenon (they can only find six examples) they call a MIXED LANGUAGE, where grammatical features are taken from multiple languages with their full complexity. Some examples:

- Michif, which combines the complex verbal morphology of Cree with the nominal morphology and syntax of French.

  Cree demonstratives are used alongside French articles, producing NPs such as *lɪ šiẽn šakwala ana* 'that brown dog' which illustrate two simultaneous types of gender agreement: *lɪ* 'the' is masculine, *ana* 'that' is animate.

- Mednyj Aleut, which retains Aleut nominal declension and non-finite verbal morphology, but takes its finite verbal morphology from Russian. A comparison of some present tense forms for 'sit':

	Bering Aleut	*Mednyj Aleut*	*Russian*	
1s	uŋuči-ku-q	uŋuči-ju	я сижу	*ja sižu*
2s	uŋuči-ku-x̣t	uŋuči-iš	ту сидишь	*ty sidiš*
3s	uŋuči-ku-x̣	uŋuči-it	он сидит	*on sidit*

- Ma'a takes most of its vocabulary, and a few structural features, from Cushitic, while the rest of the lexicon and almost all of the grammar are Bantu.

Such languages obviously arose in contact situations, but unlike pidgins and creoles, these are not a case of speakers simplifying a language they haven't learned perfectly. To create such languages, speakers must be fully bilingual. They seem to arise when there is great social pressure to learn the contact language, but a very strong desire to retain one's cultural identity.

The same drive may underlie Anglo-Romani, which uses English grammar with Romani lexicon: *Jel cause mandi's gonna del dobba* 'Go, because I'm going to hit him.' A relexified English has an obvious utility as a secret language as well as a badge of identity.

Another striking contact situation is that of the village of Kupwar (actually a pseudonym), where the local varieties of Urdu and Marathi (Indic) and Kannada (Dravidian) have modified each other to the extent that they can be seen as three lexicons sharing a single grammar and phonology. Note the word-for-word equivalence in this sample:

Ghoḍi di ya kya? *(Kupwar Urdu)*

Ghoḍi dil əs kay? *(Kupwar Marathi)*

Kudri kwaṭṭ i yan? *(Kupwar Kannada)*

horse sold you what

Did you sell the horse?

This is close enough to standard Marathi, but standard Urdu would place the question element first (*Kya ghoṛii dii?*), while standard Kannada forms questions another way, using a verbal suffix *-a*.

This linguistic situation has persisted for several hundred years, probably because the three languages are so marked socially: Kannada is the language of the Jain landowners and Lingayat craftsmen, Urdu that of Muslim landowners, and Marathi that of landless laborers (but it's also used in education and inter-caste communication).

None of the above

Around the 1960s linguists started to pay attention to pidgins and creoles. Perhaps inevitably, many people got a little too excited and started seeing creoles everywhere they looked.

It's sometimes suggested, for instance, that English is a creole. It's not; that would require that it developed from a pidgin, and there was simply never a situation when the normal genetic transmission of the language from Old English was interrupted. 50,000 or so Normans ruled over millions of English; this greatly affected English but did not pidginize it.

In any case English is by no means a unique or divergent example of language contact. It prodigiously borrows vocabulary, but Japanese and Quechua have borrowed just as much. Its morphology is simpler than German, but this is really shared with other coastal Germanic dialects... e.g. Swedish has simplified the verbal morphology even more: verbs aren't inflected by number and person— even 'to be' is *är* throughout.

A case has also been made for the period of Norse rule in England, but this was concentrated in the north of England and didn't affect standard English so much. (Nonetheless contact was intimate enough that our pronouns *she* and *they* were borrowed from Norse.)

The simplification of morphology is a common process worldwide and doesn't need to be explained via pidginization. Much of the inflectional complexity of Old English was lost before the Norman Conquest. (And it's balanced by complicating processes. It's now thought, for instance, that languages like Greek and Sanskrit *complicated* the originally simpler morphology of Indo-European.)

African-American Vernacular English (AAVE) is not a creole... though it probably developed from one. Slaves very likely developed a pidgin to communicate with each other and with their masters; some early representations of slave speech do resemble creoles. However, if slave speech was a creole, centuries of contact with whites have decreolized it, and it's best thought of as a distinctive dialect closely related to that of southern whites.

Further reading

This chapter is heavily indebted to these books, which I recommend for further reading:

Anatole V. **Lyovin**, *An Introduction to the Languages of the World* (1997)— for the description of Tok Pisin

Sarah Grey **Thomason** & Terrence **Kaufman**, *Language Contact, Creolization, and Genetic Linguistics* (1988)

Loreto **Todd**, *Pidgins and Creoles* (1974)

Life cycles

Languages have lives: they originate somewhere, they thrive for awhile, they coexist with their peers, and eventually they die. We can't take the metaphor too far but at least it allows us to put all these things in one chapter.

Proto-World

As language families have been discovered, some linguists have postulated that all languages are related and derive from "Proto-World", and some have even tried to reconstruct a few words of it.

My aim here is to discourage the idea. We know almost nothing of how language originated, but based on the size of hominid brains and on archeological remains (such as burials with evident ritual purposes), we've probably had language for 100,000 years, and perhaps twice that.

As a suggestive data point, Hans Henrich Hock offers these cognate pairs, from Hindi and English:

cakkā	*wheel*
pāñc	*five*
sī̃:g	*horn*
c^hai	*six*
pissū	*flea*

Just to ram the point home, these words are ***related***, and that's what just 6000 years of sound change did to them. After ten or twenty times that length of time, any cognates from Proto-World will be unrecognizable.

But proponents provide lists of apparent cognates! Yes they do; unfortunately, this sort of parlor game is far easier than most people imagine. Our brains love apparent patterns, and we see something like *day* vs. Latin *dies* and think they *must* be related. But such matches aren't really that close, and in a vocabulary of thousands of words there are plenty of opportunities to find random matches. [16] That's why only the

[16] I go over this in detail in "How likely are chance resemblances between languages?" on zompist.com.

COMPARATIVE METHOD (*LCK* p. 167) is considered good evidence for language relationships.

I'd also emphasize that languages, unlike people, need not derive from a common ancestor. If you're reading this book, you know that it's possible to construct a language from scratch!

Some people imagine an early situation in which some early humans, newly invented language in hand, eliminated everyone else, thus ensuring that their invention became Proto-World. It should be sufficient to point out that humans didn't even manage to wipe out the great apes, who have no language at all.

As well, we have no reason to believe that some humans had "language" and some did not. Biological advances don't work like that, and most cultural inventions don't either. Very likely the invention of language proceeded in stages, with a good deal of interchange between groups.

Primitivese

Where linguists fear to tread, of course, you the conworlder can stride in confidence: you can create Proto-Your-Planet if you like, or a sequence of communications strategies from a couple isolated signals to a fully developed language.

Most writers' attempts seem to be based on pidgins (p. 74); the irony is that these are way too sophisticated to be believable models for very early language! Consider the famous *Me Tarzan, you Jane.* Pronouns, terms whose referent varies by context, strike me as a very advanced concept. We might say the same of names— arbitrary labels for individuals, something I don't think exists in any animal signaling.

Derek Bickerton compared the (signed) utterances produced by the chimpanzee Nim Chimpsky, of which the most complex is

> *Give orange me give eat orange me eat orange give me eat orange give me you*

with Russenorsk:

> *If you buy— please four pood. If you no buy— then goodbye.*

He suggested that the pidgin is "hardly more complex", but that's hard to believe! Nim's sentence is repetitive babbling with no apparent syntax. The pidgin sentence is highly structured, has no unnecessary words, and uses complex concepts such as numerals and conditionals (as well as the ideas of sales and money).

For inspiration, we might look at various animal communication signals:

- Vervet monkeys have distinct alarm signals (and responses) for leopards, snakes, and eagles. There are other animals with species-specific alarm calls; curiously, apes don't have them. The vervets have about three dozen calls in all, including one made by a lost infant, and one called the 'anti-copulatory squeal-scream'.
- Jackdaws have distinctive signals for predators, for antisocial behaviors (e.g. nest stealing), for the desire to move out and for the desire to go home. Young jackdaws signal to their parents for food, and these signals are readopted by couples in love as endearments. Tellingly, most of these signals are provoked automatically by the right context— a bird will generate them even if there aren't other jackdaws around to hear.
- Bees have a dance which encodes the distance, quality, and direction of a food source; swarming bees use the same mechanism to signal potential colony sites.

Though these examples don't tell us much about early language, they suggest some of the topics hominids would have wanted to discuss. Nim's utterance might also be a glimpse into the world before syntax.

Animal talk

For the vervets, look up Robert Seyfarth; for the bees, Karl von Frisch. Run right out and read Konrad Lorenz's *King Solomon's Ring* for jackdaws and more.

There've been probably too many attempts to get chimpanzees to use human languages. It's more fruitful to look at how they communicate by themselves; a good place to start is Jane Goodall's *In the Shadow of Man.*

Language acquisition

Why should a conlanger study language acquisition? One reason is that if you're interested in simplicity at all, the speech of young children is a real world example of a simplified language. Another is that it offers insights into how human language works— more than one theory of language use has foundered when it can't explain the way children actually speak.

Increasing competence

Acquisition studies are conceptually simple: the parent sits around with a notebook or tape recorder and records everything the child says. The progression looks like this (ages are given as *year; month* and should be taken as averages):

0;6 – 0;9	babbling (repetitive, meaningless patterns)
0;9 – 1;6	one-word utterances
1;6 – 2;0	two-word utterances, various semantic relationships
2;0 – 2;6	multiword sentences missing most form words
2;6 +	grammatical structures appear

Infants aren't just slacking; they're learning to attend to language, to recognize phonetic patterns, to break down what they hear into phonemes, and to produce these themselves— all prerequisites to listening and talking.

The babbling stage moves from making all sorts of sounds to making only those used in the target language.

Open and back vowels like [u o a] are usually learned first, before the front vowels [i e]. Consonants seem to move the other way: labials first (presumably because it's easy to see what adults are doing when they produce these sounds), then dentals, then velars. Stops come before fricatives and affricates, and the liquids [l r] can come quite late.

Children learn vocabulary at an impressive and accelerating rate. At first (at 1;0) they learn a word a week; by 2;0 it's up to a word a day; in elementary school they chug along at 10 words a day. At all stages, comprehension far outpaces production: e.g. at 1;0 children can say about ten words but understand 100.

Children's **first words** include proper names (*Mommy, Karen*), nouns (*shoe, lunch*), verbs (*skate, kiss*), social words (*bye-bye*), and adjectives (*hot*). Sometimes it takes time to get the meaning right— e.g. *doggie* may be OVEREXTENDED to other animals, or UNDEREXTENDED to mean just one stuffed animal.

One-word utterances can be called HOLOPHRASES, to emphasize that they represent an entire communicative intention. E.g. a toddler might say *phone* to mean *the phone is ringing, I'm using the phone, that's a phone,* or *pick me up so I can talk on the phone.*

The two-word stage includes utterances like these:

doggie bark	*more milk*
mommy sit	*more sing*

put book	*ball table*
see baby	*allgone juice*
mommy gone	*all clean*
light off	*big ball*
no bed	*there daddy*

It's pretty clear that these follow regular patterns, but it's a bit controversial what those patterns are: is the child following (but failing to match) adult grammar, or using a simple grammar of her own?

After this children keep adding complexities. The following chart is based on Michael Tomasello's data and shows the typical order and age progression for English-speaking children.

negation: nonexistence, rejection (*No!*)	1;7 +
negation of sentences	2;0 +
ditransitives (e.g. *give*)	3;0
resultatives (*lick clean*)	3;0
transitive verbs	3;6
modals (*must, should)*	4;0
this, that related to closeness to hearer	4
a vs. *the*	4;6
past anterior (*when he came in I had finished)*	4;6
sentential objects (*he thinks that P*)	4 – 5
passives	4 – 5
full understanding of subjects	5 – 6
scope (e.g. understanding that in *He wanted to drive Bill's car* the pronoun can't refer to Bill)	6+

The ages refer to mastery, not first use. Mastering transitives means being able to use an entirely new transitive verb without just echoing an adult. Properly we can use *the X* only when we know the listener can identify which X we're talking about; this sort of modeling of other people's knowledge doesn't come early.

One study of three children from different families found that the children acquired negation in four stages:

- **no** + S: *no want stand head, no play that*
- NP + NEG + VP: *he no bite you, I can't catch you*
- NP + AUX + NEG + VP: *Paul can't have one, I didn't spilled it, I am not a doctor*
- adult rule— no tense on main verb: *I didn't spill it*

This is clearly the use of more and more correct rules. It's worth noting that the stages overlapped, as if the new rule was being applied tentatively.

The distinction between *The duck is easy to bite* and *The duck is anxious to bite* (p. 26) is completely missed by 6 year olds.

Cross-linguistically, questions are learned in a particular order: first *what/where*, then *who*, then *how/why*, then *when*.

Also cross-linguistically, children under 2 seem to prefer using the past tense for actions seen as TELIC (with a clear endpoint) and PERFECTIVE (p. 134)— *broke, made*— and the present or progressive for atelic, imperfective actions— *playing, riding*. This has been held to indicate that aspect comes before tense, but it's more likely that the children are just reproducing what they hear. They do quite well on tests of whether tense is correctly understood.

Do these stages vary by language? Absolutely! For instance, Turkish-speaking children start using case suffixes at around 2;0; as they're agglutinative and regular, they're learned very easily. In contrast the more complex and inconsistent case endings of Serbo-Croatian are learned later. Agglutinative case actually seems easier to learn than word order (are you auxlangers listening?).

Korean topic markers are learned soon after 2;0, followed a bit later by evidentials.

Gender systems take years to acquire. English-speaking children of 4;2 may still not be using *he* and *she* consistently. Icelandic children tested with nonsense words didn't use morphological information to assign gender before the age of 7. A very thorough study of German children found that they were applying phonological rules as early as 3;2, but hadn't mastered the whole system at 8. Dalila Ayoun finds even French adults making errors (p. 129).

Errors

Children make errors, of course, which has probably been a source of amusement back to the Neolithic. Their errors are of interest to linguists because they suggest what rules the children have and haven't learned.

In English, it's often noticed that children properly use irregular past tense forms, then lose many of these in favor of overgeneralized regular forms (*goed, runned*). Obviously, at that point they've learned that adding *-ed* is a rule.

We've seen problems with categories above; a similar problem is not quite grasping transitivity restrictions: *Don't giggle me! Go it in the box.*

It's not hard to teach them words, but they can be incredibly resistant to correction, as in this conversation collected by Martin Braine:

> *Child: Want other one spoon, Daddy.*
> *Father: You mean, you want the other spoon.*
> *Child: Yes, I want other one spoon, please, Daddy.*
> *Father: Can you say "the other spoon"?*
> *Child: Other... one... spoon.*
> *Father: Say "other".*
> *Child: Other.*
> *Father: "Spoon."*
> *Child: Spoon.*
> *Father: "Other... spoon."*
> *Child: Other... spoon. Now give me other one spoon.*

As we'll see below, one reason for this stubbornness may be that children are almost always using constructions they've used before—they're very cautious about trying out new ones. Plus, they've learned to discount a lot of what adults say! They pick up what they can understand and have to leave the rest alone.

Parents often do correct children, or provide more correct rephrasing: *Doggie bark? —Yes, the doggie is barking.* Curiously, such corrections may slow down language acquisition... not because they're not heeded, but because they're boring. A study by Courtney Cazen found that children progressed faster when parents instead offered a response or expansion: *Yes, he's trying to frighten the cat* or *Yes, tell him to be quiet.*

Young children pretty much fail at narration— setting the scene, telling stories in order. From Carole Peterson:

> *Child: He bite my leg.*
> *Adult: What?*
> *Child: Duck bite my leg.*
> *Adult: The dog bit your leg. Oh, oh, the duck. Oh boy!*
> *Child: Me go in the water.*
> *Adult: You went in the water?*
> *Child: Yeah. My leg.*

This child's age was 2;3. By five, children are able to introduce participants properly and relate incidents in order.

Both narrative and syntax (e.g. article usage) require an understanding of *what other people know*. Young children use these features based only on what *they themselves* know.

Rats, pigeons, children

B.F. Skinner suggested (in *Verbal Behavior,* 1957) that children learn language by OPERANT CONDITIONING— the association of tasks with rewards. You can easily train a rat to press a bar a certain number of times to get a food pellet; an utterance like *Please pass the bread* could be a response to a feeling of hunger. No complex mental mechanisms were needed.

Noam Chomsky's 1959 review in *Language* largely destroyed this position. For one thing, speech is not predictable in the same way that trained rat behavior is— the same feeling of hunger does not produce the same utterance. And as Roger Brown concluded from watching mother-child interactions, mothers reward true statements, not grammatical ones. There is no real reward for correct utterances at all.

Chomsky went on to show that utterances have a constituent structure, which are used by syntactic processes; e.g. to form questions in English we can move the auxiliary verb to the front:

> *The rats can handle only simple operations.*
>
> → *Can the rats handle only simple operations?*

Children handle this with great facility— they never try simpler rules like 'move the second word to the front'. This suggests that there *is* some complex internal representation going on.

He also emphasized the creative aspect of language: humans regularly produce entirely novel utterances. Operant conditioning can't produce this level of variability.

Is grammar innate?

Now, Chomsky maintains that syntax is innate– we're born with a complete UNIVERSAL GRAMMAR, and all the child has to do is figure out how to set a few switches (PARAMETERS) once she discovers that she's learning English rather than Ojibwe. He supports this idea with the POVERTY OF STIMULUS argument, which claims that there is far too little linguistic input to learn the full complexity of syntax.

But in fact children proceed very slowly, and rely heavily on the data they hear. Michael Tomasello had a rich corpus for one two-year-old, who was at the two-word stage— six weeks of data. He took the last half-hour, containing 455 distinct utterances, and compared each one to the previous weeks of data.

- 78% were word-for-word duplicates of previous utterances.
- 18% were copies of previous utterances with one minor change.
- Just 4% had two changes, though in each case the particular changes were themselves already attested.

Almost all the utterances fit simple constructions such as *Where's X, There's a X, I-wanna X, More X, I'm X-ing it, Throw X, X gone.*

That is: the vast majority of utterances were things the child had said before, or very minor variations on them. Children's resistance to correction has been taken as meaning that they don't imitate adult speech. But now we see that they don't do it because a single instance isn't enough data for them. They don't venture to use a new construction till they've heard it many times and are confident they know how to use it.

A nice confirmation of this: children learning inflectional languages don't learn the six person/number combinations at the same rate. They first master the ones with the highest frequency in adult speech– e.g. 1s before 3p. Again, they're learning by imitation, and it takes a huge amount of repetition for them to learn something. They also seem to learn each verb paradigm separately— it takes a long time before they start generalizing.

Another supposed bit of evidence that children don't imitate adult speech is that they make errors like *Her open it.* But Tomasello points out children hear plenty of expressions like *Let her open it* or *Help her open it.* They're reproducing *part* of an utterance that they've heard without understanding the whole thing. They don't make mistakes like *Mary hit I,* because that never occurs in what they hear. (Braine's *other one spoon* looks like a confusion of *(the) other one* and *(the) other spoon.*)

A child may use what seems like a complex construction, but it can be an illusion. For instance, Tomasello found that 2 years olds say *I think...* But at that age they didn't have other forms (*she thinks, you think, I don't think, I thought,* or even *I think that*). So this is not real subordination; rather, they're using *I-think* to mean *maybe.*

Now, why is all this striking? Because it doesn't fit at all with an innate, complete understanding of syntax. If all kids had to do was flip switches, they wouldn't *struggle* like this. They aren't born knowing the patterns of language; they have to laboriously acquire them, adding new features only after they've been exposed to a load of data.

Joint attentional frames

How *do* children learn language? Tomasello believes that the key is the ability, appearing at about 2 years of age, to maintain JOINT ATTENTIONAL FRAMES. That is, the child interacts with an adult, about some situation. The key word is *attention*: the child only now can understand that others have mental states, and seek to affect them. Animal language is all about *expressing states*: the animal is horny or hungry, or wants to go home, or sees a predator. Other animals may react to these expressions, but they're not intended as *communication*— in fact the animal is likely to make the same expressions when alone. What distinguishes human language is the ability to model other minds (and thus to try to affect them).

Joint attentional frames are Tomasello's response to Willard Quine's dilemma about OSTENSION: pointing to a rabbit, do we mean the rabbit, the rabbit's foot, the act of running, the color of the fur, or a bag of rabbit parts?

Ostension is of less use than we might think in language learning. Verbs, for instance, are most often used not to point out an ongoing action, but to describe one that just occurred or that's about to occur—neither of which can be pointed to. Even nouns often occur when not present (*Where's Daddy? What does a cow say?*). And you can't point at something to teach the meaning of *of* or *if*.

What the frames provide is meaning and context. Basically, toddlers learn language because it's the commentary to a situation they already understand. (To put it another way, if you leave the TV on, they won't learn about elections or *American Idol*. There's no attentional frame to give them a handle on the words from the TV, so they don't learn anything from it.) A child *won't* learn 'rabbit' from a random act of pointing. They learn the word in a familiar, information-rich context: playing with a pet, visiting a zoo, reading a book, whatever. They already understand what the adult is doing and what the utterance means, and they can use that to figure out what any unfamiliar words mean.

Item by item learning

The parameters theory implies that when a parameter is learned, a whole grammar-wide competence should click into place, and performance should improve. But looking closely at children's utterances, Tomasello found that they proceeded not feature by feature, but construction by construction.

For instance, at one point a child might use *cut* only in one simple construction (*cut X*), while *draw* might be used in several (*draw X, draw X on Y, X draw on Y, draw X for Y*). Learning *cut*, children don't really have a concept of the verb's subject and object. They learn that verb's particular slots: *cutter* and *thing cut*. It's only much later that they abstract out general syntactic categories like subject; and particular items may indeed remain as anomalies in adult speech.

Along the same lines, there may be restrictions in what can fill a slot— e.g. one child of 1;11 had a possession construction (*mummy shoe*) but the only possessors allowed were Mummy and Daddy. A month later other possessors appeared.

Some of these findings cast doubt on long-held assumptions in generative grammar, such as that questions (*Where's the rabbit?*) are transformations of statements (*The rabbit is in the box*). Tomasello points out that for many children, the first multi-word constructions they produce *are* questions: *where X, what's X?* They can hardly be transforming statements when they're not producing statements yet. Rather, they learn the questions because they hear similar questions from adults.

Gimme book!

Tomasello's *Constructing a Language* is meaty though quite technical. Jean Aitchison's *Words in the Mind* is an accessible overview. Steven Pinker's *The Language Instinct* presents a more Chomskyan viewpoint.

Eve Clarke's *The Lexicon in Acquisition* is very useful, and David Singleton's *Language Acquisition: The Age Factor* surveys the data on child vs. adult acquisition.

Bilingualism

For many Americans, it's unusual to hear someone speaking a language besides English and rare to run into someone who can't speak it. Worldwide, and over history, it's the US that's anomalous. The norm is to speak at least two languages.

There's several ways this can happen, all of which you can model in your conworld.

- People are likely to learn their **neighbors'** languages— all the more so if (say) you're a hunter-gatherer or a mountain farmer whose home community only numbers a few hundred or a few thousand people anyway.

- The country has been occupied by a small number of **invaders**, who form an elite speaking their own language— the Normans in England, the Manchu in China. As these examples indicate, the language of the majority tends to win out over the centuries.
- The country is taken over by a major metropolitan power, uniting regions that don't have a common language anyway and sending in **settlers**— the Romans in Spain and Gaul, the Spanish and Portuguese in Latin America. Here the imperial language may win out, but in premodern times the native languages may persist indefinitely outside of official contexts.

  Don't assume that the conqueror wants everyone to use their language. As Bruce Mannheim points out, the Spanish in Peru benefitted from the Indians continuing to speak Quechua, and even took measures against community leaders who spoke Spanish too well. If you don't know the conquerors' language you can't protest easily or understand the laws used against you.
- A colonial situation created a **pidgin** (p. 74) which is used for the everyday life of the nation, while the source language is used for education, the bureaucracy, and literature.
- The nation has its own language, but the **elite** learn a foreign language in order to connect with the wider world. The obvious example is English all over, but an intriguing case is the Russian Empire during the Napoleonic wars, where the nobility was often most comfortable speaking French, the language of the country they were at war with.
- A **dead language** may also be convenient, even essential, for scholarship, especially as vernaculars diverge. European elites learned Latin till the early 20th century, while Chinese learned *wényán* (classical Chinese) and Muslims learned classical Arabic.
- An **ethnic minority** has a near monopoly on trading, finance, banking, or some other useful profession, and continues to use its own language among themselves and for foreign contacts. Examples include Yiddish-speaking Jews in Slavic lands, the Chinese diaspora in southeast Asia, or the Hindu one in East Africa.
- A group may bow to the wider community and begin to use the majority language even at home— but **religion** is still special and requires the old holy language. Thus Jews preserved Hebrew, and Egyptian Christians preserved Coptic.

Where the languages are closely related (parent / vernacular; pidgin / acrolect), especially when one is greatly higher in prestige (p. 227), we refer to DIGLOSSIA rather than bilingualism. It's also very common, even in the US, for the local dialect to differ very noticeably from the standard, in which case we talk about BIDIALECTISM.

Fantasy worlds

Fantasy authors seem convinced that each species will have its own language— indeed, that nonhuman races only have one language each. In D&D they apparently pay attention to their taxonomic roots as well; we're told that gnolls also speak Troll and have a 60% chance of speaking Orcish or Hobgoblin.

As we only have one intelligent species we can't say this is wrong, but I'd advise rooting it in one of the situations described above. A people will maintain its own language if it lives separately from everyone else; conversely, it'll learn foreign tongues only if they regularly need to interact with outsiders. Do the gnolls really speak that often with humans? Or hobgoblins? If they live in isolated bands, what keeps the Gnollish language together? The *Real Academia Ñola*?

Think twice about concoctions like "thieves' cant". Special slang, sure, but if a profession has its own language it's usually because there's an ethnic minority that monopolizes the craft. Underworld slang in the real world quickly seeps into the speech of cops, entertainment districts, and slumming novelists. The worst place to keep a language secret is in a city.

What languages to speak?

If you are bilingual, what language do you speak with other bilinguals? This can be a fairly complex decision.

- It may be decided by perceived competence. Many an American venturing to speak a foreign language is upset when people respond in English. Sometimes it's just that the foreigner wants to practice too; often it's just that most people have no patience with struggling speakers and want to use the language that all parties understand best.

  (If this happens to you, you can always just keep using the foreign language. It's not like they can stop you, and it's actually a great strategy for ensuring that everyone understands everything. On the Apollo-Soyuz missions, where misunderstanding was dangerous, the Americans spoke Russian and the Russians spoke English.)

- The context may determine the language: in the home, at the workplace, at school, in the street. Or the purpose of the conversation: perhaps you discuss work in the national rather than the home language.
- The choice of language may indicate solidarity. In Paraguay, using Guaraní instead of Spanish is like switching from *vous* to *tu,* a milestone of familiarity.

Code-switching

A particularly interesting strategy is to use both languages, a practice called CODE-SWITCHING. It can involve single words, phrases, or entire sentences. Some examples from François Grosjean's *Life with Two Languages*:

> *Spanish and English*
>
> *No yo sí brincaba en el [No, I really did jump on the] trampoline. When I was a senior...*
>
> *Spanish and English*
>
> *No me fijé hasta que ya no me dijo [I didn't notice until he told me] 'Oh, I didn't think he'd be there.'*
>
> *French and English*
>
> *Now it's really time to get up. Lève-toi! [Get up!]*

Some reasons for code-switching:

- Stumbling over vocabulary. An immigrant to the US, for instance, might not know technical terms in his home language, or might not have the translations for *day care center* or *database* at the tip of his tongue.

  The first sentence above is an example. Note that after the switch to English, inertia seems to apply— the speaker continues in English.
- Quoting someone in the language they used, as in the second example.
- Group solidarity— e.g. you might ask a friend for money in your shared language, reinforcing your connection.

- Claiming authority or a more neutral role— e.g. a Luyia shopkeeper in Kenya, speaking with his sister in Luyia, switches to Swahili when the talk turns to business, as if to say that she'll be treated as a customer not as family.
- To exclude someone temporarily from a conversation. Occasionally this backfires, as the assumed outsider turns out to understand after all.

One type of code-switching that *isn't* seen: the habit of people in novels to speak fluent English except for greetings, titles, and 'yes' and 'no'. This is a cheap nod at the reader, who is likely to know only those words in the foreigner's language.

What languages to learn?

This is a topic that generates a lot of moralizing and wishful thinking. People worry that immigrants won't learn the national language, or hope that everyone will learn their auxlang which is so much better than Esperanto.

The fact is that people *try not to learn languages.* It takes many years to master a language, as well as regular exposure to speakers *who don't know yours.*

If you're reading this book, you're very likely one of those humans or gnolls who actually enjoy languages and learn them for fun. So am I. But believe me, we're a minority.

Adult speakers

Apply this principle to an immigrant in a modern country, or a gnoll in human society. They're likely to live in an enclave of their own social group, and find friendships and spouses there. Their employer might belong to the group as well; if not and it's menial work, they'll learn only just enough to get by.

The immigrant may have every intention of learning the national language, but there's no time and no teachers.

To create a situation where the adult immigrant has to learn the national language, some of these conditions must change: there is no foreign enclave, or they marry a local, or they work for an outsider in a job that requires a lot of use of the national language.

Media exposure doesn't really work on its own— even if your workmate plays salsa on the radio all day long, you won't learn Spanish from it. But it can reinforce exposure from other activities.

Conscript armies, universities, and the merchant marine are traditional levelers of language and dialect differences. Any institution that brings together people from widely varying backgrounds will facilitate the use of a common language. (For extra fun, this might not be the national language— think of medieval students at the Sorbonne who communicated in Latin, giving their name to the *quartier latin.*)

Colonizing a new land is similar. The colonizers may speak a less educated variety of the home language than the elite— e.g. the Roman legions and colonists in Gaul spread Vulgar Latin. The colonists' language may also be greatly affected by native languages encountered— e.g. Peruvian Spanish has borrowed extensively from Quechua.

Small bands or villages work differently, of course. If the people a mile away speak a different language, it's a good idea to learn their language, whether you want to trade or make war or make babies.

It's a separate question whether adult learners *master* a language. Again, it depends on opportunity more than on desire. Once there's no bad consequences for not learning more, people may just stop.

Children

Children learn languages automatically though, don't they?

No— it's just as hard *or harder* for them, and they won't learn a language without deep exposure. That could include parents, relatives, or other children in the family or the neighborhood or at school. The 'ease of learning' notion is an illusion due to psychological distance, unfortunately reinforced by Chomskyan linguistic theories which posit an innate 'language organ'.

In modern societies, immigrant children may not even pick up the parents' language— especially once they learn that the parents quite adequately understand the national language. We think of children learning their parents' language, but their peers are just as important; note that immigrant children don't pick up their parents' *accent.*

A grandmother or other caregiver who *doesn't* speak the national language is another story. Or if the child lives in an ethnic enclave there is usually enough reinforcement to retain the home language.

In premodern societies, there may be no schools, and thus children in the ethnic enclave may have no reason to learn the national language.

Children can learn different languages from each parent, but they can get confused and upset if the parent speaks the 'wrong' language! Grosjean mentions a girl named Lisa whose mother spoke German and her father Italian. Once her father spoke to her in German, and she responded, *No, tu non puoi!* ("No, you can't!") Keeping two largely unknown language systems separate is a tricky task, and associating each with different people helps: Lisa can count on knowing that whatever Daddy says is Italian. If anyone in her life could use either language at any time, the learning task would become much harder.

Kids do learn languages, of course, where adults often fail. But this isn't hard to understand. Their motivation is intense— they can't get what they want without learning to talk. They can devote their full time to learning. And their peers are nastier— other children can be vicious to a kid who speaks funny.

Avoidance strategies

Auxlangers sometimes attempt to quantify the cost of the "language problem"— e.g. they tot up the cost of translation within European companies or the Brussels bureaucracy, and compare it to the huge monolingual market in the US.

Such arguments depend on the specious impressiveness of large sums. Heck, chewing gum is a $4 billion industry in the U.S. alone. In a $15 trillion economy, it's not hard to wallop people with high numbers.

The calculations should be done per capita. How much do *I* lose by not knowing Arabic? Compare *that* to the cost of learning Arabic (or an auxlang). Then look at the cost of hiring a translator for the times I need to talk to an Arabic speaker or read Arabic media. And let's not forget the opportunity costs: the money and time it takes to learn Arabic or YourAuxlang aren't available to do something else.

I suspect that if you did all these calculations, you'd find that we're already minimizing language costs, and that spending more money on teaching a rarely-used auxlang to everyone would be uneconomical. Translators are awfully cheap, considering.

Ongoing sound change

People are aware of linguistic change, and they're against it. The usual folk theory is that it's due to slovenliness, and linguistics partially supports this, in that many sound changes make things easier to say: clusters are simplified, unvoiced stops are voiced, sounds are merged.

This can't be the whole story, as sound changes also complicate language: phonemes can be innovated; tones appear; there are fortitions (like y → dʒ); deletions create new consonant clusters.

Another common suggestion is that people imitate the leaders of society. This is not entirely wrong, as prestige dialects can expand at the expense of regional ones. But the very existence of these dialects shows that they can thrive for centuries.

So what *does* happen? The best way to learn more about the process is to look at **ongoing** sound change; no one has looked closer than William Labov. His volumes on *Principles of Linguistic Change* are full of fascinating data.

Part of the answer is COVERT PRESTIGE: non-privileged groups have their own norms. One obvious example is AAVE, the speech of urban American blacks, which largely ignores both General American and the local dialects of northern whites. Blacks and whites in the US don't want to sound like each other. (This isn't a universal– Jamaican Londoners talk like everyone else, which Labov confirmed by playing recordings of them to white folks; they couldn't tell that the speakers were black.)

The Northern Cities Shift

Do you have to find exotic languages to study ongoing sound changes? No, they're going on in the US right now. As an example, the Northern Cities Shift is proceeding among white urbanites in a huge swath of the northeastern US from Minnesota to Connecticut (but bypassing New York City).

Here's a summary of the NCS:

/æ → iə/	*have → h[iə]v*
/ɑ → æ/	*socks → sax*
/ɔ → ɑ/	*boss → b[ɑ]ss*
/ɪ → ɛ/	*Linda → Lenda*
/ɛ → ʌ/	*steady → study*
/ʌ → ɔ/	*cut → c[ɔ]t*

The first three changes form a DRAG CHAIN: as /æ/ is raised, it leaves a phonetic gap which /ɑ/ spills into, and that in turn leaves room for /ɔ/ to move forward. The final two form a PUSH CHAIN: as /ɛ/ is backed, this forces /ʌ/ to move out of its way.

Wouldn't these changes cause confusion? Certainly! Labov describes being introduced to a [dʒæn]; he looked around for a Jan before realizing that it was a John. But the problem is no worse than those between existing dialects.

Finding the culprits

To address **how** sounds change, Labov focused on **who** is changing them. The community doesn't advance uniformly. His findings:

- A phoneme doesn't change all at once; some words are leaders, some laggards. For some reason, the tensing of [æ] in Philadelphia strongly affected the word *planet*, while *Janet* remained lax. (This is reminiscent of the effect of Trojan Horse words in gender change, p. 134.)
- The leaders of sound change are almost always **women**; they're often a generation ahead of the men.
- Women keep advancing a sound change in a linear fashion; men's advance is stepwise. The obvious interpretation is that men don't pick up the change from their contemporaries, but from their mothers.

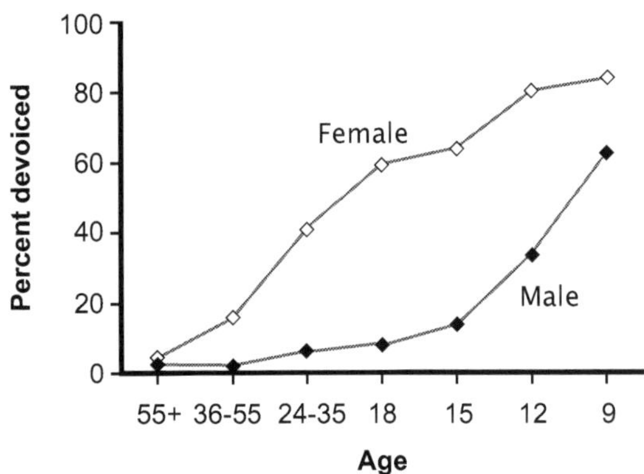

Devoicing of /ž/ in Buenos Aires (1979)

The Buenos Aires study is by Clara Wolf and Elena Jiménez.

- There's a typical curvilinear effect of class: neither the lower class nor the upper class are in the forefront of change, but those in the middle– even more specifically, the **upper working class**.

We can see this in a study from Cairo by Niloofar Haeri:

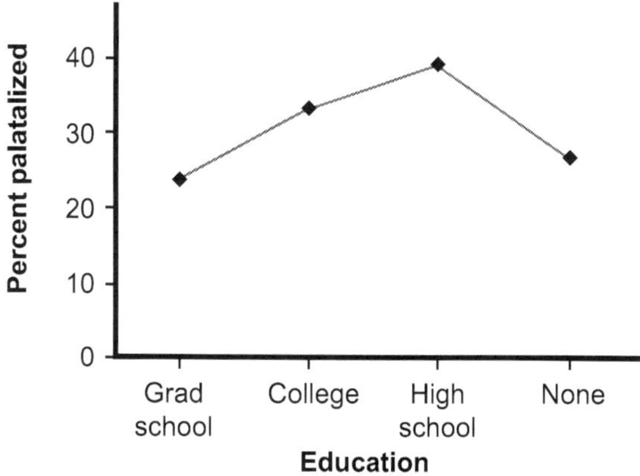

Palatalization of /t, d/ in Cairo (1996)

- Nonstandard variants often peak in **adolescence**. Indeed, older speakers may retreat from a change.
- There's only a very small contribution from ethnicity or neighborhood (except to the degree that these correlate with class).

Beyond this, Labov was able to identify **individuals** who were in the forefront of sound changes in Philadelphia. Interestingly, they shared several characteristics. They were upper working class women, with a strong nonconformist streak. Perhaps most interestingly, they were what Malcolm Gladwell calls Connectors, people who were not only intensely involved with their neighborhoods, but had strong connections to other areas as well— the perfect people to spread ideas.

This tends to falsify notions that sound change is due to ignorance or laziness; the leaders are bright and upwardly mobile. Sound changes are also not due to isolation; they're centered on the most social people. The paradox is that these women are just rebellious enough to fight social norms, but not enough to be dissipated or burned out.

The process

Labov outlines the **steps of sound change** (in particular, vowel changes like the NCS) as follows:

- Some phoneme P has asymmetrical neighbors in phonetic space: there's a bigger gap between its near neighbor N and a farther neighbor M. Phonemes are realized with a certain amount of spread; as there's more room in the direction of M, outliers in that direction are heard as valid instances of P.

- New language learners thus move the phoneme in the direction of M— in effect, they mishear the outliers as normal tokens.
- The change is taken as characteristic of younger speakers and less formal speech. It's preferentially taken up by nonconforming young women.
- Upwardly mobile women spread the change to higher and lower social classes.
- Men catch up to women in the next generation, as they pick up the now advanced sound change from their mothers.

Now, all this is **unconscious**. These are not overt markers like a regional dialect— people are generally unaware of these changes, and if they're pointed out the speakers are typically apologetic. If a change does reach public awareness, it's stigmatized. It may continue to advance (it still has appeal as a marker of nonconformity), or it may just be retained as a long-term class marker. (E.g. there's some evidence that the pronunciation of *-ing* as *-in'* goes back for centuries.[17])

If a local language variety is losing ground (generally to the standard language; this seems to be common in Europe), the leaders in this process also tend to be women.

A corollary is that people are lousy self-reporters. Labov played people recordings of words showing different stages in different sound changes; invariably people reported themselves as much closer to the standard than they were, and even claimed that "no one talked like" the more extreme variations. This should be a note of caution for linguists who rely on people's evaluations of grammatical correctness!

Another curiosity: the closest analogue to sound change may be fashion, which has also been found to be driven by the preferences of middle class, highly social women.

Labov's findings are supported by findings worldwide; studies have been done in the US, Montreal, London, Belfast, Buenos Aires, Mexico City, Hong Kong, Seoul, Cairo, and more. We don't know, of course, if his picture fully applies to earlier centuries.

---

17 We hear *-in'* more often in verbal forms, and least often in nouns (e.g. *ceiling*). Old English had a participle ending *-inde/ende* and a nominalizer *-inge/ynge*; compare German *-ende, -ung*. These merged in the written standard but never entirely did so in colloquial speech.

Long-term cycles

It's been claimed that there are long-term cycles in morphological change. (It's hard to be certain, because we don't have good ancient evidence about morphosyntax in most families.) Here are some candidates:

Degree of fusion. An inflection begins as an ordinary word, then becomes a PARTICLE (phonologically independent but bound to a phrase), then a clitic, then an affix (see p. 169). It may be fused with the root or with other affixes. Finally it's worn away to nothing.

At the whole-language level, you get a cycle something like this:

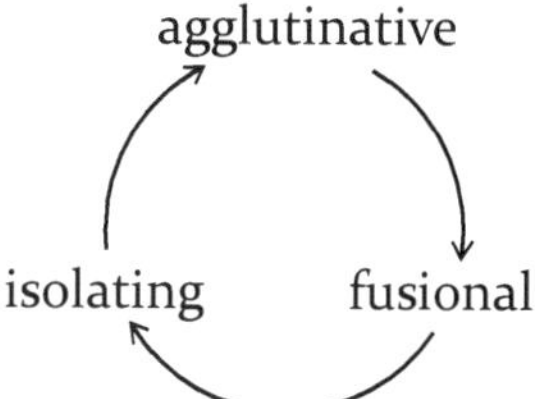

At least, kind of! The overall picture must look something like this, as we don't see any one language type 'winning'— we see complex inflections building up over here, getting lost over there.

If we look at a particular development— Latin to French, for instance— we see a more chaotic picture. (The arrows refer back to the diagram; ↺ means a feature stays where it is.)

← loss of nominal case

← passive mood replaced with synthetic passive

↺ retention of imperfect, subjunctive, many irregular verbs

↘ development of inflectional future and conditional

← simple past replaced by compound perfect

↗ cliticization of pronouns, forming verbal complex

← many verbal endings lost; pronouns required

↗ development of mandatory articles

↺ two-part negatives (*ne...pas*), then loss of *ne*

← merger of masculine and neuter gender

If we do a little vector arithmetic on the arrows, on the whole French is less fusional and more isolating than Latin. But there are exceptions to the general trend.

See also the discussion on how **gender** systems arise (p. 133).

Aspect. Indo-European is reconstructed with two past tenses, traditionally called aorist and perfect— i.e. the difference is aspectual (p. 134). Proto-Germanic merged the two into a single preterit.

Later, a new synthetic perfect was formed from an auxiliary plus a participle: *I have sung,* German *ich habe gesungen*, Swedish *jag har sjungit*. Then in Yiddish and Afrikaans the preterit was lost, leaving again one past tense. Even more recently, adverbs are used when an aspectual distinction is needed: e.g. Yiddish *ix hob šojn gezungn.*

That is, there's a cycle between one and two past tenses, with the aspectual distinction getting lost and then redeveloped.

Pronouns. Most of the European languages developed a T/V (familiar/formal) distinction in the second person. English went on this path to the extent of applying the 2p *ye / you* to individuals, but then went on to lose the 2s *thou / thee* entirely.

But some dialects have innovated a new plural pronoun. e.g. *y'all* or *youse*; even in General American *you guys* may be on its way to pronoun status. So here we have one full turn of a cycle from two pronouns to one and back to two.

In some cultures there seems to be a cycle where a formal pronoun starts to be perceived as too informal, and a new formal pronoun is developed. Portuguese *você* developed from *vossa mercê* 'your.pl mercy', but now it's a T pronoun, and a new V pronoun has developed, *o senhor*.

A very similar process happens in Japanese, resulting in regular replacement of pronouns. E.g. *boku* 'I' is now perceived as rather assertive, and suitable only for males, but it derives from Chinese 僕 'servant' (Mandarin *pú*).

Language death

Languages inevitably "die" in the sense that they change into something else. People in Italy don't speak Latin any more; they speak Italian. What we're talking about here, however, is when people stop speaking a language entirely.

You'll see news reports sometimes about the elderly last speakers of a language. Or tragicomic variants like the last two speakers of Ayapaneco— who detest each other and refuse to speak to each other.

However, now that language death has been better studied, it's clear that such languages are really already dead. Languages lose features and complexities as they're no longer used for everyday communication.

George Lakoff's book *Women, Fire, and Dangerous Things* is named for the *balan* gender category in Dyirbal (p. 125). But Dyirbal is being lost, and the last generations have progressively simplified the gender system. The second-to-last generation lost many exceptional subcategories (e.g. special rules relating to fishing, and for some speakers the 'dangerous things' subcategory of *balan*); the youngest speakers had lost one gender entirely and retained *balan* only for human females.

The languages of immigrants to the US tend to get lost in just a few generations. Even Spanish thrives only because it's reinforced by continual immigration. Young Hispanics born here, educated almost entirely in English, no longer master the details of standard Spanish and start to use not only more and more English terms but English syntax; I recall reading a college paper in Spanish whose syntax was word-for-word English (except for adjectives following the nouns).

A language becomes moribund when young speakers no longer learn it. There are other possibilities, though, such as a language being restricted more and more to certain domains— perhaps it's only used in social or family contexts, or only in religious settings.

Leonard Bloomfield describes the common case where a speaker ends up fluent in no language:

> White Thunder, a man round forty, speaks less English than Menomini, and that is a strong indictment, for his Menomini is atrocious. His vocabulary is small; his inflections are often barbarous; he constructs sentences on a few threadbare models. He may be said to speak no language tolerably.

Of the 5000 or so languages still spoken, probably half won't make it to the year 2100. The prospect upsets linguists, who after all hate to see their subject matter disappearing! Every language is an opportunity to learn something new... if languages like Hixkaryana or Apurinã had disappeared, we might never have realized that object-first languages existed.

Language death isn't limited to modern times, of course. Latin, for instance, displaced Oscan, Umbrian, Faliscan, Venetic, Etruscan, and other languages of pre-Roman Italy.

It's interesting that the best-known conlanger, J.R.R. Tolkien, expended most of his effort on dying languages— those of the elves, who were leaving Middle Earth. It may add a bit of pathos to your language if it's slowly disappearing...

Revivals

Languages can rise from the grave; the canonical example is Hebrew, which became the national and everyday language of Israel. The language was widely understood in written form, and conveniently bridged the gap between Ashkenazi and Sephardic Jews— but the majority of the settlers in Palestine spoke Yiddish. But Hebrew had the ideological edge; it was associated with the movement to build a Jewish homeland, while Yiddish was tied to the life the settlers were leaving behind.

Efforts have been made to revive other languages as well, notably Cornish and quite a few Native American languages. Generally this involves a form of conlanging: someone has to clearly set down the phonology and syntax, standardize the orthography, and fill out the lexicon.

How do you make it work? Well, it's about the same as keeping a language from disappearing in the first place. Make learning materials available; ensure that parents teach it to their children; give it a place in schools, preferably as the medium of instruction. (Bureaucratic support is often sought, but it's overrated in my view: people don't learn a language because the government grants it official status. Hebrew became dominant among Jewish settlers long before the establishment of the State of Israel.)

Studies in morphosyntax

There's nothing like curling up with a fat reference grammar— unless it's someone doing that and bringing back the good bits, which is what I've done here. All the topics relate to MORPHOSYNTAX (which is just morphology and syntax).

How do you use this chapter? I think it's all worth reading once, so you know what's here. Then re-read a section in detail when you create a conlang it's relevant to. If a section is too difficult, it's OK to skip ahead!

There's whole books on these topics, too, some of which I've noted if you want to learn more. Thomas Payne's *Describing Morphosyntax* (1997) and Bernard Comrie's *Language Universals and Linguistic Typology* (1981) are good overviews.

Latin case

Latin is the very prototype of a language with an extended, fusional nominal DECLENSION. Although it's not exotic, it's worth looking at in detail to see how such a system works.

Let's start by looking at a few PARADIGMS or sets of case forms.

		island	world	field	name
s	nom	*īnsula*	*mundus*	*ager*	*nōmen*
	acc	*īnsulam*	*mundum*	*agrum*	*nōmen*
	gen	*īnsulae*	*mundī*	*agrī*	*nōminis*
	dat	*īnsulae*	*mundō*	*agrō*	*nōminī*
	abl	*īnsulā*	*mundō*	*agrō*	*nōmine*
	voc		*munde*		
pl	nom	*īnsulae*	*mundī*	*agrī*	*nōmina*
	acc	*īnsulās*	*mundōs*	*agrōs*	*nōmina*
	gen	*īnsulārum*	*mundōrum*	*agrōrum*	*nōminum*
	dat	*īnsulīs*	*mundīs*	*agrīs*	*nōminibus*
	abl	*īnsulīs*	*mundīs*	*agrīs*	*nōminibus*

Forms

Before we look at case usage, consider the raw forms.

First, as advertised, they're FUSIONAL. There's no morpheme that means 'plural' and none that means 'genitive' or 'dative'. You can imitate this directly, by coming up with separate endings for each cell in your table of forms, or start with an agglutinative paradigm and mangle it with sound changes.

Second, Latin seems to like to double up on endings (this is SYNCRETISM). In the first column *-ae* appears in three cells. The dative and ablative are the same in all the plural cells and half the singular. Fortunately for the Romans, languages are redundant and context usually makes it clear what case is meant.

The nominative and accusative are the same for *nōmen* in both singular and plural. This is characteristic of neuter nouns in Latin and in fact in Indo-European generally.

If you look at the plural nominative endings for 'island' and 'world', they may look familiar, especially if you properly pluralize *alumna, alumnus* to *alumnae, alumni.* The genitives are easier if you know your constellations (e.g. *Centaurus* → α Centauri; *Cassiopeia* → η Cassiopeiae).

If you look across the table, you'll see the unwelcome fact that Latin has multiple paradigms or DECLENSIONS.[18] *Īnsula* is first declension, *mundus* and *ager* are second, and *nōmen* is third. (There are two more, but they have only a handful of words each.) They're not entirely chaotic, however; e.g. all the plural genitives end in *-um.*

What's that single cell with a vocative? In general only second declension nouns have a separate vocative; for all other nouns it's the same as the nominative.

The roots for *ager* and *nōmen* mutate after the first row or two. This can be blamed on sound change— the vowel in the last syllable is lost or weakened as more material is piled on. Alternations like *rex / regis* ('king' s.nom/s.gen) simply reflect devoicing of an original **regs.* Secondary roots like *agr-*, *nōmin-*, and *reg-* are called OBLIQUE roots.

Latin dictionaries give you the s.nom and s.gen, from which you can always reconstruct the rest of the paradigm. E.g. *imperātor imperātōris* 'general, emperor' tells us that the noun is the third declension, like *nōmen*, and warns us about the length change *o* → *ō* in the oblique root.

---

[18] DECLENSION is used both for a particular paradigm, and for the process of declining nouns. CONJUGATION works the same way for verbs.

Basic usage

The nominative and accusative should be easy to understand, because we have them for most of our pronouns. The NOMINATIVE is used for subjects, the ACCUSATIVE for objects.

Paulus Mariam amat.

Paul-s.nom Maria-s.acc love-3s.indic

Paul loves Maria.

Rōmānī gladiōs amant.

Roman-pl.nom sword-pl.acc love-3p.indic

The Romans love swords.

If you'd use *me* or *him* in English, use the accusative. (Unless it's after a preposition— see next page.)

You've probably heard that cases allow free word order, and indeed you can say *Mariam Paulus amat.*

The DATIVE is used for the indirect object, prototypically whoever is given something; it's named for Latin *dat* 'he gives'.

Paulus litteram Rōmānīs dāvit.

Paul-s.nom letter-s.acc Roman-pl.dat give-3s.pret.ind

Paul gave the Romans a letter.

The GENITIVE is used for the possessor of an item:

littera Pauli	**pons asinōrum**
letter-s.nom Paul-s.gen	bridge-s.nom ass-pl.gen
Paul's letter	*the bridge of the asses*

The prototypical meaning of the ABLATIVE is 'movement away', but we'll get to that when we deal with prepositions. Alone, it's used for several things, including use as an INSTRUMENTAL (*oculīs vidēre* 'see with the eyes') and placement in time (*aestāte* 'during the summer').

One of my favorite constructions is the ABLATIVE ABSOLUTE, which uses two nouns, or a noun and an adjective, both in the ablative, and can be paraphrased "with the A being B":

Turture agricolā, rārō edēmus.

turtle-s.abl farmer-s.abl rare-adv eat-1p.fut

With the turtle as farmer, we will rarely eat.

The VOCATIVE is used when addressing someone: *Paule, ī!* "Paul, go!" If you know the Catholic Mass, this is why you sometimes hear *Domine*— it's directly addressing the Lord.

With prepositions

We use a single case after all prepositions, but Latin sometimes uses the accusative, sometimes the ablative.

The ablative is used with *ab* 'from', *de* 'from', *ex* 'out of', which can all be said to imply movement away— e.g. *ab Rōmā* 'from Rome', *de profundis* 'from the depths', *ex urbe* 'out of the city'.

It's also used with *cum* 'with' and *sine* 'without': *cum gladiō* 'with a sword', *sine nōmine* 'without a name'.

The accusative is used with most other prepositions: *circum Rōmam* 'around Rome', *contra Paulum* 'against Paul', *propter litteram* 'because of the letter'.

With some prepositions, the ablative indicates location and the accusative indicates movement; the distinction is similar to our prepositions *in* vs. *into*.

in Rōmā [abl]	**in Rōmam [acc]**
in Rome	*into Rome*
super īnsulā	**super īnsulam**
above the island	*(moving) above the island*

English has borrowed many Latin phrases with prepositions. See if you can identify which of these use the ablative and which use the accusative, and why:

ā posteriōrī
ab ovō
ad hominem
cum laude
de factō
ex cathedrā
in locō parentis
in mediās rēs
prō formā
urbs in hortō

Agreement

Once you've climbed the hill of the nominal declension, you have to face the mountain of the adjectives. Adjectives not only have all the number and case forms of the nouns, but have three separate genders as well. Here's the full set for *bonus* 'good':

		m	n	f
s	nom	*bonus*	*bonum*	*bona*
	acc	*bonum*	*bonum*	*bonam*
	gen	*bonī*	*bonī*	*bonae*
	dat	*bonō*	*bonō*	*bonae*
	abl	*bonō*	*bonō*	*bonā*
	voc	*bone*		
pl	nom	*bonī*	*bona*	*bonae*
	acc	*bonōs*	*bona*	*bonās*
	gen	*bonōrum*	*bonōrum*	*bonārum*
	dat	*bonīs*	*bonīs*	*bonīs*
	abl	*bonīs*	*bonīs*	*bonīs*

Fortunately there's a lot of overlap with the nouns— in fact *bonus (m)* declines just like *mundus, bona (f)* just like *īnsula.* And *bonum (n)* only differs in three cells from the masculine.

Naturally, an adjective + noun combination must match in number, case, and gender:

Bonus Rōmānus bonās litterās amat.

good-m.s.nom Roman-s.nom good-f.pl.acc letter-pl.acc love-3s.ind

A good Roman loves good letters.

Tragœdiae bonōrum Rōmānōrum in mediās rēs incipiunt.

play-pl.nom good-m.pl.gen Roman-pl.gen in middle-f.pl.acc thing-pl.acc begin-3p.ind

The plays of the good Romans begin in the middle of things.

A fusional alternative: Russian

As another example of a fusional declension, let's look at Russian.

Though Russian is also Indo-European, the cases differ a bit.

		science		newspaper	
s	nom	наука	*nauka*	журнал	*žurnal*
	acc	науку	*nauku*	журнал	*žurnal*
	gen	науки	*nauk^{j}i*	журнала	*žurnala*
	dat	науке	*nauk^{j}e*	журналу	*žurnalu*
	instr	наукой	*naukoj*	журналом	*žurnalom*
	prep	науке	*nauk^{j}e*	журнале	*žurnal^{j}e*
pl	nom	науки	*nauk^{j}i*	журналы	*žurnalɨ*
	acc	науки	*nauk^{j}i*	журналы	*žurnalɨ*
	gen	наук	*nauk*	журналов	*žurnalov*
	dat	наукам	*naukam*	журналам	*žurnalam*
	instr	науками	*naukami*	журналами	*žurnalami*
	prep	науках	*naukax*	журналах	*žurnalax*

The INSTRUMENTAL indicates that something is used as an instrument— we're trying to conlang наукой 'with science'.

The PREPOSITIONAL is used with certain prepositions— e.g. на столе 'on the table'. Despite the name, it's not used with all prepositions, and indeed as in Latin, the choice of case helps determine the meaning:

в школе [prep]	**в школу [acc]**
in the school	*into the school*
на плошади	**на плошадь**
at the square	*into the square*

With prepositions indicating *movement away*, the genitive is used: из школы 'out of the school'.

Журнал has identical nominative and accusative forms. Speakers must have found this confusing when referring to people and animals, because the convention is to use the genitive endings for these. Thus the accusative for Иван 'Ivan' is Ивана.

Note the null ending for pl. gen. in the first column, as seen in Академия Наук 'Academy of Sciences'.

An agglutinative alternative: Quechua

Finally, to underline that a non-fusional language really doesn't fuse the case endings, here's how nouns are declined in Quechua:

	house		
	s	pl	
nominative	*wasi*	*wasikuna*	
accusative	*wasita*	*wasikunata*	
genitive	*wasipa*	*wasikunapa*	of
dative	*wasipaq*	*wasikunapaq*	for
instrumental	*wasiwan*	*wasikunawan*	with
ablative	*wasimanta*	*wasikunamanta*	from
locative	*wasipi*	*wasikunapi*	at
distributive	*wasinka*	*wasikunanka*	for each
illative	*wasiman*	*wasikunaman*	to
causative	*wasirayku*	*wasikunarayku*	because of

The last column gives the English preposition which roughly corresponds to each case. The ILLATIVE is used for the recipient of a transfer or the goal of a movement; the dative gives the beneficiary.

Personal endings can be added before the case ending, with a possessive meaning— e.g. *wasiy* 'my house', *wasiyki* 'your house', *wasin* 'his/her house', *wasinta* 'his/her house (acc.)', *wasiykunapi* 'at my houses'.

In some contexts these endings can be combined. E.g. *taytaypa* 'of my father' can be used as a substantive— compare English "We're going to my father's." As such it can take a locative, too: *taytaypapi* 'at my father's [place]'.

Alignment

MORPHOSYNTACTIC ALIGNMENT deals with how verbal arguments are organized— e.g. the famous ERGATIVITY. This can affect several things:

- The choice of **case** on nouns
- Verbal **agreement**
- **Word order**

Arguments

We just considered one alignment, nominative-accusative, but it was described by comparing it to English. To be more precise we need to define some terms.

Abstractly, verbs have ARGUMENTS that specify the key players, much as in predicate calculus (p. 41).

The number of arguments is the VALENCE (p. 140). For now we're only interested in valences of one or two:

- INTRANSITIVE verbs have one argument; let's call it the EXPERIENCER or **e**.

  The window broke.

  Jesus wept.

  The nation prospered.

- TRANSITIVE verbs have two arguments. The AGENT or **a** is the more active role (**bolded**); the other is the PATIENT or **p** (<u>underlined</u>):

  The boys *broke* <u>*the window*</u>.

  Jesus *cursed* <u>*the fig tree*</u>.

  The linguist *inspected* <u>*the case system*</u>.

  The rice soup *pleased* <u>*the critic*</u>.

These are syntactic roles, and yet there's a clear correlation with semantics: the prototypical transitive verb involves someone *doing something* to someone or something. But many verbs are far from the prototype. The soup, for instance, isn't much of an agent; it's just sitting there. Just as a syntactic imperative may not be an order, a syntactic agent may not be active or even animate.

Such mismatches may be unstable. The last example in Spanish is *La sopa de arroz gustó al crítico;* the Portuguese *O crítico gostou da sopa de arroz* has 'corrected' the verb to treat the human as an agent rather than a patient.

Some linguists prefer to use the abbreviations. I think that makes the roles harder to grasp, and worse yet Bernard Comrie uses **S** for the experiencer, which invites confusion with *subject* (or *sentence*).

In English we're used to verbs which can be either transitive or not; these are AMBITRANSITIVE or LABILE. We can divide these in two categories:

- AGENTIVE (experiencer = agent)

  We ate / We ate the sushi
  Caleon won / Caleon won the war
  Do you follow? / Are you following me?

- PATIENTIVE (experiencer = patient).

  The ice melted / The heat melted the ice
  The window broke / The zombie broke the window
  Her bodice ripped / Fabio ripped her bodice

Some languages, such as Latin or Dyirbal, have no or few ambitransitives.

Languages don't always agree on ambitransitivity. E.g. we can say *the book is selling well*, but in French you'd switch to the reflexive: *le livre se vend bien.* On the other hand, French *descendre* can be used transitively: *descends-moi mes lunettes* 'bring my glasses down'.

The major alignments

Now that we have the terms we need, we can clearly define the different alignments.

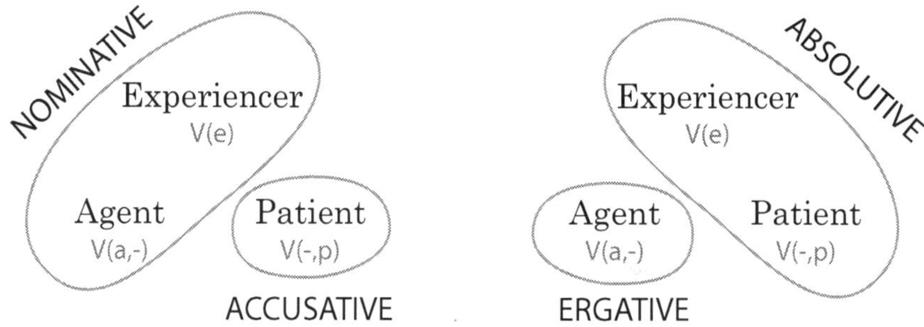

(The predicate calculus notation is a mnemonic, and a reminder that all these roles are defined in terms of verb arguments. The order is not always **a, p** though **p, a** is rare.)

In a NOMINATIVE-ACCUSATIVE alignment, like English, Latin, Russian, and Quechua,

- **experiencer and agent** take the nominative
- patients appear in the accusative

In an ERGATIVE-ABSOLUTIVE alignment, like Dyirbal and Basque,

- **experiencer and patient** take the ABSOLUTIVE
- agents take the ERGATIVE

(*Ergative* comes from Greek ἔργον 'work', as in *ergonomics.* You can think of the agent as the one doing the work.)

If you're used to nom/acc languages, ergativity takes some getting used to. In sentences like *The window broke* vs. *The boys broke the window*, the window obviously has the same *semantic* role (it's the breakee), so it's logical to use the same case. But both systems are common, as they both solve the problem of distinguishing the two arguments of transitive verbs.

Alignments need not involve case; they may be deduced from word order alone. E.g. even if we ignore pronouns, English treats experiencer and agent NPs alike by placing them before the verb, as subjects, while patients appear after the verb, as objects.

An example from Dyirbal showing ergative-absolutive alignment:

> **Balan d^{y}ugumbil baŋgul yaṛaŋgu balgan.**
>
> f.abs woman-abs m.erg man-erg hit
>
> *The man hit the woman.*
>
> **Balan d^{y}ugumbil banin^{y}u.**
>
> f.abs woman-abs came.here
>
> *The woman came here.*

The also-rans

There are three other logically possible alignments:

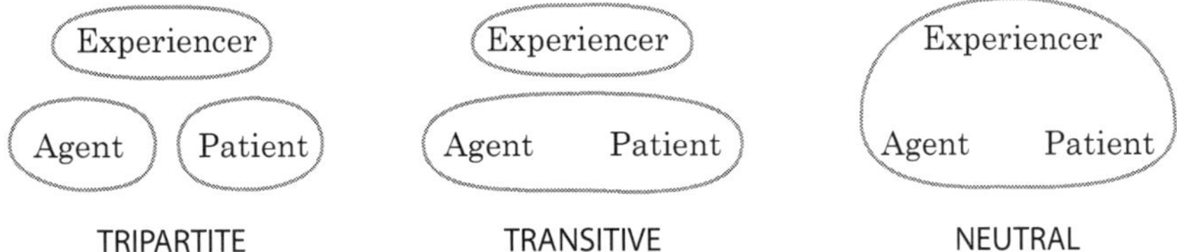

TRIPARTITE TRANSITIVE NEUTRAL

- TRIPARTITE, where each role gets its own case. In Nez Percé, the agent takes the ergative ending *-nim*, the patient takes the accusative *-ne*, and the experiencer takes no ending (this is the INTRANSITIVE case).
- TRANSITIVE, or Monster Raving Loony as Justin Rye puts it: experiencer gets one case, agent and patient the other. This is found in the Iranian language Rushani, but said to be unusual even there.
- DIRECT or NEUTRAL: no role distinctions are made at all, even with word order.

These systems are very rare, probably because they provide either too much or not enough information. It's useful to distinguish the two arguments of a transitive verb. It's less useful to never distinguish them, or to pedantically distinguish them from the experiencer role too.

Split systems

Alignments can be partly nominative-accusative and partly ergative-absolutive, and in several different ways.

Split intransitivity

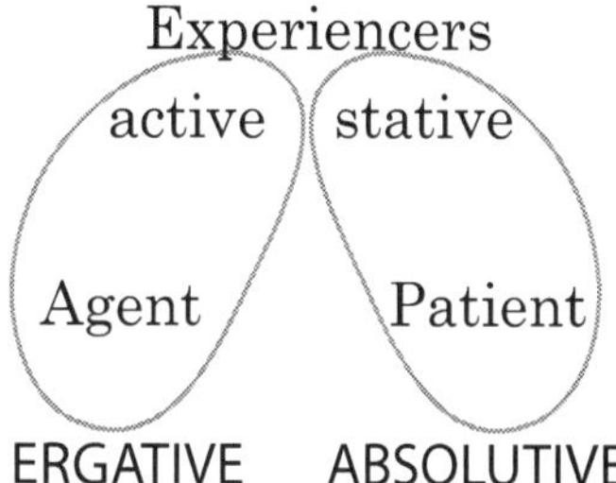

Not all transitives are alike: the experiencer in *John swerved* is a lot more active than the one in *The window broke.* ACTIVE-STATIVE or SPLIT-S languages treat the more active experiencers like agents, the less active ones like patients.

In Lakhota, intransitive verbs can be ACTIVE or STATIVE; compare the 1s affixes in active and stative verbs with the agent and patient markers on transitive verbs:

ACTIVE	STATIVE
wa-hí 'I came'	*ma-háŋske* 'I am tall'
wa-wáčhi 'I dance'	*ma-híŋȟpaye* 'I fall'
TRANSITIVE	
a-wa-pȟe 'I hit him'	*a-má-pȟe* 'he hit me'

In Tsova-Tush a verb can go either way (it's FLUID-S), depending on how much control the experiencer is felt to have:

So vož-en-so.	**As vuiž-n-as.**
1s.abs fall-aorist-1s.abs	1s.erg fall-aorist-1s.erg
I fell (by accident)	*I fell (on purpose)*

The case names are arbitrary here; rather than labeling them ergative and absolutive, we might call them AGENTIVE and PATIENTIVE.

The agentivity hierarchy

Dyirbal, as we've seen, has ergative-absolutive case marking on its nouns. But 1st and 2nd person pronouns are nominative-accusative!

Ŋad^{y}a banin^{y}u.	**Ŋinda banin^{y}u.**
1s.nom came.here	2s.nom came.here
I came here.	*You came here.*

Ŋad^{y}a ŋinuna balgan.

1s.nom 2s-acc hit

I hit you.

Such splits aren't arbitrary; they follow the AGENTIVITY HIERARCHY:

verbal agreement (1 > 2 > 3)
pronouns (1 > 2 > 3)
proper nouns
nouns— humans
nouns— animates
nouns— inanimates

That is, if you have both alignments going, the split will be located somewhere on this list, with nom/acc above and erg/abs below.

- In Dyirbal, the split is on the "pronouns" line: 3rd person pronouns, and everything below, are erg/abs.
- The Papuan language Managalasi has nom/acc for verbal agreement only.
- The Australian language Ritharngu has nom/acc for pronouns, a tripartite system for humans and higher animals, and erg/abs for everything else.

The hierarchy makes sense if we note that *accusative* and *ergative* are the more likely to be explicitly MARKED. Then a split along the hierarchy means we're marking *departures from expected agentivity.* That is:

- arguments likely to be agents (i.e. those higher in the hierarchy) are marked accusative if they instead turn out to be patients
- arguments likely to be patients (those lower in the hierarchy) are marked ergative if they turn out to be agents

What if we relied on the agentivity hierarchy most of the time, and just marked the violations? That's precisely what the Algonquian languages do. You normally use the DIRECT affixes, while the INVERSE forms signal that the lower-agentive argument is actually the agent. An example from Fox:

Ne-waapam-aa-wa.	**Ne-waapam-ek-wa.**
1s-see-direct-3s *I see him.*	1s-see-inverse-3s *He sees me.*

In Algonquian languages, when you have multiple third person referents, one must be foregrounded by using PROXIMATE markings, while the rest are backgrounded by using the OBVIATIVE. Again, the inverse form can be used if the obviatives are getting above themselves and acting as agents.

Tense/aspect-based splits

Another type of split, very rare, is within the verbal paradigm: different tenses use different alignments. For instance, in the Chibchan language Guaymí, the ergative marker *-kwe* appears only in the past tense.

As an exercise, look at these Georgian examples and decide what alignment is used in each tense:

Present

> **Xe izrdeba.**
>
> tree-A grow-pres.3s
>
> *The tree is growing.*
>
> **Glexi tesavs siminds.**
>
> peasant-A sow-pres.3s corn-B
>
> *The peasant is sowing corn.*

Aorist

> **Xe gaizarda.**
>
> tree-C aor-grow-3s
>
> *The tree grew.*
>
> **Glexma datesa simindi.**
>
> peasant-D aor-sow-3s corn-C
>
> *The peasant sowed corn.*

Perfect

> **Xe gazrdila.**
>
> tree-E grow-perf.3s
>
> *The tree has grown.*
>
> **Glexs dautesia simindi.**
>
> peasant-F aor-sow-3s corn-E
>
> *The peasant has sown the corn.*

The tree is an experiencer, the peasant an agent, and the corn a patient. So the alignment is nom/acc in the present, and erg/abs in the aorist and perfect.

If you compare the endings, you can see that cases A, C, and E are the same. In Georgian grammar this is the nominative, and as you can see it acts as an absolutive as well. That makes case D an ergative.

Case F ought to be an ergative too, but it's identical to case B, which was acting as an accusative! In Georgian grammar it's called the dative. Despite the unusual case usage, note that agents and patients always appear in different cases.

Intriguingly, both Georgian and Guaymí are also split-S languages. So active experiencers appear as ergatives:

> **Bavšvma itamaša.**
>
> child-erg aor-play-3s
>
> *The child played.*

On the topic of subjects

In English and most Indo-European languages, we can define a SUBJECT as having these overlapping qualities:

- it takes nominative case (***I** saw you*)
- it triggers verbal agreement (*he **sees** you*)
- it's either an agent or an experiencer
- it's the TOPIC of the sentence (that is, it usually isn't used for the comment or new information)
- it appears before the other arguments of the verb (the OBJECTS)

But these don't have to line up. Ergative-absolutive languages are one exception; topic-prominent languages are another (see the description of Mandarin, p. 157).

We can use **transformations** as the tiebreaker, as often they apply only to certain roles. If there are many transformations that group experiencers and agents, we can group those as the subject (and talk about nom/acc syntax).

English RAISING is an example: experiencers and agents can be raised from a subclause—

> *I want [he leaves] → I want him to leave.*

I want [he kisses the girl] → I want him to kiss the girl.

but not patients:

*I want [he kisses the girl] → *I want her to he kiss.*

The rule is easily stated by saying that the subject (= **e** or **a**) of the sub-clause becomes the object of the main clause.

In Chukchi, there's a construction that **relativizes** clauses with negative participles, e.g.:

E-tipʔeyŋe-kə-lʔ-in nevəćqet raɣtəɣʔi.

neg-sing-neg-part-abs woman-abs 3sf.went.home

The woman who was not singing went home.

This relativization works with experiencers or patients, but not agents; it's an instance of erg/abs syntax. So we might define Chukchi subjects as **e** or **p**.

Another syntactic test: look at **deletion of coreferential NPs under conjunction**. This is best explained with an example:

The girl hit the boy and disappeared.

Who disappeared? For an English speaker it's obviously the girl. That is, a missing *experiencer* is assumed to match the *agent* of the previous clause.

So again, English is treating agents and experiencers alike, and we can say that the syntax is nom/acc.

Now let's look at Dyirbal:

Balan dʸugumbil baŋgul yaṛaŋgu balgan, baninʸu.

f.abs woman-abs m.erg man-erg hit came.here[19]

The man hit the woman and [she] came here.

Who came? Speakers will agree that it's the woman, not the man. Thus it's the absolutives in Dyirbal that are the subjects. Interestingly, this is still the case when pronouns (whose morphology is nom/acc) are used:

Ŋadʸa ŋinuna balgan, baninʸu.

1s.nom 2s.acc hit came.here

I hit you, and [you] came here.

---

19 There's no overt conjunction; concatenation implies conjunction.

Sometimes this test is ambiguous— e.g. in Chukchi *either* NP might be coreferential with the omitted NP in the conjoint.

Gender

There's more to say about GENDER, beyond the brief description in the *LCK* (p. 68). This section is greatly indebted to Greville Corbett's *Gender* (1991).

Gender is defined by AGREEMENT with other items. Besides the usual adjectives, demonstratives, articles, participles, and numerals, this can include verbs, possessives, relative pronouns, adverbs, and adpositions.

Adpositions? Sure, here are some examples from Abkhaz:

Àxra yə-zə̀	**a-žaħ°à à-la**
Axra 3sm-for	the-hammer 3sn-with
for Axra	*with the hammer*

Semantic gender systems

Genders may be assigned purely **semantically**— that is, the gender depends only on facts about the referent. The most common categories are sex and animacy, but many other categories occur: shape, importance, size, age, food, valuable things (as in Grebo), liquids (Fula), insects (Andi), hunting weapons (Ngangikurrunggurr), reflectiveness (Anindilyakwa), etc.

Tamil has three genders, which are assigned purely semantically:

male humans (and gods)
female humans (and goddesses)
everything else

English gender has roughly the same categories, though it only applies to the 3s pronouns *he, she, it.* The Nigerian language **Defaka** has the same three-way pronoun-only system.

Zande, a Niger-Kordofanian language, has four:

male humans
female humans
other animate
everything else

The gender system of **Dyirbal**, from Australia, is discussed in George Lakoff's book on classification, *Women, Fire, and Dangerous Things*; the title is a description of Dyirbal's second gender. (However, the rules were worked out by R.M.W. Dixon.) A schematic of the system:

I	male humans, non-human animates
II	female humans, water, fire, fighting
III	non-flesh food (honey, fruit, vegetables)
IV	everything else

There are quite a few unexpected assignments, but they are due to association of ideas. For instance:

birds, seen as spirits of female ancestors → II
light, sun, stars, associated with fire → II
moon is the husband of the sun → I
stinging nettle, hawks, gar fish are dangerous → II
fishing line, associated with fish → I
storms, rainbow, seen as mythical men → I

Ojibwe, an Algonquian language, has two genders:

animates (including spirits and trees)
inanimates

There are puzzling exceptions— e.g. *aagim* 'snowshoe', *anang* 'star', *miskomin* 'raspberry', and *akik* 'pot' are all animate. Mary Black-Rogers suggests that what's common to the animates is 'power'— a difficult notion to explore, she says, as power is not to be openly discussed!

Analyzing another Algonquian language, Penobscot, Conor Quinn found a number of clusters of nouns sharing animacy— e.g. fluid containers, big fleshy fruits, bodily swellings, thornlike items, cordage. These could be learned by analogy; e.g. if you know that *káskimin* 'red plum' is animate, you can correctly guess that *ssòmin* 'fox grape' and *psáhk'ətemin* 'blackberry' are too.

The base meaning of ANIMATE is easy— living things— but languages differ on the precise boundaries. E.g. plants are often excluded, while powerful natural forces like fire may be included. For a conlang, it's an opportunity to show off the metaphysics of your speakers (or their ancestors).

Semantic/formal gender systems

The opposite of a semantic gender system would be a FORMAL one—genders are assigned based on the **form** of the word. No natlang gender systems are purely formal; there's always a semantic assignment as well.

Indo-European

The classical Indo-European languages all had three genders, called MASCULINE, FEMININE, and NEUTER, but there was never a purely semantic classification. Rather, some words were assigned semantically, and the rest are assigned by DECLENSION (i.e. a particular pattern or paradigm of noun endings).

There are four such paradigms in Russian, two of which we saw above (p. 113). Here they are, with default gender assignments:

I	журнал 'newspaper'	masculine
II	наука 'science'	feminine
III	ночь 'night'	feminine
IV	слово 'word'	neuter

The rules for Russian gender are both semantic and morphological:

1. Male humans and higher animals → masculine
2. Female humans and higher animals → feminine
3. Everything else: go by the paradigm

That is, where the semantic and morphological rules conflict, follow the semantic rule. Thus дядя 'uncle' is masculine though the morphological rule points to feminine, while words like врач 'doctor' *when applied to a female* are feminine.

Be careful here; *declensions* are defined by their endings, *genders* by agreement. Even professors can get this wrong, e.g. calling declension II 'feminine'. If you think of declensions rather than words as gendered, the correct gender agreement as in this sentence will seem odd:

> **Мой добрый дядя читал.**
>
> my-s.nom.m good-s.nom.m uncle-s.nom read-past.m[20]
>
> *My good uncle was reading.*

---

[20] Russian verbs in the past tense inflect for gender, not person— compare я читал 'I (m.) read', я читала 'I (f.) read'. That's because historically they derive from participles.

Languages like Latin and Greek work much the same way as Russian, and I've imitated this system in Almea's Eastern family, including Verdurian.

Swahili

Swahili has seven genders, as summarized below:

Gender	*Noun*		*Verb*		*Contents include*
1/2	*m-*	*wa-*	*a-*	*wa-*	animates
3/4	*m-*	*mi-*	*u-*	*i-*	plants
5/6	*(ji-)*	*ma-*	*li-*	*ya-*	fruits; augmentatives
7/8	*ki-*	*vi-*	*ki-*	*vi-*	diminutives; small objects
9/10	*N-*	*N-*	*i-*	*zi-*	animals
11/10	*u-*	*N-*	*u-*	*zi-*	long objects; abstractions
15	*ku-*		*ku-*		infinitives

Scholars numbered the agreement prefixes, but counted singular and plural separately. Thus genders have names like 1/2, meaning that prefix 1 (*m-*) indicates the singular, prefix 2 (*wa-*) the plural. The numbering applies to all Bantu languages; as you can see Swahili has lost a few.[21]

The Verb columns give the singular and plural agreement affixes for the verb; these may differ from the noun prefixes.

An example:

Mwezi mmoja utatosha.

3-month 3-one 3-fut-sufficient

One month will be enough.

The verbal affixes are used for both subject and object concord:

Watoto walikisoma kitabu hiki.

2-child 2.pl-past-7-read 7-book this

The children read this book.

Gender 5/6 usually has no prefix in the singular (e.g. *yai* 'egg', *shauri* 'advice'), but *ji-* appears before one-syllable words (*jicho* 'eye') and *j-* before a vowel (*jambo* 'thing'). The N- in genders 9/10 and 11/10 sometimes appears as an *n-* (*ndege* 'bird'), sometimes as *m-* (*mbwa* 'dog'), but more often disappears (*fedha* 'money', *siku* 'day', *asali* 'honey').

---

[21] Bantu genders are sometimes called NOUN CLASSES, but there's no need to make a distinction.

The gender assignment rules are, like Russian, partly semantic and partly morphological:

1. Augmentatives → 5/6
2. Diminutives → 7/8
3. All other animates → 1/2
4. Everything else: follow the morphology

The important bit is rule 3, which overrides morphological gender for animates. E.g. *kiboko* 'hippopotamus', *jogoo* 'rooster', *tembo* 'elephant' form their plurals according to their morphological gender (*viboko* 'hippos'), but have 1/2 (animate) **agreement**: *kiboko mkubwa* 'a big hippo', *viboko wakubwa* 'big hippos'. This is exactly parallel to Russian дядя.

Very likely the original Bantu system was entirely semantic; that's why we still see regularities like plants abounding in gender 3/4 (e.g. *mpunga* 'rice', *mtama* 'millet', *muhogo* 'cassava'). But we find plants in other genders too (e.g. *embe* 'mango', *tunda* 'fruit' in 5/6), and agreement follows the morphological form.

Godie

Godie, a Kru language of Ivory Coast, has four genders, which can be identified by their 3s pronouns *ɔ, ɛ, a, o*. The first is assigned semantically, the others according to the frontness of the final vowel of the stem.

ɔ	humans
ɛ	nouns ending in front vowels *i ɩ e ɛ*
a	nouns ending in central vowels *ɨ ʉ ə a*
o	nouns ending in back vowels *u ʊ o ɔ*

E.g. *nyʉkpɔ* 'man' takes the pronoun and agreement marker *ɔ* as it's human; *li* 'spear' ends in a front vowel and so takes *ɛ*; *nyú* 'water' ends in a back vowel and takes *o*.

French

French has two genders, having merged the masculine and neuter from Latin:

masculine
feminine

It's long been the poster child for arbitrary gender, and learners are told to suck it up and remember the gender for each word. However, French gender is quite predictable. As with all the languages we've reviewed, it starts with semantic rules: words referring to male humans are masculine (*père* 'father', *blond* 'blond man', *instituteur* 'teacher'), those referring to female humans are feminine (*mère* 'mother', *blonde* 'blond woman', *institutrice* 'teacher').

The rest are assigned based on the last few phonemes of the root. G. Richard Tucker, Wallace E. Lambert, and André Rigault, in their 1977 monograph *The French speaker's skill with grammatical gender,* provided rules accounting for the genders of 85% of the *Petit Larousse*'s 30,000 nouns.

They started with final phonemes; e.g. 94% of nouns ending in /ʒ/ are masculine (*mirage, juge*); 90% of those in /-z/ are feminine (*cause, valise*).

In equivocal cases (e.g. /-ɔ̃/ is 30% feminine), they looked at earlier phonemes. E.g. 92% of words in /-jɔ̃/ *(nation, opération*) are feminine. This improves to 99% if we just take /-sjɔ̃, -zjɔ̃, -ʒjɔ̃, -tjɔ̃/, which leaves out masculines like *camion, sillon.*

But! There's often a *but* in linguistics, or in this case a *mais.* Dalila Ayoun (2007) has tested native speakers on 93 masculine and 50 feminine nouns, and they did *terribly.* They agreed on just 17 of the masculines, just *one* of the feminines. Adults did better than teenagers; less than half of the teens got the feminine nouns *alcôve, crypte, idole, oasis* right. More work is needed, but perhaps this is a case where linguists have found regularities that native speakers are not necessarily aware of.

Gender and number

Gender structure often looks different in different NUMBERS. **Russian** is a striking example: gender differences are neutralized in the plural. (Adjective endings are shown; the initial vowels look different after a palatalized consonant.)

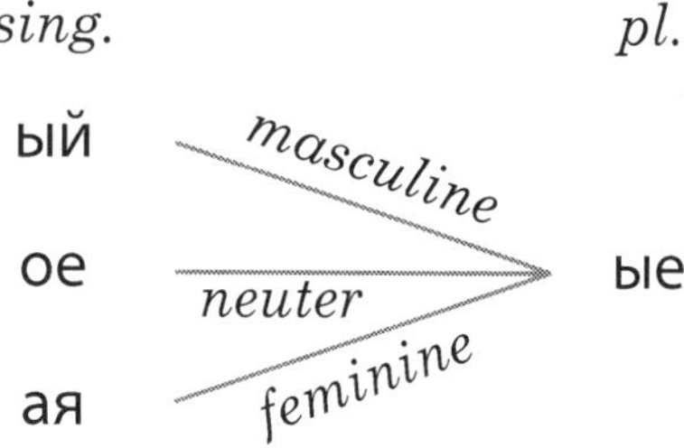

Tamil merges masculine and feminine in the plural. (It's a purely semantic system, so there are no associated endings.)

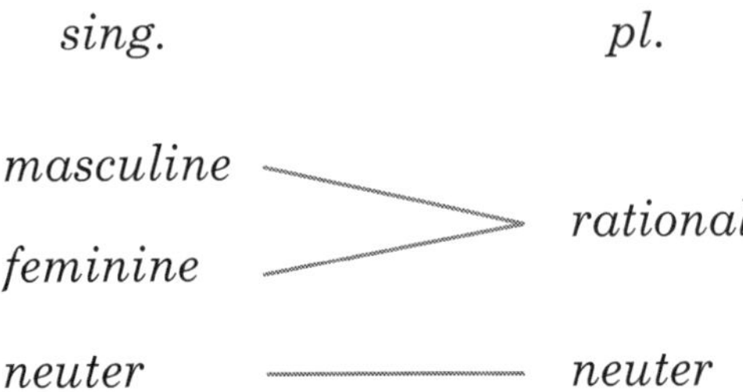

Romanian has just two forms in the singular and two in the plural—but these appear in three combinations, so there are three genders.

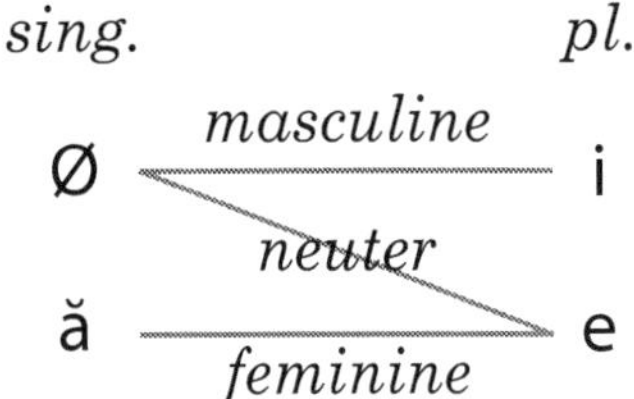

In such cases the agreement forms are TARGET GENDERS; the gray lines are CONTROLLER GENDERS. Thus we could say that Romanian has two target genders in the singular (masculine-neuter and feminine) and two in the plural (masculine and feminine-neuter), but three controller genders.

Here's a neat system— the **Somali** definite article, which shows POLARITY (the markers switch meanings in the plural):

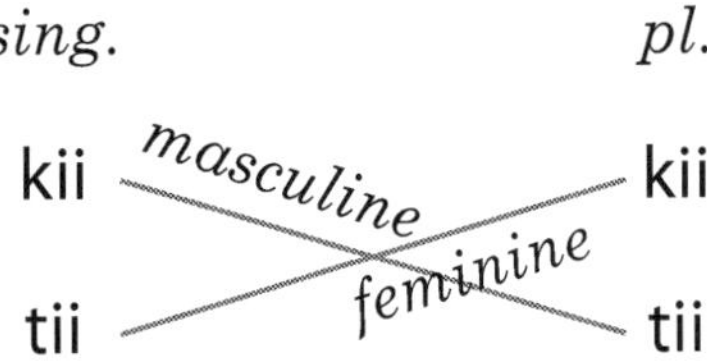

Tsova-Tush, a North Central Caucasian language, has eight genders, with this impressive system:

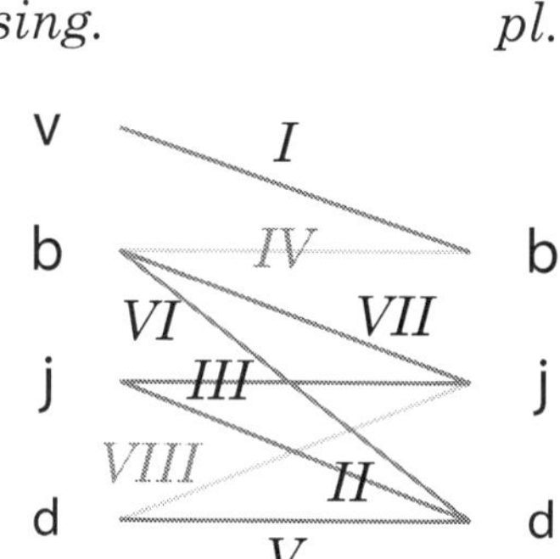

Difficulties

Counting all possible patterns may lead to a high number of genders. A few terminological niceties can tidy this up.

For instance, in Tsova-Tush gender IV has just two members, gender VIII just four. We can just treat these as exceptions—INQUORATE genders. French has a few nouns (notably *amour* 'love') which are masculine in the singular and feminine in the plural. If there were hundreds of them, it would look like Romanian and we'd call this a separate gender. But there are just three, so it's simpler to consider them irregular.

If we looked at Russian like a Martian, we'd find no less than six genders. However, the difference can be stated as a simple rule:

> For animate nouns, if the accusative would normally be identical to the nominative, use the genitive instead.

E.g. это журнал 'this newspaper' is the same in nominative and accusative. For 'this professor' the nominative is это профессор, but the accusative is этого профессора, which is identical to the genitive.

As the differences are confined to one case, we say that журнал and профессор live in separate SUBGENDERS— masculine inanimate and masculine animate.

In Kolami, a Dravidian language, there are two genders, male human and other; but the numerals 2, 3, 4 have three forms (male, female, other). Rather than say that the language has three genders, we say that these numerals have OVERDIFFERENTIATED targets.

HYBRID words can live in more than one gender. For instance, Spanish *artista* is masculine for male artists, feminine for female ones. Swahili *kiboko* 'hippo' is gender 1/2 when it refers to the animal, but if it's a toy, it follows its morphological gender 7/8.

Agreement may waver between semantic and phonological rules. Semantic agreement is more likely as we move up the AGREEMENT HIERARCHY:

> personal pronouns (*the artist painted, and she...)*
> relative pronouns *(the artist who...)*
> predicative adjectives *(the artist is good)*
> attributive adjectives (*the good artist)*

For example, the Spanish title *Su Majestad* is feminine, and takes feminine attributives (*Su Majestad suprema*), but predicatives and personal pronouns are masculine. In the West Atlantic language Landuma, animals like *abok* 'snake' follow their morphological gender (here 3/4) with adjectives, but take animate (gender 1/2) pronouns:

> **Abok ŋŋe, i-nəŋk kɔ lɛ.**
>
> snake this.3 1s-see 3s.acc.1 focus
>
> *This snake, I've seen it.*

The agreement hierarchy is reminiscent of the agentivity hierarchy (p. 119), though it ranks agreement targets rather than arguments. The overall principle seems to be the same: the more agentive something is, the more it's likely to take semantic agreement.

Gender mismatches

If there are sex-linked genders, which is used for an **unknown person**? Often the masculine is used, but in languages ranging from Maasai (Africa) to Seneca (N. America) to Goajiro (S. America), the feminine is used. English can use *they;* Polish uses the neuter singular. Zande has a special personal pronoun *ni* which can be used for people of unknown gender. In Dyirbal the feminine may be used for a mixed group if the majority, or the oldest members, are women.

There may be a NEUTRAL AGREEMENT FORM for things that don't have a gender. The Jane's Addiction album *El ritual de lo habitual* is a Spanish example; adjectives don't have genders so the special form *lo* is used. *Lo* is also used for sentential objects, which also have no gender: *No lo creo* 'I don't believe it.'

A similar problem is how to refer to **conjoints** of differing genders. There are a number of options:

- Have the verb agree with the **nearer** conjoint, as in Swahili:

Kti na mguu wa meza umevunjika.

7-chair and 3-leg of table 3-pres.perf-break-stat

The chair and the leg of the table are broken.

- Use the **neuter** form, if you have one, even for people; Icelandic is an example.
- **Disallow** conjoints of different genders. E.g. in Tamil you can't conjoin animate and inanimates; if you want to say something like "Raman and the dog came", you use an alternative like "Raman came, with the dog."
- **Choose** one gender arbitrarily— usually the masculine, but in the Omotic language Zayse it's the feminine.

Origins of gender

If you want to develop a gender system from scratch, Corbett suggests a recipe:

- Start with measure words, as in Mandarin (p. 160). These in turn start as nouns, as in English *a grain of rice, a sheet of paper.*
- Fuse the measure words with the demonstratives, forming demonstratives that make gender distinctions.
- Turn the demonstratives into 3s pronouns.
- For verbal agreement, cliticize these onto the verbs. (Compare Tok Pisin *Bill i luk-im mi.*)
- For nominal agreement, turn the demonstratives into definite articles (as happened going from Latin to Romance). Then fuse these with the noun.
- Hide your tracks with sound changes, so the agreement markers don't all look the same. (The loss of final /ə/ in French made gender assignment quite difficult.)

The above process is clear in many languages, but Indo-European seems to have followed a different route. As Winfred Lehmann explains, early Indo-European didn't have genders so much as endings: *-s, -m,* and *-h,* the latter marking a collective.

In Hittite, the *-h* disappeared, and there were just two genders, animate and inanimate. This was apparently a pure semantic system: all the inanimates really were inanimate.

In the other branches, the *-h* disappeared but lengthened the previous vowel, increasing the contrast with the consonantal endings. This ending became associated with feminine referents, while the *-s* ending was increasingly associated with masculines.

An insight into how such association may arise comes from languages where a single word in the 'wrong' gender functions as a **Trojan horse**, realigning the meaning of the genders. E.g. in the Indic language Konkani, *čeḍũ* 'girl' is neuter, and has led to the 'neuter' being used for all young women, the feminine for older women. Similarly, nicknames in certain Polish dialects are neuter (e.g. *Zuzię* for *Zuzia*), which has led to a similar usage of the neuter for unmarried women, even for self-reference: *jo poszło* 'I went' (neuter agreement on the verb).

Aspect

Aspect was discussed in the *LCK* (pp. 74, 117). But it's worth looking at in more detail.

A major pitfall is that the names of tenses often conflict with the technical terms. Traditional grammarians could object that they came up with their terms first; but the modern terminology is more precise. Forms called "perfects" are often really perfectives (or something else entirely).

Plus, even if a language's form largely meets one of these definitions, it will have other uses that go beyond it.

Perfective

As a first approximation, the PERFECTIVE treats an event or state as an instance in time— as an **unanalyzed whole**; the IMPERFECTIVE treats it as a process with a beginning, duration, and end:

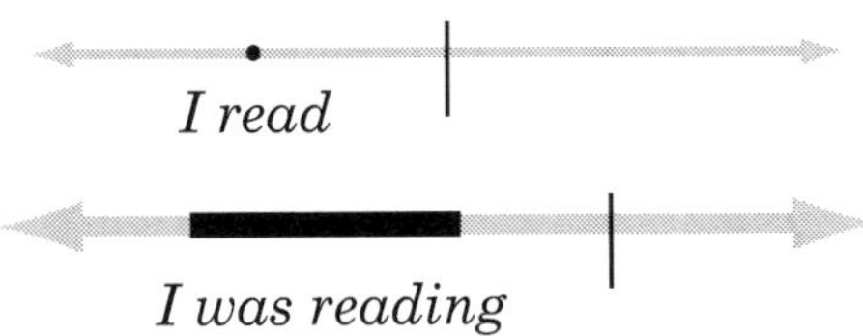

It's not the length of the event that's key, it's the perspective. In French, the same long event could be described with either aspect:

Henri IV régna 21 ans. [perfective]

Henri IV régnait 21 ans. [imperfective]

Henri IV ruled for 21 years.

The first formulation treats the reign as a whole; it would be appropriate if we were looking at the whole sweep of French history, or comparing different kings. The second considers the reign as a process, or a background; it would be appropriate for discussing events within the reign.

Either the perfective or imperfective may be the UNMARKED or default form. E.g. я читал in Russian is unmarked for aspect— it's 'I read' or 'I was reading'; the perfective я прочитал is marked. In French, by contrast, it's *je lus* which is unmarked, contrasting with the imperfective *je lisais* 'I was reading'.

Aspect is normally expressed on the verb, but not always. E.g. Finnish sometimes marks aspect with the choice of case:

Hän luki kirjan.

he read book-acc

He read the book.

Hän luki kirjaa.

he read book-partit

He was reading the book.

Beginning and end

Latin *perfectus* means 'complete', and grammarians evidently felt that the most important thing about an event seen perfectively was that it was over with. Often it is, but a form which focuses on the **end** of an event is really a COMPLETIVE.

Russian has some derivational completives, e.g. отужинать 'finish supper', which are to be distinguished from the perfective ужинать 'have supper'.

Bulgarian verbs mark **both** perfective/imperfective and completive/incompletive (in Bulgarian grammar called AORIST[22]/imperfect). The aorist always expresses that an event began and ended, but it's still possible to treat it as a whole (perfective) or as a process (imperfective).

A form which focuses on the **beginning** of an event is INCEPTIVE or INCHOATIVE. There may be a separate derivational form; compare also English constructions like *burst out laughing*.

---

[22] The AORIST in Classical Greek was a perfective, but as this example shows, the term is used in quirky ways in other languages.

A perfective may suggest completion— *I cleaned the kitchen* may announce that you're done— but attention may be focused on the start, too, as in this Spanish example:

> **Conocí a Juan hace treinta años.**
>
> *I got to know Juan thirty years ago.*

Repetitions

The HABITUAL aspect emphasizes that a situation was characteristic of the time in question; e.g. English *used to:*

> *He used to read to me every night.*

The English past habitual has an IMPLICATURE (p. 44) that the situation no longer holds: if I say *Bill used to be a member of the Communist Party* you can assume that he isn't a member now. (But it's not an IMPLICATION, as I can deny it without contradiction: *...and he still is.*)

A habitual action is often but not always ITERATIVE, i.e. divided into separate, repeated instances. The reading example is also an iterative, but *This used to be a Wendy's* is not.

Many languages have a FREQUENTATIVE, usually in the derivational morphology, which expresses repeated action— e.g. Latin *dīco* 'I say' → *dicto* 'I say often'. The English suffix *-le* (cf. *dab/dabble, daze/dazzle, crumb/crumble, prate/prattle, scud/scuttle*) was originally a frequentative.

Retrospective

PERFECT aspect refers to past or future events **with present relevance**; to put it another way, it draws attention to the **consequences** of the action.

As this term is easily confused with the perfective, and often conflicts with traditional terminology, I prefer RETROSPECTIVE for past events (*I've had an idea)* and PROSPECTIVE for future ones (*He'll have finished cleaning*).

The English perfect has several uses:

- The PERFECT OF RESULT, which unlike the simple past implies that the condition still obtains:

  John has arrived [and he's still here].
  I've had a bath [so I'm clean].
  I've told you before [and I'm telling you again].
  She's finished eating [and didn't start up again].

I've lost my pen [and haven't found it yet].
I've eaten lunch [so I'm not hungry].

I prefer to talk about implications or consequences than relevance, since as Grice tells us, people usually only say what is relevant. But note that the implication can vary by circumstances— e.g. that John has arrived may mean that we can start the party; that I've eaten lunch may mean that I'm free for an event.

In Swahili this is the infix *me-: umesoma* 'you've read'.

- The EXPERIENTIAL PERFECT, which asserts that the action has occurred at least once:

  The queen has been to Utah.
  I've watched C-beams glitter near the Tannhauser Gate.

- The PERFECT OF PERSISTENCE, which emphasizes continuity from the past to the present:

  We've lived here for ten years.

- The PERFECT OF RECENCY, where part of the message is in fact how recent the event is:

  I've just learned that the election was rigged.

  Irish has a transparent form for this, e.g. *Táim tar éis teacht isteach* 'I just came in', literally 'I'm after coming in,' which can be borrowed into Irish English.

When does recency expire? *I've seen my mother this morning* is fine if said during the morning; in the evening we'd be more likely to say *I saw my mother this morning*. But Spanish *He visto a mi madre esta mañana* would still be OK. In French the recency requirement of the perfect (*Je l'ai vu*) was so relaxed that it simply became the colloquial past tense.

In English, a diagnostic of the perfect— *except* for the perfect of persistence— is that it resists assignment to a specific time: **She's finished eating at 7:30.*

The PAST ANTERIOR or PLUPERFECT is a perfect where the relevance, experience, recency etc. apply to the narrative past rather than the present: *John had arrived, so we could party. We'd studied at Beauxbâtons. We'd lived there for ten years.* But sometimes it serves as a remote past tense, describing events before the time of the narrative:

> *Earlier that day I had taken the bus, where a man in a strange hat with a cord for a band had argued with another passenger.*

All four types can occur in the **future**, with the same nuances— e.g. *John will have arrived* implies that he'll still be there, or that the party can start; *we'll have lived here for ten years* means that the action goes up to the postulated future time.

Progressive

The PROGRESSIVE specifically expresses ongoing action. The English progressive (*I was studying, I'm cooking*) is a good example.

In English, we are happy to use the ordinary present for STATIVE verbs (*I know you are confused*), but for events we almost always use the progressive (*I'm writing a book, my wife is sleeping*), leaving the present for habitual uses (*I write every day, she snores loudly*). Spanish *Escribo un libro* can be used more generally.

We do use the progressive with stative verbs, either to emphasize the process *(I'm understanding aspect better every day!*) or to underline that a situation is temporary (*I'm living in a van*).

In Spanish, you can combine perfective and progressive:

> **Estuve leyendo en casa todo el día.**
>
> *I was reading in the house all day long.*

Estuve 'I was' is perfective; the whole day's event is thus bounded, seen as a unit, and yet it consisted of an ongoing process (reading). The imperfective, by contrast, would set the scene for an event:

> **Estaba leyendo en casa cuando llegó.**
>
> *I was reading in the house when he arrived.*

In many languages the progressive derives from **locatives**. This is a neat application of the TIME IS SPACE metaphor (*LCK* p. 114). E.g. Icelandic *Ég er að lesa* 'I'm reading', literally 'I am in reading'. Cf. Italian *sto leggendo,* where the verb originally meant 'stand'.

Chopping up time

A few more aspects, all of which express various very particular relationships between the event and the timeline:

- A state that's always or universally true (*kittens are cute*) can be called GNOMIC. Swahili's *a-* tense can be considered gnomic, as opposed to *na-* which implies ongoing action.

- A PUNCTUAL aspect refers to an event which only takes an instant. Russian has this as a derivational form; compare кашлять 'cough' with кашлянуть 'cough for a moment'.
- A DELIMITATIVE expresses that an action was only done for a short period: *He cleaned up a little.*
- The DURATIVE emphasizes that an event took some time, though it can still be viewed as a whole (i.e. placed in the perfective). This is also derivational in Russian; compare Он стоял 'he stood', Он постоял там час 'he stood there for an hour'.

Telicity

A TELIC activity is one with an inherent product or achievement, as in *walk home* or *make a conlang* or *eat up the Doritos.* Two tests of telicity:

- Whether you can add *in an hour.*

  I walked home in an hour.
  I made a conlang in an hour,
  **I sang in an hour.*
  **We browsed porn in an hour.*

- Whether the progressive implies the simple past. *I was browsing porn* implies that *I browsed porn*, but *I was making a conlang* doesn't imply *I made a conlang.*

English 'persuade' is ATELIC, but Russian уговаривать is not:

> **Он уговаривал меня, но не уговорил меня.**
>
> he persuade-impfv.past-3sm I.acc but not persuade-pfv.past-3sm I.acc
>
> *He was persuading me, but didn't convince me.*
> *[lit., didn't persuade me]*

There can be derivational affixes for telicity. Compare German *kämpfen* 'fight', *erkämpfen* 'achieve by means of a fight', or Latin *facere* 'do', *conficere* 'complete'.

Aspect and time

The present is an instant— something can be going on right now, but few events can really happen in the present. That is, the present tense is inherently imperfective. (In English the present usually has a habitual meaning for event verbs: *Don't worry if I write rhymes; I write checks.*)

If you have a morphological perfect, then, it's likely to take on a future meaning— that is, it becomes a prospective. This has happened in Russian (я напишу 'I'll write') and other languages, such as Georgian.

Often aspects are distinguished only in the past, like the French imperfect. English habitual *used to* only works in the past—you can't say **Next year I'll use to read to you every night.*

Some languages **don't mark tense**, only aspect. Yoruba has no tense markers, but instead relies on a variety of aspect markers: *ń* progressive, *ti* retrospective, *yó* prospective, *máa* inceptive/iterative. These can be combined:

> **Èmi yó ti máa kọ́lé.**
>
> 1s.emph prosp retro incep build.house
>
> *I will have started building a house.*

For more, see Bernard Comrie's *Aspect* (1976), which I've relied on heavily here.

Also see the section on Mandarin aspect (p. 164).

Valence

VALENCE (or valency) is a verb's number of arguments (p. 115). Languages often provide ways to increase or decrease valence:

eat(s)	1	*The soup is eaten*
eat(m, s)	2	*Mafalda eats soup*
eat(r, m, s)	3	*Raquel made Mafalda eat soup*

The semantics are the same— it's the same soup-eating— but the pragmatics are different. Valence-changing operations in general allow foregrounding a non-agent, or backgrounding (or omitting) an agent.

They can also facilitate linking up sentences. As we saw above, shared subjects can often be eliminated after a conjunction:

> *The soldier hit the sniper then ran away.*

If it's the sniper who fled, we can use the passive to make him the subject:

> *The sniper was hit by the soldier then ran away.*

Valence-changing operations may work in several ways:

- **Lexically**: a separate verb encodes the situation with more or fewer arguments. Compare *Jill teaches Julie* vs. *Julie learns, Morgan eats mutton* vs. *Morgan dines*
- **Morphologically**: an affix changes the verb's valence
- **Analytically**: a syntactic construction is used, like the English causative or passive

Decreasing valence

Passives

In nominative-accusative languages, the PASSIVE promotes the object into a subject.

In Latin, there are separate endings for the passive, with several tenses—this part of the morphology is called passive VOICE.

Nūllīus illōs capit.

none-s.nom that-m.pl.acc seize-3s

Nobody is catching them.

→ **Capientur ā nūllō.**

seize-passive.3p by none-s.abl

They are caught by nobody.

Note that the verb agrees with the new subject; also that if you want to keep the old subject, it's placed in a prepositional phrase. Of course, one of the reasons to use the passive might be that you want to leave out the old subject entirely:

Cerevisia potātur in tabernā.

beer-s.nom drink-passive.3s in tavern-abl

Beer is drunk in a tavern.

Latin has a rather neat form, the GERUNDIVE or future passive participle, which we see in expressions like *quod erat dēmonstrandum* 'which was to be demonstrated', or the name *Amanda* '(she who is) to be loved'.

Some languages have a MIDDLE voice alongside the passive. Prototypically these envision the action as a process affecting the subject rather than something done to it by someone. E.g. in K'iche, *xch'aay* 'be hit (by someone)' contrasts with *xch'aayik* 'get hit' (with no focus on the agent). Ancient Greek had a similar voice, but it was also used for reflexives. Latin has a few verbs called DEPONENTS which are conjugated like passives but have an active meaning, e.g. *nāscor* 'I am born', *vereor* 'I'm afraid', *hortor* 'I urge', *lōquor* 'I speak'.

An agentless form can also be called an ANTICAUSATIVE, as in Amharic:

> **Bər-u tə-kəffətə.**
>
> door-def passive-open.perf.3m
>
> *The door opened.*

Could a language contrast anticausatives and passives? English does: *the door opened* vs. *the door was opened.* Note that you can add an agent to the second sentence but not the first.

Antipassives

In ergative-absolutive languages, the ANTIPASSIVE turns the agent (the ergative argument) into an experiencer (marked by the absolutive). If you're used to the nom-acc system this sounds like a demotion, but as we've seen the 'subject' in erg/abs languages is arguably the absolutive.

An example from Dyirbal:

> **Balan d^{y}ugumbil baŋgul yaṛaŋgu balgan.**
>
> f.abs woman-abs m.erg man-erg hit
>
> **→ Bayi yaṛa bagun d^{y}ugumbilgu balgalŋaŋu.**
>
> m.abs man f.dat woman hit-antip
>
> *The man hit the woman.*

The gloss is the same, but the man is now an absolutive, while the woman is relegated to the dative. This sentence foregrounds the man, and also allows the sentence to be conjoined to another where the man appears in the absolutive (e.g. *the man left*).

Reflexives

A REFLEXIVE is simply an action where the subject and object are the same, e.g. *I washed myself.* (It can be seen as valence-reducing because the number of *distinct* arguments is lower.) In logic this is no big deal, but languages often have special forms to mark it.

- English has an analytic reflexive (using special pronouns: *I dressed myself*), or it can omit the object (*I dressed for dinner*).
- Russian adds a suffix to the verb: e.g. Я купаю 'I bathe (someone)', Я купаюсь 'I bathe myself.'

A related concept is the RECIPROCAL: *they killed each other.* (For the oddity of the English construction see p. 27.) In Spanish, the reflexive and reciprocal use the same form: *se mataron.*

Impersonal expressions

Often we'd like to just omit the subject, either because we don't know who it was or we just don't care. In English we can use the passive, or an existential construction (*There will be dancing*), or general 'they' or 'people'.

Spanish often uses the reflexive in impersonal expressions: *Se habla castellano* 'Spanish is spoken here'.

In Russian you can use 3p forms with no expressed subject:

> **В России мало играют в теннис.**
>
> in Russia-prep little play-3p in tennis
>
> *In Russia they don't play much tennis.*

In French a special pronoun *on* is used: *On n'aime pas les tricheurs* 'People don't like cheaters'.

Nishnaabemwin, as we'll see later, has a special ending (the 3x) for unspecified actors.

Increasing valence

Causatives

Logically, a CAUSATIVE has the meaning *cause(x, V(y))*; that is, *x* causes the situation *V(y).*

Quechua has a **morphological** causative; that is, it can turn any verb into a causative using the suffix *-chi*:

> **puñura** *he slept* → **puñuchirani** *I made him sleep*

Often this allows Quechua to save on roots:

> **mikuy** *eat* → **mikuchiy** *feed*
>
> **qaway** *see* → **qawachiy** *show*
>
> **wañuy** *die* → **wañuchiy** *kill*
>
> **yachay** *know* → **yachachiy** *teach*

The former subject is normally demoted to an accusative:

Luwis waqan → Luwista waqachini.

Luis-nom cry-3s / Luis-acc cry-caus-1s

Luis is crying / I'm making Luis cry.

But if there was already an object, rather than having two accusatives, Quechua prefers to put the former subject into another case:

Wasiyta qawanqa.

house-my-acc see-3s.fut

He will see my house.

→ **Wasiyta payman qawachisaq.**

house-my-acc 3s-illative see-caus-1s.fut

I'll make him see my house.

This sort of case rearrangement is common, but some languages are happy with double accusatives, e.g. Korean:

Nay-ka ku yeca-lul simpwulum-ul sikhi-ess-ta.

1s-nom the woman-acc errand-acc make-past-decl

I made the woman do an errand.

English has an **analytic** causative. Note the lowering of the original subject to be the object of the causative:

She did it → I made her do it.

(Really we have multiple causatives— *make, cause, force, order, let* imply various levels of responsibility and coercion.)

French is similar, but the old subject becomes a dative:

Il a obéi. → Je lui ai fait obéir.

3s have.3s obey-past.part / 1s 3s.dat have.1s make-past.part obey

He obeyed → I made him obey.

There are also **lexical** causatives— that is, words with an inherently causative meaning. Of course, to the users of the language, these look like ordinary transitive verbs! Only a logician cares that *He dropped the ball* is equivalent to *He made the ball fall.*

Ambitransitives can be considered a regular class of lexical causatives:

cause(Chris, melt(cheese)) → Chris melted the cheese.

cause(Marie, work.hard(employees)) →
Marie worked her employees hard.

John Haiman suggests that the progression

analytic causative
morphological causative
lexical causative

implies a more direct or active type of causation. So *Cat killed Wubie* means Cat was fully in control; *Cat caused Wubie to die* might have been an accident. Similarly, Korean has both a morphological and an analytic causative; the latter is used for mere persuasion or enabling.

Applicatives

An APPLICATIVE takes a peripheral argument and promotes it to direct object. Here are some examples, showing the original case of the promoted argument:

instrumental
Amharic

Aster mət'rəgiya-w-ɨn dəǰǰ t'ərrəgə-čč-ɨbb-ət.
Aster broom-def-acc doorway sweep.perf-3f-inst-3mo
Aster swept the doorway with a broom.

benefactive
Kinyarwanda

Umugóre a-ra-kor-er-a umuhuungu igitabo.
woman she-pres-read-applic-asp boy book
The woman is reading the boy the book.

reason
Nomatsiguenga

Pablo i-kisa-biri-ke-ri Juan.
Pablo he-angry-applic-past-him Juan
Pablo was angry on account of Juan.

locative
Ainu

Poro cise e-horari.
big house applic-live
He lives in a big house.

In these examples there's an affix on the verb (underlined) that marks the applicative and its type. However, a promoted argument might also be marked simply by position, as in the English DATIVE SHIFT:

Nyarlathotep gave the Necronomicon to Lara.

→ *Nyarlathotep gave Lara the Necronomicon.*

Measures can act as objects in English: *She walked a mile; that shelf weighs a ton.* These might be better classified as applicatives than transitives, especially as they can't be passivized: **A ton is weighed by that shelf.*

Dative of interest

Colloquial French has what might be called an unexpected benefactive— a personal argument (usually *moi* 'me') that doesn't seem to contribute to the meaning of the sentence:

> **Goûte-moi c'te chocolat!**
>
> taste-2s.imper-1s.acc that chocolate
>
> *Taste that chocolate!*

We might translate *Taste that chocolate for me*, but the speaker is not asking for a favor, but communicating the intensity of their own experience.

The DATIVE OF INTEREST in Spanish is similar, but works as an anti-benefactive— this happened to my detriment.

> **Se me rompió el condon.**
>
> refl 1s.dat break-past.3s the.s.m condom
>
> *The condom broke on me.*

Modality

MODALITY is concerned with the status of a proposition— how true it is, and whether it's subject to obligations and intentions.

For more see F.R. Palmer's *Mood & Modality* (2001). He offers this overall classification (but I've changed a few of the terms):

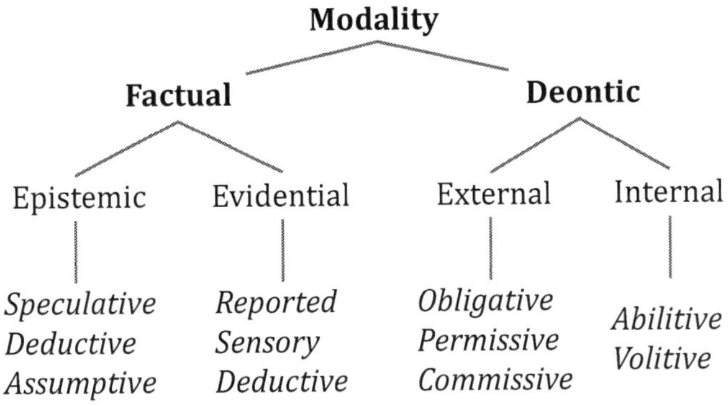

(Deductives may appear in either the epistemic or evidential branch; languages tend to have only one of these branches.)

As with aspect, be aware that the clear-cut theoretical distinctions may be messy in a particular language. Modals tend to accumulate multiple meanings. (For that matter, a particular marker can mix tense, aspect, and mood.)

The morphology of mood

Modality can be expressed in various ways:

- Lexically, e.g. by adverbs: *He's certainly a Sith Lord.*
- By auxiliary verbs, as in English: *Sith Lords can attack with electric blasts.*
- By agglutinative inflections, such as the Quechua evidential clitics: *Mariyaqa wiksayoqsi* 'I hear Maria is pregnant.'

  The latter two types can be grouped as MODAL SYSTEMS.
- As a dimension of verbal morphology; here we talk about MOODS, either subjunctive vs. indicative or irrealis vs. realis; e.g. French *Je veux* (ind.) *que tu partes* (subj.) 'I want you to leave'.

It's possible to have both moods and auxiliaries, as in the Romance languages (but note that the subjunctive has been declining for centuries).

If you use auxiliaries, note that English's modals have some peculiar morphological limitations other languages don't share. E.g. English modals don't have infinitives (**He wants can swim*), but this isn't true of German or French (*Il veut savoir nager*). 'Must' doesn't have a past tense in English, but *müssen* and *devoir* do.

Factual modality

FACTUAL (Palmer's PROPOSITIONAL) modality has to do with the **reliability** of statements. Languages tend to approach this in one of two ways:

- EPISTEMIC modality is concerned with the **factual status** of statements. English is an example:

  SPECULATIVE: *It can rain today.*

  DEDUCTIVE: *The old lady must be dead.*

  ASSUMPTIVE: *The book will be out by now.*

- EVIDENTIAL modality deals with the **source of knowledge**, such as hearsay or sensory perception. Deductives can appear in this branch too.

Deductives aren't simply a matter of confidence: *She must be dead* is more than just *She is certainly dead.* 'Must' implies inference, and in fact it's often accompanied by a reason: *It's been hours since she went in after the golem, she must be dead.* By contrast the assumptive doesn't require any reasoning.

Some evidential systems

Quechua has three basic evidentials:

-mi personal knowledge
-si hearsay
-cha probability

These are clitics, and have the secondary function of indicating the COMMENT (the new information in the sentence, as opposed to the TOPIC).

In Spanish, Quechua speakers often use *diz que* 'they say that' as a rough equivalent to *-si.*

The three clitics can combine with the suffix *-iki* with slightly different meanings:

-miki general knowledge; also makes an excuse: *Warmakunaqa achkatamiki* 'Children eat a lot, you know.'
-siki takes a bit more responsibility for the assertion— insists on it despite the indirect knowledge: *Kanansiki chayamunqa* 'I'm told he's arriving today'
-chiki reduces the improbability, or expresses resignation: *Risaqchiki, imanasaqtaq* 'I have to go— what can I do?'

They also combine with the emphatic suffix *-á*, with strengthened meanings:

-má absolute certainty: *Manamá rinqakuchu* 'I'm certain they won't go'
-sá still hearsay, but very reliable
-chá reduces the doubt: *Hamunqachá* 'I believe he'll come'

Central Pomo has a system of five clitics:

č^{h}éemul unmarked: *It rained*
č^{h}éemul- ma? established fact *(everyone knows...)*
č^{h}éemul- ya visual cxperience *(I saw it)*

čʰéemul- nme·	auditory experience *(I heard it)*
čʰéemul- ʔdo	hearsay *(I'm told)*
čʰéemul- ʔka	deduction *(everything's wet, so...)*

Hidatsa concentrates more on who knows what about the proposition:

ski	speaker knows it's true
c	speaker believes it's true
wareac	it's something everyone knows
rahe	hearsay
—	question: speaker doesn't know, but listener does

The type of hearsay may be further broken down: **Fasu** *-pakae* is used if the speaker heard the news from a direct witness; but *-ripo* if it came from a more remote source.

Lega distinguishes good from weak evidence: the particle *ámbo* marks reported or doubtful statements, while *ampó* means the statement is highly trustworthy.

Makah distinguishes certain and uncertain visual experience:

čapac	*I see it's a canoe*
čapaccaqil	*It looks like a canoe*

If you have evidentials, think about whether they're **required** and what happens if they're not given.

- Quechua requires evidentials on all statements.
- Central Pomo (above) has an unmarked (DECLARATIVE) form. Ngiyambaa has a marked declarative form for when the source of knowledge isn't given.
- In Huichol, the unmarked form is used for questions.

Questions may use the same evidentials as statements, or have their own forms. Latin has three ways of asking a question, depending on what you think the answer is:

Guess	*Example*
None	**Ursusne in tabernam introit?** *Does a bear go into a bar?*
'No'	**Num cerevisia mala est?** *Beer isn't bad, is it?*
'Yes'	**Nōnne ursus animal implūme bipēs?** *A bear is a featherless biped, right?*

Khezha has no less than eight ways of asking a question, depending on whether the speaker

- knows the answer, but expects confirmation
- has reliable info, but wants confirmation
- is uncertain
- thinks the info is correct, but isn't sure
- assumes the listener will agree
- is amazed at the idea, wants a reaffirmation
- heard a strange rumor, wants verification
- doubts an unusual event, wants reaffirmation

Deontic modality

DEONTIC modality has to do with obligation and permission. It can be subclassed based on the source of the compulsion:

- EXTERNAL factors:

  OBLIGATIVE: *You must marry the prince.*

  PERMISSIVE: *You may kiss the bride.*

  COMMISSIVE: *You will bring me the diamond.*

- INTERNAL factors:

  ABILITIVE: *I can conlang!*

  VOLITIVE: *I will take the Ring.*

(Palmer calls all this EVENT modality, which seems uninformative. He calls the subdivisions deontic and DYNAMIC.)

Emotional reactions to statements may also be considered modals—e.g. DESIDERATIVE for things wanted, TIMITIVE for things feared. The BENEFACTIVE (e.g. Quechua *-pu*) indicates that something was done for someone's benefit.

Again, actual modals often have multiple meanings. English *can* is also used as a permissive and even as a speculative (p. 147). *Will* usually has at least some commissive or volitive force, but it's also as close as English comes to a future tense (*The drought will end someday*).

In Modern Greek, μπορώ agrees with its subject only for deontic meanings:

Τα παιδιά μπορεί να φύγουν αύριο.

Ta peðjá borí na fiɣun ávrio.

the children may.3s that leave.3p.pfv tomorrow

The children may leave tomorrow [possibility].

Τα παιδιά μπορούν να φύγουν αύριο.

Ta peðjá borún na fiɣun ávrio.

the children may.3p that leave.3p.pfv tomorrow

The children may leave tomorrow [permission].

Many languages distinguish knowing how to do something (e.g. French *il sait nager* 'he knows how to swim') from having the physical ability *(il peut voler* 'he can fly').

Negative deontics

When you negate a modal statement, are you negating the *statement* or the *modality*?

Mandarin takes the logical approach that you should negate the modal or the main verb— or both— depending on what you mean:

Wǒ bu néng qù.

1s not can go

I can't go. = *¬can(go)*

Wǒ néng bu qù.

1s can not go

I'm capable of not going. = *can(¬go)*

Wǒ bu néng bu qù.

1s not can not go

I'm not capable of not going. = *¬can(¬go)*

It's quite common, however, for negating the modal to be taken as negating the proposition:

English

I mustn't go. = *must(¬go)*

French

Il ne faut pas partir.

Kinyarwanda

Ntagomba kwinjira.

This is sometimes called NEG HOPPING, as the negative hops like a bunny over the auxiliary (semantically it's *must* ¬*go* but syntactically it's ¬*must go*).

But we still need to negate the auxiliary itself sometimes; in English this can be done by changing the verb. Compare:

Kim may not be a Cylon. = *may(¬Cylon)*
Kim can't be a Cylon. = *¬may(Cylon)*

You must not open the Necronomicon. = *must(¬open)*
You need not open the Necronomicon. = *¬must(open)*

The irrealis

If modality is incorporated into your verbal morphology, and must be expressed, it's considered a MOOD.

E.g. Spanish *hablo* and *hable* are the indicative and subjunctive of 'I speak'; marking the mood is just as obligatory as marking person, number, and tense. Compare Tamil *avan pēca* 'He speaks' with *avan pēcalām* 'He can speak': modal affixes *can* be added to a sentence but aren't obligatory, so Tamil doesn't have moods.

Realis/irrealis systems

The prototypical REALIS form is used for simple past or present events. IRREALIS forms are used for 'less real' events, but the exact system varies by language. Let's look at a few classifications.

Latin

Realis (indicative): past, present, and future events, including negatives and interrogatives

Irrealis (subjunctive):

JUSSIVES[23]: *naviget,* let him sail

volitives: *ut Morbōniam abeās,* (I wish you'd) go to hell

obligatives: *sed maneam etiam,* but I should still stay

speculatives: *iam apsolutos censeas,* you may think they were already paid off

presuppositions: *Forsitan malē tē dīcat,* perhaps he's speaking ill of you

plus quite a few uses in subclauses— for instance, in both halves of an *if* clause: *Sī ursus essem, ursus fābulāns essem* 'If I were a bear, I'd be a talking bear'

Manam

Realis: past, present, habitual

Irrealis: future, imperatives, warnings, counterfactuals

Caddo

Realis: future, future intentions, imperatives

Irrealis: negation, prohibition, obligation, conditionals, simulative, infrequentative, admirative, temporal negatives, generic conditional, negative conditional

Central Pomo

Realis: imperfective, perfective

Irrealis: conditional, imperative, future

Amele

Realis: habitual past, remote past, yesterday's past, today's past, present[24]

Irrealis: future, imperative, hortative, prohibitive, counterfactuals, apprehensive

Generalizations tend to fail. The future is usually irrealis, but not in Caddo, or Latin/Romance. The habitual past is irrealis in Bargam, realis in Manam. Imperatives are often irrealis, but not in Caddo and Maricopa...

---

[23] Or HORTATIVES: non-2nd person imperatives.

[24] Take a moment to admire that array of past tenses.

Because of such variation, some scholars (e.g. Joan Bybee) have doubted that irrealis is a useful typological category. As so often, I think the problem disappears if we think in terms of prototypes (*LCK* p. 118). The prototypical realis is a simple event known to have occurred or to be occurring. The prototypical irrealis is something not known to be real; different languages focus on different kinds of unreality.

Once you have the distinction, it can be extended in all sorts of ways. E.g. in **Alamblak**, the bare imperative is realis; switching to the irrealis is more polite.

I've included the SUBJUNCTIVE here, though some see this as a slightly different kind of irrealis. (E.g. the subjunctive co-occurs with tense, while the irrealis is usually tenseless.[25]) However, it seems to be a matter of terminological preference, by region: 'irrealis' is used for Native American and Papuan languages, while 'subjunctive' is used for Indo-European and African languages.

There are a few **three-way** distinctions. **Dani** distinguishes real, likely, and potential events (e.g. *Wathi* 'I killed him', *Wasik* 'I'll kill him', *Waʔle* 'I may kill him'.) **Seneca** has a factual for direct perception or memory (i.e. realis), a future, and an optative (for obligations or possibilities).

More complicated systems exist, e.g. **Maricopa** with irrealis (future, possibilities, counterfactuals), realis (present, past), perfective, incompletive, desiderative, visual evidential, and non-visual evidential. This is something of a grab bag, and should perhaps be considered a modal system instead.

Joint and non-joint systems

Most often there are subdivisions of the irrealis, and the irrealis marker co-occurs with some more specific affix or particle; Palmer calls these JOINT systems, as the irrealis is functioning along with another marker.

Hixkaryana is a straightforward example.

- The realis can be used alone: *nomokyaha* 'he's coming'.
- The irrealis alone forms a question: *nomokyano?* 'will he come?'

---

25 But this parenthetical requires a footnote: in colloquial French it's rare to see anything but the present subjunctive. Another claimed difference is greater fusion in the IE subjunctive; but you can't get much more fusional than the suppletive irrealis forms in Takelma (e.g. 'run', realis *yowo-*, irrealis *yu-*). And Caddo has fusional affixes, e.g. *ci-* for 1s.agent.realis, *t́a-* for 1s.agent.irrealis.

- Adding the particle *ha* changes the meaning slightly: with the realis it forms an obligative ('he must come'); with the irrealis, a speculative ('he may come').
- Another particle after *ha* refines the irrealis meaning:

ha-ɨ	hearsay
ha-na	possibility
ha-mɨ	deduction
ha-mpe	skepticism

- Finally, *ha-mpɨ-nɨ* after the realis forms a warning: 'he's coming, be worried'.

NON-JOINT systems, where the irrealis doesn't co-occur with other tense or modal markers, are rarer, but **Manam** is an example:

U-nóʔu.

1s.real jump

I jumped.

Úra i-pura-púra.

rain 3s.real-come-come

It's raining.

Úsi né-gu mi-ásaʔ-i.

loincloth poss-1s 1s.irr-wash-3s.obj

I will wash my loincloth.

Go-moanáʔo.

2s.irr-eat

Eat!

Use of other tenses as irrealis

It's also worth noting that tense can be used as a stand-in for modality. English uses the past tense in a few non-past ways:

- To weaken a modal: *I could buy that for you; Greg might know a stripper.*
- To weaken requests: *I wanted to ask you a question.*
- To add more doubt to an *if* clause: *If Neil came, I'd be in heaven.*

The French imperfect can be used as a jussive: *Si nous allions?* 'Shall we go?'

The past is used for a sense of unreality in Tigre:

> **London wa-gəsko, wa-mətko.**
>
> London cond-go.1s.perf cond-die.1s.perf
>
> *If I went to London, I would die.*

The Russian 'subjunctive' is really just the past tense with an additional particle бы:

> **Хорошо было бы поесть.**
>
> good-s.n.nom be.past-3s.n subj eat-inf
>
> *It'd be nice to have something to eat.*

The future can be used as an assumptive or deductive in French:

> **Ce sera mon ami Nicolas.**
>
> that be.fut-3s my.m friend.m Nicolas
>
> *That must be my friend Nicolas.*

Modality on things besides verbs

Modality is usually a verbal category, but some languages mark it on other elements. Supyire has two sets of 1st and 2nd person pronouns, one for declarative sentences (1s *mìi*, 2s *mu*), one for non-declaratives (1s *na*, 2s *ma*).

> **Mìi à pa.**
>
> 1s.decl perf come
>
> *I've come.*
>
> **Taá ma kɛ-ɛ-gé ke?**
>
> where 2s.nondecl go.impfv loc.q
>
> *Where are you going?*

Kayardild marks modality on both the verb and on NPs. And then there's Chamicuro, which encodes *tense* on the *definite article* (it's *ka* for the past, *na* for present and future).

Mandarin syntax

Whenever someone suggests that languages without inflections are easy, I like to hit them with a copy of *Mandarin Chinese: A Functional Reference Grammar* (by Charles Li and Sandra Thompson, 1981), which is nearly 700 pages and leaves quite a welt. And it doesn't even address the writing system.

In this section I'll give some of the touristic highlights. (This is by no means a full grammatical sketch of Mandarin.) Besides Li and Thompson, Jerry Norman's *Chinese* and Robert Ramsey's *The Languages of China* are excellent overviews.

Subjects and topics

Mandarin is probably best described as TOPIC-FIRST. This is made clear by sentences where the topic is explicitly stated but is not the subject of the sentence:

> **Yànméi yǎnjing hěn dà.**
>
> Yanmei eye very big
>
> *As for Yanmei, her eyes are large.*
>
> *Yanmei's eyes are large.*
>
> **Zhèi bān xuéshēng tā zuì yúchǔnde.**
>
> this class student 3s most stupid-of
>
> *As for this class of students, s/he's the stupidest.*
>
> *S/he is the stupidest of this class of students.*
>
> **Lánqiú nǐ dǎ de bu tài hǎo.**
>
> basket-ball 2s play sub not too good
>
> *You don't play basketball too well.*
>
> **Lúzi lǐ de huǒ wǒ ràng tā zìji miè-diào.**
>
> stove in of fire 1s let 3s self extinguish-off
>
> *The fire in the stove, I'll let it go out by itself.*

The structure of all these sentences is <topic> <S>; the relationship of the subject to the topic is not explicit, but obvious.

(Don't confuse *Yànméi yǎnjing* for an NP; the NP 'Yanmei's eyes' would be *Yànméi de yǎnjing*.)

Time and locative expressions are also fronted, and can be considered topics.

Qiáng shang pá zhe hěn duō kūnchóng.

wall on climb dur very many insect

That wall has a lot of bugs crawling on it.

Now when we see a sentence like

Nèi gè nǚzi wǒ yǐjing kàn-guo le.

that MW girl 1s already see exp perf

That girl, I've already seen her.

we can see it fits the same pattern, and not leap to the conclusion that Chinese is OSV. SVO occurs too; in this case there is still a topic, but it's identical to the subject:

Tā xiě le liǎng fēng xìn.

3s write pfv both MW letter

S/he wrote two letters.

A sentence can include a fronted object and no subject; we can translate these as passives but they're just one more instance of the <topic> <S> construction:

Fángzi zào hǎo le.

house build finish perf

Someone's finished building the house.

A sentence may lack a topic if it's understood from the context (e.g. it answers a question, or it's an imperative), or in a PRESENTATIVE sentence:

Yǒu rén zài dǎ diànhuà gěi Yànméi.

exist person dur hit telephone give Yanmei

There's someone calling Yanmei on the phone.

Word-building

Though it's the classic example of an isolating language, Mandarin does have a couple of **inflections**.

One is the suffix *-men* used to form **plural** pronouns, which means there are just three roots needed:

	s.	*pl.*
1	*wǒ* 'I'	*wǒmen* 'we'
2	*nǐ* 'you'	*nǐmen* 'you'
3	*tā* 'he/she'	*tāmen* 'they'

Interestingly, it can be applied to other nouns referring to people— e.g. *lǎoshīmen* 'teachers'.

The Chinese got by for centuries without distinguishing sex for 他 *tā* and still do in speech; but in the 20th century, under European influence, they started writing 她 for 'she' (using the 'woman' radical) and 它 for 'it' (using the character for an old word *tuó* 'other').

The other inflection is the **diminutive** *-r*, which (very unusually for Mandarin) modifies the previous syllable, eating its final consonant: *yìdiǎnr* 'a little' is pronounced *yìdiǎr*.

Beyond this, Mandarin has a number of **derivational inflections**, such as:

dì-	ordinal	*dì-yī*	first
kě-	ability	*kě-ài*	lovable
hǎo-	good to X	*hǎo-chī*	good to eat
nán-	hard to X	*nán-chī*	unpalatable
-xué	study	*yǔyánxué*	linguistics
-jiā	professional	*kēxuéjiā*	scientist

There are also very productive forms of **compounding**. Here are a few common patterns, with examples:

N + N	locative	*tián-shǔ*	field-mouse
	container	*nǎi-píng*	milk bottle
	additive	*fù-mǔ*	father-mother = parents
	product	*fēng-là*	bee-wax = beeswax
	source	*yóu-jǐng*	oil well
V + V	resultative	*dǎ-pò*	hit-broken = break
		xià-sǐ	frighten to death
	direction	*sòng-lái*	send-come = send over
	narrowing	*cāi-zháo*	guess-target = guess right
S + V		*tóu-téng*	head-ache
V + O		*lǐ-fǎ*	arrange-hair = haircut
A + A	quality	*dà-xiǎo*	big-small = size
A + N	description	*rè-xīn*	hot-heart = enthusiastic

The V + O combinations should perhaps be described as *almost* compounds. Aspect particles or numerical qualifiers may intrude in between (*lǐ-guò fǎ* 'to have ever had a haircut'). *Kàn-shū* literally means 'look.at books' but it just means 'read', without any reference to a particular book or even to books as opposed to other reading matter; this can be considered an example of noun incorporation (p. 180).

One reason Mandarin relies so heavily on compounds is that sound changes have eliminated many phonetic distinctions, creating a high degree of homonymy. Using a compound narrows the meaning enough to avoid problems.

Old Chinese (*wényán*) style was highly aphoristic, and Mandarin is still very fond of four-character sayings which don't follow modern syntax. A few examples:

画蛇添足	**huà shé tiān zú**
	draw snake add feet
	ruin by adding unnecessary details
以卵击石	**yǐ luǎn jī shí**
	use egg hit stone
	fight hopelessly against a strong enemy
一针见血	**yī zhēn jiàn xiě**
	one prick see blood
	get right to the point
忙中有错	**máng zhōng yǒu cuò**
	busy in have error
	haste makes waste

Measure words

Numbers or demonstratives must be followed by a MEASURE WORD, which gives the general class of object. We have these in English: *a grain of rice, a bottle of beer, three head of cattle, four sheets of paper*. But we restrict them to MASS nouns; Mandarin uses them for COUNT nouns as well. (Measure words were only rarely used in classical *wényán*, but by the 4th century they were obligatory.)

yī zhāng zhǐ	one sheet of paper
liǎng zhī niǎo	two birds
sān tóu niú	three cows
sì lì mǐ	four grains of rice
zhè bēi chá	this cup of tea

něi gè rén	which person

Measure words started as ordinary nouns: *tóu* means 'head'; *zhī* is 'branch'; *lì* is 'grain'. *Zhāng* means 'open out, display'; the derived meaning 'sheet' seems to survive only in its use as a measure word. The default classifier *gè*, a lifesaver for the foreigner as it can be used with almost any noun, originally meant 'bamboo stalk'.

Some of the most common measure words:

tiáo	long narrow things	road, skirt...
gēn	stick-like things	string, match...
zhāng	flat surfaces	paper, table, bed...
kē	small round things	pearl, soybean...
bǎ	things held in the hand	knife, umbrella...
zuò	large, imposing things	mountain, building...
zhī	small animals, insects	mouse, fly...
shuāng	pairs of things	shoes, chopsticks...

Measure words thus form a set of categories, much like genders. They don't comprise a gender system because they don't cause agreement—though it may be moving that way, as measure words can be used anaphorically:

—Nèi běn shū shì shéi de?

that MW book be who of

Who does that book belong to?

—Něi běn? Shì zhèi běn ma?

which MW / is this MW q

Which one? Do you mean this one?

That is, on second reference, it's the noun rather than the measure word that can be omitted.

Containers count as measure words; note that these all specify a different quantity:

wǔ dī jiǔ	five drops of liquor
wǔ bēi jiǔ	five glasses of liquor
wǔ píng jiǔ	five bottles of liquor
wǔ shēng jiǔ	five liters of liquor

However, when you're counting containers, they need a separate measure word!

liǎng gè píngzi	two bottles

Words referring to time normally don't take measure words: *liǎng nián* 'two years'.

Pivots

The pivot construction is a neat syntactic trick, allowing the object of one sentence to serve as the subject of another. The pivot is underlined in the examples.

> **Tāmen qǐng <u>wǒ</u> chī Fǎguó cài.**
>
> 3p invite 1s eat French-country food
>
> *They're inviting me to eat French food.*
>
> **Méi yǒu <u>rén</u> bù xǐhuan Zhōngguó cài.**
>
> not exist people not like China food
>
> *There's no one who doesn't like Chinese food.*
>
> **Xiǎo háizi xiào <u>tā</u> shì yī ge dà pàngzi.**
>
> small child laugh 3s be one MW big fat-dim
>
> *The children laugh at him/her for being a big fatty.*

Let's look at the first example again. Its structure is something like this:

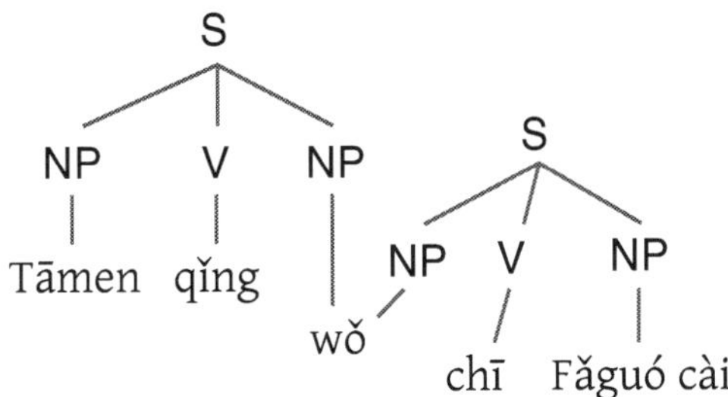

Compare to the English glosses— Mandarin manages this melding with no extra syntactic glue. Note that it probably couldn't get away with this if it had case marking— *wǒ* serves for both 'I' and 'me'.

Subordination

I really like Mandarin's main method of subordination: a sentence, NP, or adjective is subordinated to a noun simply by adding the particle *de*. (I borrowed the idea for Kebreni; see the *LCK* p. 237.)

Nà shì shū [wǒ gěi nǐ shū].

that be book [1s give 2s book]

→ **Nà shì wǒ gěi nǐ de shū.**

that be 1s give 2s sub book

That's the book I gave you.

Wǒmen dōu ài chī yú [lǎo Wáng zuò yú].

1p all love eat fish [old Wang cook fish]

→ **Wǒmen dōu ài chī lǎo Wáng zuò de yú.**

1p all love eat old Wang cook sub fish

We all love eating the fish old Wang cooks.

The order within a subclause is normally SVO— compare

wǒ ài de rén people I love

ài wǒ de rén people who love me

If you subordinate an NP, the meaning is genitive: *wǒ de chéng-li* 'my city', *Yànméi de jiā* 'Yanmei's family'; *Zhōngguó de shǒudū* 'China's capital'.

The head of a *de* construction can be omitted, in which case it can be taken as 'things' or 'people':

Nà sān běn shū shì Yànméi de.

that three MW book be Yanmei of

Those three books are Yanmei's.

This is one way of forming a 'person who does' nominal: *mài yú de* '(person) who sells fish = fishmonger'.

'Adjectives' in Mandarin are really a kind of verb; they don't require a copula (*lǎo Wáng hěn pàng* 'old Wang is quite fat'), and they can take aspect particles (*lǎo Wáng pàng le* 'old Wang got fat'). Thus the normal way to attribute them to a referent is with a *de* phrase: *pàng de rén* 'fat people', *xiǎo de shū* 'a small book'.

These expressions too can be headless: *pàng de* 'fat ones', *xiǎo de* 'small ones'.

Single-character adjectives can be combined directly with nouns, e.g. *hóng huā* 'red flowers'.

Aspect

Mandarin is an example of a language without tense markers. Instead, it has an array of aspect particles.

-le	perfective
-guo	experiential
zài	progressive
-zhe	durative
reduplication	delimitative
le	perfect

Perfective

Perfective *-le* appears just after the verb, before any objects. Recall that perfectives (p. 134) view an event as a whole; as Li and Thompson put it, *-le* is used if the event is "*bounded* temporally, spatially, or conceptually." This is easily done by specifying a duration:

Yànméi shuì-le sān ge zhōngtóu.

Yanmei sleep-pfv three MW hour

Yanmei slept for three hours.

but also by other quantities:

Zhèi huǐ kǎoshì wǒ dé-le bā-shí fēn.

this time exam 1s obtain-pfv eight-ten point

I got eighty points on this exam.

or by contrasting it to a later event:

Tā kāi-le mén, nǐ jiu jìn-qu.

3s open-pfv door / 2s then enter-go

When s/he opens the door, you go in.

That last sentence also illustrates that the perfective isn't a tense; the opening of the door is in the future.

The perfective is usually used when the direct object is DEFINITE; markers of definiteness in Mandarin include names, demonstratives, pronouns, and relative clauses:

Tā xiě-cuò-le nèi ge zì.

3s write-wrong-pfv that MW character

S/he wrote <u>that</u> character wrong.

Some verbs are viewed as inherently bounded (e.g. *sǐ* 'die', *wàng* 'forget', *huài* 'break') and thus appear in the perfective. (Unless they refer to hypothetical events— e.g. *Tā yào sǐ* 'S/he wants to die'.)

Experiential

The experiential aspect (with *-guo*) expresses that the situation has been experienced before:

Wǒ chī-guo Rìběn fàn.

1s eat-exper Japan food

I've eaten Japanese food [at least once].

Progressive

Verbs representing an activity (rather than a state) can take the marker *zài* before the verb, to indicate that the activity is in progress:

Wǒ xiànzài zài xuéxí zhōngwén.

1s now prog study Chinese-language

I'm studying Chinese right now.

Durative

The durative *-zhe* is used in several ways. One is with verbs of posture or location:

Tā zài chuáng shàng tǎng-zhe.

3s at bed on lie-dur

S/he is lying on the bed.

With some verbs, it's used to express the state resulting from an activity. Compare:

Tā zài chuān yī tiáo hóng qúnzi.

3s prog put.on one MW red skirt

She's putting on a red skirt.

Tā chuān-zhe yī tiáo hóng qúnzi.

3s put.on-dur one MW red skirt

She's wearing a red skirt.

Finally it can be used to describe an action which takes place when another occurs:

Tā tǎng-zhe kàn bào.

3s lie-dur look paper

S/he was lying down reading the newspaper.

Delimitative

The delimitative expresses that an action is done just a little, or for a short period of time. It's formed by reduplication.

Wǒ wèn yi-wen zài juéding.

1s ask one ask then decide

I'll decide after I inquire a little.

As a perhaps inevitable extension, it can be used to mark an action as tentative, or soften an imperative:

Nǐ wènwen lǎo Wáng ba.

2s ask-ask old Wáng suggestion

You go and ask old Wang a bit.

Perfect

In addition to the perfective particle *-le*, which follows the verb, there's a sentence-final particle *le* which marks the perfect. (You might hope that the writing system disambiguates these, but no luck, they're both 了.)

Li & Thompson describe *le* as signaling a **currently relevant state**—which is more or less a perfect (p. 136). E.g. you want to see a friend next month, but he responds:

Xià ge yuè wǒ jiu zài Rìběn le.

next MW month 1s then at Japan perf

Next month I'll be in Japan.

The *le* tells you that your friend's trip is currently relevant—i.e. because of it, he can't meet you.

Li & Thompson break down uses of *le* into five categories.

- A change of state— compare *wǒ zhīdào* 'I know' with *wǒ zhīdào le* 'I know now = I just learned it'.
- Correcting a false assumption— e.g. *wǒ chī-guo le* 'I've eaten (= so I don't need to eat more)'.

- Bringing someone up to date on an activity or situation:

  Wǒ zài nàli zhù-le liǎng ge yuè le.

  1s at there live-pfv both MW month perf

  I've lived there for two months already.

- Mentioning a situation with immediate (usually unstated) consequences for what's about to happen.

  Xiǎo Huáng jiù yào lái le.

  small Huang soon will come perf

  Little Huang is about to arrive.

  The English gloss sounds merely descriptive, but the Mandarin is anticipatory— it implies something, like "Get ready!" or "So put your pants on!"

- Finally, it may end a speaker's turn (here the "current relevance" is that someone else can speak).

Polysynthesis

Many conlangers, I think, have the ambition of creating a POLYSYNTHETIC language before they die. At the risk of hastening their deaths, let's look at what that means.

The DEGREE OF SYNTHESIS is simply the typical number of morphemes per word. It's a continuum, with isolating languages at one end and polysynthesis at the other. It's very easy to find words in polysynthetic languages that represent what would be an entire sentence in English.

As a rough guide, if your degree of synthesis averages 1–3 you probably have an isolating language; a dozen is polysynthetic; and somewhere in between is neither. To put it another way, (poly)synthesis is a matter of degree, not a binary state.[26]

We can also talk about the DEGREE OF FUSION. In Latin *rogāminī* 'you were asked', the morpheme *-āminī* fuses 2nd person, plural, imperfective, indicative, and passive (and also signals that the verb is first conjugation). But fusing (say) a dozen morphemes isn't really practical. Thus

---

[26] Mark Baker does think it's binary, but a) his 'polysynthesis parameter' works only within Chomsky's parameters theory, and b) it leads to odd conclusions such as Yup'ik not being polysynthetic.

polysynthetic languages tend to be agglutinative, though they may include some fusion.

How do they rack up the morpheme count? One or more of these ways, which I'll describe below:

- Polypersonal agreement
- A wide array of prefixes and suffixes on the verb
- Noun incorporation

To get a flavor for what they're like, here's a few examples:

Nishnaabemwin

Gii-bi-mdaaswi-shi-niizhdaabaan'gizwag.

past-come-ten-and-two-be.carload-3p

They came in twelve carloads.

Greenlandic

Aliikusersuillammassuaanerartassagaluarpaal-li...

entertainment-provide-semitrans-one.good.at-copular-say.that-rep-fut-sure.but-3p>3s -but

However, they will say that he is a great entertainer, but...

Koasati

Ostohimilááchihalpíísalahoolimáámimpayon...

go.and-inst-distrib-3dat-arrive-pl-ability-irr-deduc-hearsay-consequential-different.subj:focus

They say that they all might be able to go and bring it to him, but on the contrary...

Words

To count morphemes per word, we need to be clear on what a WORD is. To linguists, it's one or more of these overlapping concepts:

- A phonological unit— e.g. something with one stress accent or one pitch contour; or a unit within which intervocalic stops get voiced.
- The abstraction underlying a morphological paradigm (e.g. *write* underlies *write, writes, writing, written, wrote*).
- An element which can stand alone (e.g. in response to a suitably chosen question), as suffixes or BOUND MORPHEMES cannot.

- A morphological unit you can't insert other morphemes into (e.g. *black dog* is not a word since you can change it to *black, tired dog*; but you can't turn *blackbird* into *blacktiredbird*).
- An expression with a conventional meaning— something that has to be defined in the mental lexicon (this sense is also called a LEXEME).

What we *don't* do is define it typographically, as whatever appears between spaces. That would be useless for unwritten languages, and can be misleading as languages change. E.g. arguably the colloquial French verbal complex as in

Je le lui ai pas donné.

1s.nom 3sm.acc 3s.dat have.pres.indic.1s not give-past.part

I didn't give it to him.

is a single word; it's pronounced as a unit, the parts can't stand alone, and it resists addition of other material.[27] (Ignoring fusion, I count about 18 morphemes— probably enough to make a case that spoken French is polysynthetic!)

It's possible to apply these concepts to Mandarin; that's why my sketch included compounds like *Zhōngguó* 'China' and *yìdiǎnr* 'a little'. There's even a Mandarin term for these— *cí* 'phrase, compound' as opposed to *zì* 'character'. However, it's fair to say that due to the psychological dominance of the writing system, the Chinese 'think in *zì*'. Even indivisible words like *pútáo* 'grape' are treated as compounds.

Edward Sapir claimed that his informants had no trouble agreeing on word boundaries in polysynthetic languages like Nuuchahnulth; in general it doesn't seem to be a source of controversy for such languages.

CLITICS are morphemes that phonologically attach to another word, but apply to an entire noun or verb phrase rather than a word. English examples include the articles *a* and *the*, and possessive *'s*; Spanish has pronominal clitics as in *díga<u>me</u>* 'tell me'; Quechua's evidential suffixes are clitics.

(You may have heard that *'s* was a case ending— as it once was. But it attaches to entire NPs, not to nouns, as in *the queen of England's corgis.*

---

[27] If *je* is a bound morpheme, how do you reply to a question like *Who said that?* You use the stressed form *moi.* You also use this for emphasis, as you'd use *yo* in Spanish: *Moi je le lui ai pas donné / Yo no se lo dí* '<u>I</u> didn't give it to him.'

That is, the possessor is the NP *the queen of England*, not the noun *England*.)

Polypersonal agreement

This refers to the verb agreeing with both subject and object, or more. As it doesn't add much to the morpheme count, it doesn't make a language polysynthetic in itself, though polysynthetic languages generally include it.

The Swahili system is particularly simple:

	subject	*object*
1s	ni-	-ni-
2s	u-	-ku-
3s	a-	-m-
1p	tu-	-tu-
2p	m-	-wa-
3p	wa-	-wa-

The overall order is subject + tense + object + root:

Ninakupenda	*I love you*
Unanipenda	*You love me*
Nilikuona	*He saw me*
Tutawaona	*We will see them*

As we've seen, when the arguments are nouns, the gender agreement prefix is used instead: *Nina<u>ki</u>ona kitabu* 'I see the book'.

There are often special forms for reflexives; in Swahili it's *-ji*: *Nilijiona* 'I saw myself'.

Quechua and Nishnaabemwin forms are given in the next section.

Some languages mark the indirect object on the verb as well; e.g. Basque:

Eman d-i-da-zu.

given 3s.abs-have-1s.polite.dat-2s.erg

You have given it to me.

The French example given above also includes a dative (*lui*).

Head-marking

Many phrases have a HEAD: a verb is the head of its arguments; a possessed item is the head of the possessor.[28] HEAD-MARKING languages signal grammatical relationships on the head, while DEPENDENT-MARKING ones modify the dependent. And some do both.

Compare these translations of *the boy's parents*, with the head (the parents) underlined and the marking bolded:

Nishnaabemwin	wgitzi**iman** gwiiwzens	*head*
Quechua	maqta**pa** taytamama**n**	*both*
Latin	parentēs puer**i**	*dependent*

Polysynthetic languages tend to be head-marking. If you apply this to the verb-noun relationship you get polypersonal agreement and nouns without case, as in Nishnaabemwin or Ainu. But this isn't an absolute—e.g. nouns *are* marked for case in Yup'ik, Lake Miwok, and Quechua.

Extreme verbs

The best way to see how a polysynthetic verb works is to look at some examples. We'll warm up with Quechua and proceed to Nishnaabemwin. And for yet more see the section on the NW Causasian languages (p. 184).

Quechua verbs

I'm not entirely comfortable calling Quechua polysynthetic, because in actual texts, the verbs are not really more complex than in Spanish. Here's an example, with the verbs divided into morphemes:

> **Chaysi ni-sqa suwakunaqa: "Ay haqay payaqa sumaqtaraq allqutapas uywa-chka-n, wiray-wirayta! Chaychus mana suwa-mu-sun-man?"**
>
> this-hsy say-past thief-pl-topic / ay that old.woman beautiful-adv-still dog-acc-also raise-prog-3s, fat-fat-acc / this-Q-hsy not steal-toward-1pi-cond
>
> *The thieves said, "Oh, that old lady cares for those dogs too much, they're so fat! Shouldn't we rob her for that?"*

However, the potential for very hairy verbs is there. The overall verb template is this:

[28] That's not backwards. The head of *Morgan's cat* is *cat*, the thing that can participate in the rest of the sentence; *Morgan* is a modifier.

verb root	derivational & modal affixes	tense/ aspect	personal endings	discourse particles

Tense/aspect can include past *-ra* and progressive *-chka*, which can be combined (*-rachka*).

The basic personal endings (shown for *rimay* 'speak') are these:

1s	**ni**	rimani	*1px*	**ni-ku**	rimaniku
			1pi	**n-chik**	rimanchik
2s	**nki**	rimanki	*2p*	**nki-chik**	rimankichik
3s	**n**	riman	*3p*	**n-ku**	rimanku

In the second column we see two pluralizers, *-chik* which includes the listener and *-ku* which excludes them. (*1px* and *1pi* are exclusive and inclusive 'we'.)

Quechua has polypersonal agreement, but it's distressingly incomplete, as can be seen from this table.

	object			
subject	*1s*	*2s*	*1p*	*2p*
1s		-yki		-ykichik
2s	-wanki		-wankiku	
3s	-wan	-sunki	-wanku (*excl*) -wanchik *(incl)*	-sunkichik
1p		-ykiku		
2p	-wankichik			

The endings (if present) replace the ordinary personal endings; thus *rimawanki* 'you speak to me', *rimayki* 'I speak to you'.

The shaded cells are covered by the reflexive *-ku*, as in *rimakuni* 'I speak to myself'.

Pronouns can be used if there's no polypersonal suffix: *paykunata rimankichik* 'you (pl.) are speaking to them'.

To keep things from being too simple, there is a separate set of endings *and* polypersonal markers for the future tense.

The conditional affix *-man* follows the person endings and *-chik*, but precedes *-ku*.

I won't fully explain the derivational and modal suffixes, but I'll list them in their required order. More than one can occur, and certain combinations have fusional forms (e.g. *-pu* + *-ku* = *-paku*).

-pa	repeated action
-paya	insistent action
-raya	prolonged or repeated action

-tiya	rapid repetition
-kacha	same, but with some disapproval
-cha	affectionate diminutive
-ri	dismissive diminutive
-yku	beyond the norm; surprise
-ru	personal interest or urgency
-na	reciprocal action
-chi	causative
-ysi	with someone's help
-pu	benefactive
-ku	reflexive
-mu	movement toward
-lla	courtesy; fear, lamentation

The discourse particles aren't exclusive to verbs; they can appear on any word in the sentence. They include the topic particle *-qa*, the evidentials, *-raq* to mark a condition still in force, and *-ña* to indicate that a situation has changed.

Nishnaabemwin

J. Randolph Valentine's *Nishnaabemwin Reference Grammar* devotes 264 pages to verbal morphology, so this is just a small sampling.

Transitive and intransitive verbs behave differently, and within each class animates and inanimates do too. I'm only going to cover the **animate intransitives**.

Inflection

First let's look at verb conjugation. The template for INDEPENDENT (non-subordinated) verbs is:

1s, 2s	**verb stem**	negative	1p, 2p, 3s	mode	3p

The negative affix is *-sii*, and the mode can be one of *-ban* preterit, *-dig* dubitative or *-goban* preterit dubitative.

The personal affixes are boldfaced in these examples:

	'make a fire'	'arrive'
1s	**n**boodwe	**n**dagshin
2s	**g**boodwe	**g**dagshin
3s	boodwe	dgoshin
4	boodwe**wan**	dgoshn**oon**
3x	boodwe**m**	dgoshn**am**
1px	**n**boodwe**mi**	**n**dagshin**ami**
1pi	**g**boodwe**mi**	**g**dagshin**ami**

2p	gboodwe**m**	gdagshin**am**
3p	boodwe**wag**	dgoshn**oog**

4 is the obviative; 3x is used for an unspecified actor; 1px and 1pi are exclusive and inclusive we.

The stem for *dgoshin* looks like it's out of control. The etymological form, still heard in other dialects of Ojibwe, is *dagoshin*. But Nishnaabemwin has a SYNCOPE rule which deletes every other short vowel, starting at the beginning of the word: *n~~i~~-dag~~o~~shin* → *ndagshin*. (The last vowel in the word isn't affected.)

Let's pause to admire some other examples of syncope, applied to the word 'shoe' (which you should recognize; English *moccasin* was borrowed from Algonquian):

m~~a~~kizin → *mkizin* 'shoe'
m~~a~~kiz~~i~~nan → *mkiznan* 'shoes'
n~~i~~-mak~~i~~zin → *nmakzin* 'my shoe'

If you want a simple sound change that wreaks havoc on the entire morphological system, borrow Nishnaabemwin syncope.

There is a separate set of affixes, called CONJUNCT form, for subordinated verbs. Here are the forms for 'make a fire':

1s	boodwe**yaanh**
2s	boodwe**yin**
3s	boodwe**d**
4	boodwe**nid**
3x	boodwe**ng**
1px	boodwe**yaang**
1pi	boodwe**ying**
2p	boodwe**yeg**
3p	boodwe**waad**

An example, showing that no explicit subordinator is needed:

Giizhgaate<u>nig</u> giiwenh wganwaabmaan niwi giisoon.

day.bright-0.obv.conj hsy looks-3s>4 4 moon.4

Once, when it was shining brightly, he looked at the moon.

(This is an inanimate verb, which Valentine marks as 0 since person is not marked in their conjugation.)

Conjunct forms are also used for relative clauses, as in *ge-giigoonykejig* '(those) who will fish'.

Polypersonal inflections

Let's glance over at the transitive animates, just to see the affixes for polypersonal agreement. The unsyncopated forms are given.

The – indicates where the verb stem goes. Thus ***g****waabm****imin*** 'you see us' (2s>1px), ***n****waabm****ig*** 'he/she sees me' (3s>1s).

	object			
subj	*1s*	*2s*	*3s*	*4 (if ≠ 3s)*
1s		g–in	n–aa	
2s	g–i		g–aa	
3s	n–ig	g–ig	w–igoon*	w–aan
in.s	n–igon	g–igon	w–igon	
1px		g–igoo	n–aanaan	
1pi			g–aanaan	
2p	g–im		g–aawaa	
3p	n–igoog	g–igoog		w–aawaan
in.p	n–igonan	g–igonan	w–igonan	
3x	n–igoo	g–igoo	–aa	–aawan

subj	*1px*	*1pi*	*2p*	*3p*
1s			g–inim	n–aag
2s	g–imin			g–aag
3s	n–igonaan	g–igonaan	g–igowaa	w–igowaan*
in.s	n–igonaan	g–igonaan	g–igonaawaa	w–igonaawaa
1px			g–igoom	n–aanaanig
1pi				g–aanaanig
2p	g–imin			g–aawaag
3p	n–igonaanig	g–igonaanig	g–igowaag	
in.p	n–igonaanin	g–igonaanin	g–igonaawaan	w–igonaawaan
3x	n–igoomin	g–igoomin	g–igoom	–aawag

The *in.s* and *in.p* forms are just inanimate third person singular and plural. All other persons are animate.

Reflexives, formed with a derivational suffix *-idizo*, are used when the subject and verb are identical (shaded cells).

The other empty cells are explained by the principle that agent and patient must be disjoint. E.g. there is no form for 1s>1p since the speaker is included in both groups.

The *3s* row is used for 4 (obviative) too; the * indicates that the given form is only used for an obviative subject. (If the subject is 3s you use the reflexive.)

Many of the forms include either the DIRECT suffix *-aa* indicating an agent acting down the agentivity hierarchy, or the INVERSE suffix *-ig* indicating the reverse. Compare 1s>3s *n–ig* vs. 3s>1s *n–aa*, as well as the Fox forms on p. 120.

Only one object can be marked on the verb. However, the object slot is sometimes used for a beneficiary or recipient, with the associated patient given in the sentence but not marked on the verb.

Derivation

The verb stem that we met in the previous section is itself built from smaller parts. The basic pattern is

- an initial that provides a quality, object, or adverbial
- a medial that is usually a body part, classifier, or goal
- a final which specifies the action and verb type.

The initials are an open-ended class; the medials and finals are numerous but limited.

Here are some of the basic patterns. The components are given in unsyncopated form. I haven't glossed them, but the meanings should be clear from the category and the meaning of the combined form— e.g. *dakw aabiig izi* below has initial 'short', a medial classifier for string-shaped objects, and a final 'be'.

BE SOMETHING; BE A QUALITY

anishinaabe wi → *nishnaabewi* be an Indian
aniniw wi → *niniiwi* be(come) a man
mashkikiw wi → *mshkikiiwi* be medicine
dendewi be a bullfrog

biin izi → *biinzi* be clean
gonaad wi → *gnaajwi* be pretty
mashkaw aji → *mshkawji* freeze, be frozen
niigaan ii → *niigaanii* be at the start, head of line

ATTRIBUTE PLUS MEDIAL CLASSIFIER

dakw aabiig izi → *dkwaabiigzi* be short (string-shaped)
dakw aakw izi → *dkwaakzi* be short (pole-shaped)
dakw aabik izi → *dkwaabkizi* be short (metal, stone)
ginw aabik izi → *gnwaabkizi* be long (metal, stone)
dakw eg bizo → *dkwegbizo* wear a short dress

DIRECTION

anim ose → *nimse* walk away
babaam batoo → *bbaambatoo* run around
babaam aajimo → *bbaamaajmo* spread a rumor
biid bizo → *biijbizo* arrive by driving
biid aajimo → *biidaajmo* bring news
biid aaso → *biidaaso* bring a pile of things
bim ose → *bmose* walk along
bim aaboozo → *bmaaboozo* float along

ADVERBIAL

apiit aapi →*piitaapi* laugh to some extent
biin inaagzi → *biinnaagzi* look clean
dak izi → *dkizi* be cold to the touch
gtimi jiizo → *gtimjiizo* be lazy because of the heat
minw itaagzi → *mnotaagzi* sound good
miskw aaso → *mskwaaso* be sunburned (i.e. reddened)
mtaakzhebtoo run around naked

VERB + QUANTITY

niizh i → *niizhi* be two
niizh gon endi → *niizhgonendi* be absent for two days
niizh wewaan'gizi → *niizhwewaan'gizi* be paired

POSSESSION

bezhgoogzhiimi have a horse
nahaangshiimi have a son-in-law

VERB (FINAL) + OBJECT

anishinaabe mo → *nishnaabemo* speak Nishnaabemwin
aniniw aapne → *niniiwaapne* be man-crazy
gookoosh aadzi → *gookooshwaadzi* live like a pig
miskw konay e → *mskokon'ye* wear red clothes

VERB (INITIAL) + OBJECT

gziibiig ninjy e → *gziibiigninjii* wash one's hands
gziibiig isag inig e → *gziibiigsagnige* wash the floor
nanda aangzhe → *ndawaangzhe* look for a job
nanda apiny e → *ndapiniiwe* look for potatoes
naad miijim e → *naajmiijme* fetch food
naad aabikw e → *naadaabkwe* fetch one's money

VERB + BODY PART MEDIAL

> *book aawgan* → *bookwaawgan* break one's back
> *book gwew shin* → *bookgweshin* fall and break one's neck
> *book jaan e* → *bookjaane* break one's nose
> *mashkaw jaan waji* → *mshkawjaanewji* have a frostbitten nose
> *minw bwaam e* → *mnobwaame* have nice thighs

ASPECT

> *boon aabi* → *boonaabi* stop looking
> *maad aabi* → *maadaabi* start looking
> *maad angizo* → *maadgizo* be the beginning of the month

For some finals, there is a variant for inanimates— e.g. animate *mskozi*, inanimate *mskwaa* 'be red'.

There are also finals that can apply to another verb, e.g. detransitive *-ge*, passive *-igaazo*, reflexive *-idizo*, reciprocal *-idi*, *-kaazo* 'pretend to V', and *-ishki* 'be addicted to Ving'.

Preverbs

And we're not done yet! There are also preverbs, prefixes that precede the entire verb stem. Some examples:

subordinators	*a-* 'where'
	e- that, who
tense, mode	*gii-* past tense
	nji- recent past
	wii- future (will or desire)
	da- future (obligation, consequence)
	daa- possibility, necessity
directional	*bi-* come (movement to speaker)
	ni- go (movement away)
	b(i)mi- go by, go along
	b(i)baa- go around
relational	*(a)ko-* since
	(i)zhi- in a certain way
	d(a)so- many or every time
aspectual	*de-* able to
	g(a)gwe- try to
	maajii- begin to
	shkwaa- end
	(o)shki- for the first time
manner, quality	*aabji-* constantly
	baakji- prematurely, irreversibly

g(a)giibaaji- badly, foolishly
wiinge- carefully

Nuuchahnulth

As another example, here's a list (mostly from Matthew Davidson) of some of the lexical suffixes of the Wakashan language Nuuchahnulth (Nootka). These are all bound morphemes, and they're just a sampling—there's over 400 possibilities.

- *-ʔayim̓č* 'presage weather': *wiiʕayim̓čʔaała* 'it's a sign of bad weather' (root *wiiq* 'bad')
- *-y̓iiḥa* 'die from': *c̓axy̓iiḥa*, '[people are often] speared to death' (root *c̓axʷ-* 'hurl point-foremost')
- *-ḥsaa* 'desiring to eat ...'
- *-awił* 'expecting'
- *-cḥi* 'married to': *masčimcḥinƛ* 'she had married a commoner"' (root *masčim* 'commoner')
- *-iic* 'belonging to': *ʔiiḥtuupiicukʷaḥ*, "[this tama song of mine] belonged to a whale" (root *ʔiiḥtuup-* 'whale')
- *-(n)aanak* 'having ... along with one out at sea'
- *-aatuk* 'sounding like'
- *-cʔakʷ* 'acting like'
- *-cy̓ak* 'dressed in; appearing like'
- *-ʕiƛ* 'find, come upon'
- *-ʔinḥi* 'waiting for'
- *-maap* 'paying attention to'

Lexical suffixes can make extremely precise indications of location, space, orientation, direction, and movement:

- *-kʷist* 'move away (perfective)': *hičkʷisan̓ap̓aƛ* 'illuminate-move.away.perf-on.beach.caus.perf = they startled them off the beach with a light'
- *-ʕaaʔatu* 'move down': *c̓itkʕaaʔat̓asʔaƛ* 'it rolled downhill' (root *c̓itk*, 'roll')
- *-cswii* 'through': *kuḥswiiʔakweʔin* 'they say [their beams] have holes through them' (root *kuḥ-* 'hollow')
- *-sy̓uč* 'exposed, extending out, in view': *huuʔaksy̓učičim* 'be up (out of bed) early!' (root *huuʔakʷ-* 'early')
- *-is* 'on the beach'
- *-ʔaaʔa* 'on the rocks, in the fire': *m̓ałʔaaʔamaʔaała* 'it's always cold on the rocks' (root *m̓ał-* "cold')
- *-n̓aaqi* 'up on a height'
- *-ʔimł* 'at the ear'

-aat 'move downstream, out of the woods'
-inʕatu 'up the coast'
-w̓isa 'come out of one's hands, escape'
-c̓as 'at the crown of the head'
-(k)swiʔii 'at the teeth'
-pii 'on the back'
-stiił 'at the collar bone'
-p̓iqa 'on the knee'
-asuu 'under, in liquid'
-caqs 'at the side of a vessel'
-wiiʔis 'at the bow'
-ałc̓a 'at a vertical surface'
-(q)ḥsa 'at the edge, bank'
-misa 'on top'

A sample sentence showing some of the possibilities:

ƛiqwiis c̓axy̓ak̓ ƛaatmaqan̓ołʔi.

stick.in.vertical.crosswise.position-extend.there-on.beach spear stick-like.object.sticking.up-extending.downward-tree-caus

the spear, which was (long and) made of yew wood, went clear through him on to the beach.

Looser word order

Because so much information is marked on the verb, polysynthetic languages can have relatively free word order. Nishnaabemwin, for instance, allows all orderings of S V and O, though it has a preference for placing transitive verbs first. (However, Ainu is consistently SOV, as is Quechua.)

Some languages allow discontinuous phrases, as in this Nishnaabemwin example where the numeral lives far from the noun it modifies:

<u>Bezhig</u> eta ngii-nsaa <u>saawe</u>.

one only 1s-killed-3s perch

I only caught one perch.

Noun incorporation

NOUN INCORPORATION involves a noun used as an affix on the verb. This can be considered a form of valence reduction, as the noun loses its grammatical information (case, number), and typically the verb becomes intransitive. It can also be seen as a form of compounding.

Marianne Mithun reports that

- if a language incorporates nouns of just one morphosyntactic role, it'll be patients
- if two, they'll be patients and experiencers
- instruments and locations are also frequently incorporated

It seems that no languages allow incorporating agents.

Here's some examples from Ainu showing independent and incorporated objects, with a decrease in valence.

Inaw a-ke. → **Inaw-ke-an.**

symbol 1s.trans-make symbol-make-1s.intr

I make a wooden prayer symbol.

Asir cise ci-kar kor...

new house 1px.trans-make and

We made a new house and....

Ney ta cise-kar-as.

there at house-make-1px.intr

We made a house there.

Ainu even allows oblique nouns to be incorporated— if they're first promoted to direct objects with an applicative:

Nea cep a-pone-ko-kuykuy.

that fish 1s.trans-bone-applic-bite

I bit that fish with its bones.

Incorporated nouns may have simplified or suppletive forms. For instance, the Nishnaabemwin medial for 'firewood' is *-is,* seen in *mnise* 'chop firewood'; the independent stem (without syncope) is *mis-*. The medial *-aabikw* 'money' relates to the stone/metal classifier *-aabik* but not to the ordinary word for money, *zhoon'yaa.*

Some languages allow multiple nouns to be incorporated; this Cuiba verb has three:

Na-maxi-péri-na-dobóba-me.

refl-arm-skin-hair-take.off-2s

You take off the hair of the skin of the arm.

A language can be polysynthetic without being incorporating. E.g., Siberian Yup'ik allows only one lexical morpheme per word:

Angya-ghlla-ng-yug-tuq.

boat-augm-acquire-desiderative-3s

He wants to acquire a big boat.

'Boat' is the only lexical morpheme here; the other morphemes are grammatical. (This isn't a case of noun incorporation, but of verbalization: *angya-ng* 'acquire a boat' works like *idol-ize* 'make into an idol'.)

In Zuni, a noun may be incorporated syntactically but not phonologically:

ʔī-kih ʔaš-ka.

reciprocal-ceremonial.brother make-past

They make each other ceremonial brothers.

ʔī- is a verbal element, so the noun is grammatically part of the verb complex; but *ʔī-kih* and *ʔaš-ka* each have initial stress and thus are separate phonological words. This may be a stage on the path to full incorporation.

Four reasons to incorporate

Mithun lists four types of incorporation, in a hierarchy— if a language has one of these, it'll have the earlier ones too:

1. To narrow the focus of a verb. In this example, the incorporation gives the type of chopping involved:

   Yucatec Maya

   Tinch'akah che'

   compl-1s-chop-it-perf tree

   I chopped a tree.

   → **Ch'akche'nahen**

   chop-tree-antip-perf-1s

   I chopped wood.

2. To allow an oblique argument to be promoted to subject or direct object.

Blackfoot

No'kakíni áisttsiwa.

1s-back dur-pain-3s

My back hurts.

Nitáisttso'kakíni.

1s-dur-pain-back

I have a backache.

The original statement is about my back; the incorporated version is about me.

3 To background an argument after it's introduced. In this Koryak text, for instance, a whale is introduced as a freestanding NP; but subsequent statements use incorporation (where English uses pronominalization).

Wutču iñinñin yuñi qulaivun.

this.time.only such whale 3sin.come

This is the first time that such a whale has come near us.

Malyuñi. Gayuñyupenyilenau.

good-whale / 3p-whale-attacked

It's a good one. They attacked it.

4 Incorporation can be used as a classifier, as we've seen in Nishnaabemwin. Again, this may make it clear what's being referred to in secondary references.

English has a few rare compounds that incorporate nouns— *fingerprint, babysit, stress-test, window-shop*— which can be put in the first of these categories (narrowing the focus of a verb), as could Mandarin's verb-object compounds like *kàn-shū* 'read'.

(We much more freely compound nouns with participles: *back-breaking, man-hating, pub-crawling, paint-spattered, store-bought.* Curiously, a few of these incorporate the agent: *employee-run, ghost-written, moth-eaten.*)

Modifying the noun

A common question is: what if you want to modify or relativize the incorporated noun? If you consider Mithun's categories, you can see that you normally don't want to. The action is being generalized or backgrounded, so either there is no specific referent or there's no need to add information about it.

However, some languages do allow incorporating modifiers too; e.g. Chukchi:

T-meyŋə-levtə-pəɣt-ərkən.

1s-big-head-ache-imperf

I have a fierce headache.

Another approach is to add a modifier next to the verb which applies to the incorporated verb, as in Southern Tiwa:

Wisi bi-seuan-mu-ban.

two 1s-man-see-past

I saw two men.

The NW Caucasian verb

This section contributed by ***Steven Foley***

The Northwest Caucasian family, spoken in Georgia and Russia, is notable for the complexity of its verbs, which we'll focus on here.

This section is fairly technical, so please warm up on alignment (p. 115) and valence (p. 140) first. The reward however is some truly awesome verbal morphology.

Examples are from Abkhaz unless otherwise indicated.

Overall verb structure

The only obligatory morpheme is the root. The verb may consist of a single root, or of a string of over a dozen morphemes:

Adyghe

k^{w}'a

go.imper

Go!

Kabardian

Ø-q'ə-s-x^{w}ə-w-a-j-a-ʁa-a-t-ə-ʒə-aʁ-q'm

3.abs-hor-1s.erg-can-2s-dat-3-agt-caus-con-give-trans-back-past-neg

I was unable to make him give it back to you.

The NW Caucasian verb agglutinates morphemes marking polypersonal agreement, tense, aspect, mood, polarity, directionality, finiteness, subordination, and other grammatical information. The overall verb template is as follows:

ABS person marker	directional/ adverbial/ aspectual prefixes	DAT person marker	ERG person marker	CAUS, NEG prefixes	**verb root**	tense, mood, adverbial suffixes	NEG, Q, COMP, suffixes

Almost any lexical element can function as a root:

Abaza

də-l+pa-p'

3s.abs-her+son-pres.stat

He is her son.

də-ʃt'a-p'

3s.abs-at.the.base-pres.stat

S/he is prostrate.

Case markers

As the template suggests, the Northwest Caucasian languages are morphologically ERGATIVE (p. 117).

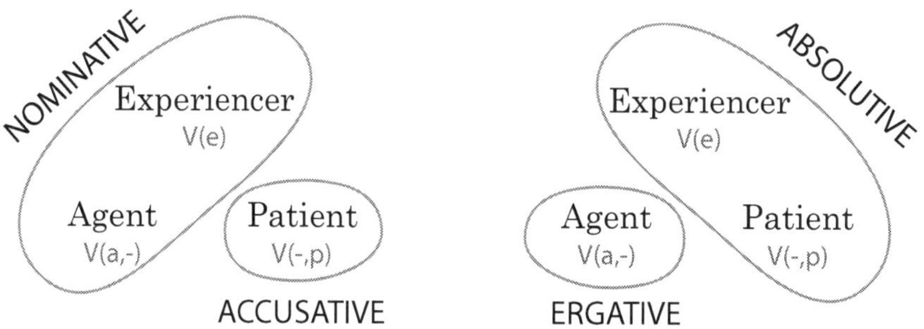

The absolutive prefix is underlined in these examples; note that it always begins the verb, and the ergative affix if any comes later.

Kabardian

sə-q’a-fanəwɕ

1s.abs-hor-will.dance

I will dance.

wə-q’a-fanəwɕ

2s.abs-hor-will.dance

You will dance.

sə-q’a-w-ɬaːʁʷəʁaɕ

1s.abs-hor-2s.erg-saw

You saw me.

wə-q’a-s-ɬaːʁʷəʁaɕ

2s.abs-hor-1s.erg-saw

I saw you.

The DATIVE marker (for **indirect objects**) comes before the ergative marker:

Adyghe

sə-w-j-a-tə-Ø

1s.abs-2s.dat-3s.erg-dyn-give-pres

S/he gives me to you.

w-ja-s-atə

2s.abs-3p.dat-1s.erg-gives

I give you to them.

Indirect objects are not just found in ditransitives like ‘give’. Many intransitive verbs select an absolutive argument and a dative one, and certain copular roots take a dative as their only argument.

Kabardian

Ø-q’ə-sa-apɬ-ha

3p.abs-hor-1s.dat-look-pl

They are looking at me.

l-akʷ’ə-m jə-z-dzaxə-z

3s.f.dat-is-neg 3.nh.abs-rel.erg-sew-rel

She was not the one who sewed it.

Such a construction may be used where we might expect a transitive verb:

jə-sə-ma-wp’

3.nh.abs-1s.dat-have-pres.stat

I have it.

jə-l-taxə-wp'

3.nh.abs-3s.f.dat-want-pres.stat

She wants it.

The affixes that encode person/number/gender for oblique arguments in verbs also encode those features for possessors and for postpositions.

a-pħʷəs a-fatʷ' Ø-lə-s-ta-jt'

art-woman art-food 3s.nh.abs-3s.f.dat-1s.erg-give-aor

I gave the food to the woman

a-pħʷəs lə-ɥnə

art-woman 3s.f.poss-house

the woman's house

a-pħʷəs lə-q'əntʷ'

art-woman 3s.f-from

from the woman

All three constructions thus show head-marking (p. 171).

Tense, Aspect, and Mood

The NW Caucasian languages can encode a great variety of tenses, aspects, moods, and adverbial notions into their verbs. Such inflection is highly regular, but the full range is only found in DYNAMIC verbs, which express actions. STATIVE verbs, which denote properties and states, are much more limited in their inflectional flexibility. In Abkhaz, for instance, the dynamic verb paradigm produces ten basic tense-mood inflections while the stative one has only two.

DYNAMIC

s-tsa-wajt' 1s.abs-go-pres.dyn *I'm going, I go, I will go*	**stsa-wan** 1s.go-impfv *I was going*
stsa-jt' 1s.go-aor *I went*	**stsa-n** 1s.go-pind *I went (and then...)*

stsa-p'
1s.go-fut1
I will go (if...)

stsa-rən
1s.go-cond1
I would (have) go(ne)

stsa-ʂt'
1s.go-fut2
I will (probably) go

stsa-ʂan
1s.go-cond2
I would (probably) (have) go(ne), I'll have (no doubt) gone

stsa-xʲajt'
1s.go-perf
I have (already) gone

stsa-xʲan
1s.go-plu
I had (already) gone

STATIVE

sə-q'a-wp'
1s.abs-be-pres.stat
I am

səq'a-n
1s.be-past.stat
I was

Other tenses can be derived from a stative by adding a dynamicizing morpheme and treating it like a dynamic verb.

sə-q'a-zaː-p'
1s.abs-be-dyn-fut1
I will be (if...)

sə-q'a-zaː-ʂt'
1s.abs-be-dyn-fut2
I will (probably) be

Negative polarity is marked in the verb. Here are the negative versions of both paradigms above. (The negative marker may appear before or after the verb root.)

DYNAMIC

s-tsa-wa-m
1s.abs-go-pres.dyn-neg

s-tsa-wa-mə-zt'
1s.abs-go-impfv-neg-impfv

sə-m-tsa-jt'
1s.abs -neg-go-aor

sə-m-tsa-zt'
1s.abs -neg-go-pind

s-tsa-rə-m
1s.abs -go-fut1-neg

s-tsa-rə-mə-zt'
1s.abs-go-cond1-neg-cond1

s-tsa-ʂa-m

1s.abs.go-fut2-neg

s-tsa-ʂa-mə-zt'

1s.abs-go-cond2-neg-cond2

sə-m-tsa-ts

1s.abs -neg-go-perf

sə-m-tsa-tsəzt'

1s.abs -neg-go-plu

STATIVE

sə-q'a-m-Ø

1s.abs-be-neg-pres.stat

sə-q'a-mə-zt'

1s.abs-be-neg-past.stat

The verb complex is potentially very expressive in terms of aspectual, modal, and adverbial nuance:

Abaza

də-nxa- rk^{w}'a-wan

3s.abs-work-cont-impfv

S/he was continuing to work.

də-tsa-la-jt'

3s.abs-go-hab-pres.dyn

S/he goes (regularly/frequently).

d-(ata)-jə-s-x-t'

3s.abs-(again)-3s.f.erg-hit-again-aor

She hit him/her again.

jə-g^{j}-jə-ma-dza-m-zt'

3s.abs-emph-3s.m.dat-have-emph-neg-past.stat

He really didn't have it at all.

d-g^{w}ərɣ^{j}a-g^{w}ʃa-p'

3s.abs-rejoice-poor.thing-fut1

S/he will rejoice, poor thing.

jə-tsk^{j}a-ʕ^{w}əʃ^{w}a-p'

3.abs-clean-completely-pres.stat

It's completely clean.

sə-j+pħa-nda

1s.abs-his+daughter-opt-pres.stat

I wish I were his daughter / If only I were his daughter.

ħ-gʲə-z-najx-wa-m

1p.abs-neg.fin-pot-go.back-pres.stat-neg

We won't be able to go back.

Kabardian is unusual cross-linguistically in overtly marking the affirmative:

Ø-q'at'asha-ʁa-ɕ

3.abs-sit.down-past-aff

He sat down.

Valence

VALENCE (p. 140) refers to the number of arguments a verb commands. Having polypersonal agreement, the NW Caucasian languages mark each of these arguments on the verb.

The family employs a number of operations to decrease or increase valence. For example, **causative** constructions **increase** a verb's valence by one. The marker for the new argument (the causing agent) usually follows the ergative slot.

Abaza

də-tsa-jt' → d-sə-r-tsa-jt'

3s.abs-go-pres.dyn /
3s.abs-1s.agt-caus-go-pres.dyn

S/he goes → I make him/her go; I send him/her.

d-a-pxʲa-jt' → d-a-sə-r-pxʲa-jt'

3s.abs-3s.nh.erg-read /
3s.abs-3s.nh.erg-1s.agt-caus-read-pres.dyn

S/he reads it → I make him/her read it.

In Abaza, Kabardian, and Adyghe, any verb can be causativized, including trivalent ones. Thus, tetravalent verb forms are possible:

Abaza

jə-lə-w-t-t' → jə-lə-wə-s-rə-t-t'

3.abs-3s.f.dat-2s.erg-give-aor /
3.abs-3s.f.dat-2s.erg-1s.agt-caus-give-aor

You gave it to her → I made you give it to her.

Double causatives are possible too.

Abaza

jə-lə-j-s-r-rə-fa-jt'

3.abs-3s.f.erg.3s.m.agt-1s.agt-caus-caus-eat-pres.dyn

I make him make her eat it.

Applicative constructions (p. 145) are another valence-increasing strategy. They promote an adjunct (a nonobligatory element) to an oblique object (an obligatory element). Often the operation is essentially the incorporation of a postposition and its pronominal affix.

a-pħ^{w}əs a-xats'a jə-zə a-xarp Ø-lə-dʑ^{w}dʑ^{w}a-jt'

art-woman art-man 3s.m-for art-shirt 3s.abs-3s.f.erg-wash-aor

The woman washed the shirt for the man. (adjunct)

→ apħ^{w}əs axats'a axarp Ø-jə-zə-lə-dʑ^{w}dʑ^{w}a-jt'

— — — 3s.abs-3s.m.dat-ben-3s.f.erg-wash-aor

The woman washed the shirt for the man. (argument)

a-xats'a a-ħ^{w}əzba a-la a-k^{w}'ət'ə Ø-j-ʃə-jt'

art-man art-knife 3s.nh-with art-chicken 3s.abs-3s.m.erg-kill-aor

The man killed the chicken with the knife. (adjunct)

→ axats'a aħ^{w}əzba ak^{w}'ət'ə Ø-a-la-j-ʃə-jt'

— — — 3s.abs-3s.nh.dat-inst-3s.m.erg-kill-aor

The man killed the chicken with the knife. (argument)

A verb may also have more than one applicative:

Kabardian

Ø-q'ə-w-f'ə-ha-da-s-ʃə-aʁ-ɕ

3.abs-hor-2s.dat-adver-3p.dat-com-1s.erg-marry-aor-aff

With their help I married her despite you (no adjuncts)

Applicatives and causatives may freely combine.

Kabardian

sjə dəsa-r Ø-q'ə-w-xʷ-s-a-w-ʁa:-na

my gold-abs 3.abs-hor-2s.dat-ben-1s.erg-pres-prog-caus-remain

I am making my gold remain for you; I'm leaving you my gold.

There are also strategies to **decrease** a verb's valence. The **passive voice** is one option. A stative passive is achieved by deleting the ergative person marker from a dynamic verb and adding stative tense suffixes. Dynamic passives must be expressed periphrastically, or with causatives.

Abaza

də-r-ʃə-t' → d-ʃə-p'

3s.abs-3p.erg-kill-aor / 3s.abs-kill-pres.stat

They killed him/her → S/he is killed. (stative)

A simpler technique is simply omitting person markers from the verb complex. This method of decreasing valence is not possible for all verbs.

jə-pə-s-tʂə-jt' → jə-p-tʂə-jt'

3s.nh.abs-pv-[1s.erg]-break-aor

I broke it → It broke.

Should the initial absolutive argument be deleted, the ergative marker is replaced by the equivalent absolutive one.

jə-zə-ɥ-wajt' → sə-ɥ-wajt'

3s.nh.abs-1s.erg-write-pres.dyn /
1s.abs-write-pres.dyn

I am writing it → I am writing.

In the following example, a dative argument (the indirect object) is deleted.

Kabardian

Ø-q'a-j-s-tə-ʒə-aʁ-ɕ → Ø-q'a-s-tə-ʒə-aʁ-ɕ

3.abs-hor-[3.dat-]1s.erg-give-again-past-aff

I gave it again to him/her → I gave it again.

The valence can further be reduced, but for this verb another device must be employed. Here a change in the stem's vowel marks valence reduction and intransitivization (which also triggers the horizon of interest morpheme to disappear). This vowel alternation is unique to Kabardian and Adyghe, but in these languages it is widespread.

sə-ta-ʒə-aʁ-ɕ

1s.abs-give.intr-again-past-aff

I gave again.

In this language family it is important to distinguish VALENCE and TRANSITIVITY. A verb is only transitive if it takes an ergative argument; it is thus necessarily at least bivalent. As the data above suggest, however, a bivalent verb is not necessarily transitive. In fact, trivalent intransitives are possible:

Abaza

s-wə-z-lə-ts-tsa-jt'

1s.abs-2s.dat-ben-3s.f.dat-com-go-pres.dyn

I'm going with her for you.

Some intransitive verbs are vacuously bivalent: they necessarily govern a meaningless indirect object, which is always 3rd person singular.

Kabardian

s-ja-s-aʁ-ɕ

1s.abs-3s.dat-swim-past-aff

I swam.

Changing transitivity need not change valence. E.g. Kabardian's method of expressing capability or potentiality:

səmadʒa-m mə?aresa-r Ø-j-a-ʃx^j

sick.man-obl(erg) apple-abs 3.abs-3s.erg-pres-eat

The sick man eats the apple.

səmadʒa-m mə?aresa-r Ø-Ø-x^w-aw-ʃx^j

sick.man-obl(dat) apple-abs 3.abs-3s.dat-pot-pres.intr-eat

The sick man can eat the apple.

In both sentences the verb is bivalent, but only the first is transitive. This operation also triggers inverse marking, but because the Kabardian ergative case marker is homophonous with the dative, alone the nouns create an illusion of transitivity. However, the tense morpheme /aw/ is only found in verbs with 3rd person subjects that are intransitive.

Bivalent intransitive verbs may also denote incomplete actions or activities, as in the second of these pairs of examples:

Kabardian

ha-m qʷ'əpʃxʲa-r Ø-jə-dzaq'a

dog-obl(erg) bone-abs 3.abs-3s.erg-bite

The dog bites the bone (to the marrow, completely).

ha-r qʷ'əpʃxʲa-m Ø-ja-aw-dzaq'a

dog-abs bone-obl(dat) 3.abs-3s.dat-pres.intr-bite

The dog is biting/nibbling at the bone.

ç'a:la-m txʲəɬ-ər Ø-j-a-dʒ

boy-obl(erg) book-abs 3.abs-3s.erg-pres-read

The boy reads the book (to the end, completely).

ç'a:la-r txʲəɬ-əm Ø-ja-aw-dʒa

boy-abs book-obl(dat) 3.abs-3s.dat-pres.intr-read

The boy is reading the book (and is not finished).

In Kabardian there are only a few verbs, termed LABILE or DIFFUSE, which can function as transitive or intransitive with no modification (e.g., no vowel root alternation, transitivizing suffixes, differing tense markers, etc.).

a:- r ma-a-va

3s-abs 3.abs-pres-plow

He plows.

a:-bə ʃʔə-r Ø-j-a-va

3s-erg ground-abs 3.abs-3s.erg-pres-plow

He plows the ground.

Nonfinite Forms

The Northwest Caucasian languages employ a number of nonfinite verbal forms, the specific mechanics of which vary from language to language. For instance, the verbal noun in Abkhaz is a MASDAR, roughly equivalent to the English gerund. Its arguments are expressed with possessive prefixes and postpositional phrases.

a-tsa-ra → l-tsa-ra

art-go-masd / her-go-masd

going → her going

a-ba-ra → sə-la bə-ba-ra

art-see-masd / 1s-by.2s poss-see-masd

seeing → my seeing you (lit. your seeing by me)

The equivalent form in Kabardian is better characterized as an infinitive. Its arguments are marked in the verbal complex just as in finite verbs.

Kabardian

Ø-sə-tx^{j}ə-n	**Ø-ja-dʒa-n-ha**
3.abs-1s.erg-write-inf	3.abs-3p.erg-learn-inf-3p
(... for) me to write it	*(...for) them to learn it*

Another nonfinite construction is the CONVERB, which expresses adverbial subordination. Many sophisticated syntactic structures involve converbs, but the simplest ones express an event which is simultaneous or anterior to that of the main clause. Depending on their form and environment, converbs may or may not display full person marking.

a-kalpad (Ø-l-)pa-wa də-px^{j}a-wan

art-sock (3s.abs-3s.f.erg-)knit-sim 3s.abs-read-impfv

(While) knitting the sock, she was reading.

akalpad pa-nə də-tsa-jt'

– knit-ant 3s.abs-go-aor

Having knitted the sock, s/he left.

Clause variety

Marked clause types— e.g. relative, adverbial, conditional, and interrogative clauses— are formed not with independent function words, but with morphemes within the verbal complex.

Relative clauses, for instance, are formed by replacing the person marker of the relativized argument with a special affix and using different tense suffixes that mark subordination.

a-pħʷəs rts’aɥə-s də-q’a-wp’

art-woman teacher-pred 3s.abs-be-pres.stat

The woman is a teacher.

→ də-j-dər-wajt’ rts’aɥəs jə-q’a-w apħʷəs

3s.abs-3s.m.erg-know-pres.dyn teacher-pred rel.abs-be-pres.stat.sub art-woman

S/he knows the woman who is a teacher.

a-xats’a apħʷəs də-j-ba-jt’

art-man — 3s.abs-3s.m.erg-see-aor

The man saw the woman.

→ dəjdərwajt’ axats’a jə-j-ba-Ø apħʷəs

— — rel.abs-3s.m.erg-see-aor.sub —

S/he knows the woman who the man saw.

Relativized clause as subject:

a-xatsʷa a-pħʷəs də-r-ʃə-jt’

art-men art-woman 3s.abs-3p.abs-kill-aor

The men killed the woman.

→ a-pħʷəs də-z-ʃə-Ø axatsʷa Ø-aː-wajt’

— 3s.abs-rel.erg-kill-aor.sub — 3.abs-come-pres.dyn

The men who killed the woman are coming.

Indirect objects can be relativized:

axats’a apħʷəs a-ʃʷqʷ’ə Ø-lə-j-ta-jt’

— — art-book 3s.abs-3s.f.dat-3s.m.erg-give-aor

The man gave the woman the book.

→ axats’a aʃʷqʷ’ə Ø-zə-j-ta-Ø apħʷəs də-z-der-wajt’

— — 3s.nh.abs-rel.dat-3s.m.erg-give-aor.sub — 3s.abs-1s.erg-know-pres.dyn

I know the man who the woman gave the book to.

As can applicatives:

a-waɥ a-ħʷəzba a-kʷʼətʼə Ø-a-la-j-ʃa-jtʼ

art-man art-knife art-chicken 3s.nh.abs-3s.nh.dat-inst-3s.m.erg-kill-aor

The man killed the chicken with the knife.

→ **awaɥ akʷʼətʼə Ø-z-la-j-ʃ-Ø aħʷəzba Ø-z-ba-jtʼ**

— — 3s.nh.abs-rel.dat-inst-3s.m.erg-kill-aor.sub — 3s.nh.abs- 1s.erg-see-aor

I saw the knife the man killed the chicken with.

Complement clauses are formed with the same subordinate tense endings as relative clauses, but retain all person markers and add a complementizer morpheme.

Aqʷʼa-qʼa s-axʲ-tsa-wa s-a-r-gʷəɣʲa-wajtʼ

Sukhumi-to 1s.abs-comp-go-pres.dyn.sub 1s.abs-3s.nh.agent-caus-rejoice-pres.dyn

The fact that I'm going to Sukhumi makes me happy.

d-ʂə-tʃmazaɥə-z s-a-kʷʃʷa-jtʼ

3s.abs-comp-sick.person-past.sub 1s.abs-3s.nh.dat-realize-aor

I realized that s/he was sick.

A wide variety of subordinate **adverbial** meanings can be encoded into the verb. As in relative clauses, the verbs heading these constructions take a different set of tense-markers than those of unmarked clauses, but the insertion of the appropriate subordinating morpheme is less predictable.

d-anə-tsʷa-w a-wəs Ø-z-w-wajtʼ

3s.abs-when-sleep-pres.stat.sub art-work 3s.nh.abs-1s.erg-do-pres.dyn

When s/he sleeps, I do work.

d-an-aː-lakʲʼ-Ø a-fatʷʼ Ø-lə-s-ta-la-wan

3s.abs-whenever-come-whenever-aor.sub art-food 3s.nh.abs-3s.f.dat-1s.erg-give-impfv

Whenever she came, I would give her food.

də-ʂə-j-ba-tsʷʼqʲʼa-z də-tsa-jtʼ

3s.abs-as.soon.as-3s.m.erg-see-as.soon.as-pind.sub 3s.abs-go-aor

As soon as he saw him/her, he went.

də-ʂə-z-ba-z də-q'a-wp'

3s.abs-how-1s.erg-see-pind.sub 3s.abs-be-pres.stat

S/he is as I saw her/him.

dəpʂdzanə a-ʃʷa Ø-ʂə-l-ħʷa-wa-gʲə lə-bʒə Ø-s-gʷapxa-wam

beautifully art-song 3s.nh.abs-however-3s.f.erg-say-pres.dyn.sub-however 3s.f.poss-voice 3s.nh.abs-1s.dat-like-pres.dyn.neg

However beautifully she sings, I don't like her voice.

a-ts'a-ra bzəjanə Ø-axʲə-j-ts'a-waz a-zə, ajħabərats'ara d-aː-na-xʷa-jt'

art-study-masd well 3s.nh.abs-because-3s.m.erg-study-impfv.sub it-for, institute 3s.abs-pv-3s.nh.erg-admit-aor

Because he studied well, the institute admitted him.

a-mra Ø-pxa-wa-zargʲə Ø-xʲta-wp'

art-sun 3s.nh.abs-shine-impfv.sub-even.though 3s.nh.abs-cold-pres.stat

Although the sun is shining, it's cold.

There are a number of strategies used to express a PROTASIS (an **if clause**) depending on the reality or irreality of the conditional phrase.

də-z-ba-Ø-r, jərlasnə s-aː-wajt'

3s.abs-1s.erg-see-aor.sub-if, quickly 1s.abs-come-pres.dyn

If I see him/her, I'll come quickly.

b-tsa-Ø, Ø-b-taxə-zar

2s.abs-go-imper 3s.abs-2s.dat-want-if.pres.stat.sub

Go if you want to!

jatsə də-z-ba-z-tgʲə, jə-ba-s-ħʷa-wan

yesterday 3s.abs-1s.erg-see-pind.sub-if, 3s.abs-2s.dat-1s.erg-tell-impfv

If I had seen her yesterday, I'd have told you.

Interrogative clauses too have unique verb forms. The production of yes-no questions is relatively simple: use the subordinate tense endings and add an interrogative suffix.

Abaza

jə-w-ba-t’ → jə-w-ba-Ø-ma

3.abs-2s.erg-see-aor /
3.abs-2s.erg-see-aor.sub-q

You saw it/them → Did you see it/them?

jə-g^{j}ə-w-m-ba-t’ → jə-g^{j}ə-w-m-ba-Ø-ma

3.abs-neg-2s.erg-neg-see-aor /
3.abs-neg-2s.erg-neg-see-aor.sub-q

You didn’t see it/them → Didn’t you see it/them?

Content questions are formed by replacing the questioned argument’s person marker with a relativizer morpheme (if applicable) and adding an interrogative pronoun, either into the verb itself or as an independent word.

d-aː-jt’ → j-aː-da-Ø

3s.abs-come-aor / rel.abs-come-who-aor.sub

S/he came → that came

→ j-aː-Ø d-arban

rel.abs-come-aor.sub 3s.abs-who

Who came?

jə-b-ɥə-z-zəj

rel.abs-2s.erg-write-pind.sub-what

What did you write?

jə-z-fa-x^{j}a-da / jə-z-fa-x^{j}aw darban

3.abs-rel.erg-eat-perf.sub-who / 3s.abs-rel.erg-eat-perf.sub who

Who has eaten it/them?

d-anba-tsa-waz

3s.abs-when-go-impfv.sub

When was s/he going?

d-aba-tsa-x^{j}aw

3s.abs-where-go-perf.sub

Where has s/he gone (already)?

də-z-tsa-zə-z

3s.abs-why-go-q-pind.sub

Why did s/he go?

ʂaq'a ħʷa Ø-a:-w-xʷa-Ø-j

how.many pig 3.nh.abs-pv-2s.erg-buy-aor.sub-what

How many pigs did you buy?

Directionality

Besides postpositions, which are added to nouns, a great variety of verbal affixes can express locative and directional meaning. These morphemes (often called PREVERBS) take dative person markers much like applicatives. They may add directional/locative meaning to a verb, or act alone as a stative root.

Adyghe

sə-p-ta-s-Ø

1s.abs-2s.dat-on-sit-pres

I'm sitting on you.

wəna-m s-jə-s-Ø

house-obl 1s.abs-3s.dat-sit-pres

I'm sitting in the house.

Preverbs often have no discernible etymology or nonverbal use (a), but they can be homophonous with postpositions (b).

(a) d-a-v-s-wajt'

3s.abs-3s.nh.dat-by-pass-pres.dyn

S/he passed by it.

(b) ħa-ɥnə a-za:jgʷa də-nxa-wajt'

2p.poss-house it-near 3s.abs-live-pres.dyn

S/he lives near our house.

d-a-za:jgʷa-xa-jt'

3s.abs-3s.nh.dat-near-become-aor

He became near it; he approached it.

If more than one preverb occurs, it can denote a changing directionality.

Kabardian

ç'aƙa-r q^{w}əħa-m psə-m Ø-q'ə-Ø-də-Ø-x^{j}ə-a-x^{j}əx^{w}a-ʁa-ç

youth-abs boat-obl water-obl 3.abs-hor-3.dat-out-3.dat-in-dat-fall.down-past-aff

The youth fell out of the boat and into the water.

Some preverbs carry a remarkably specific meaning.

a-ɥnə də-ɥnə-sə-jt'

art-house 3s.abs-in.a.house-pass-aor

S/he passed through the house.

a-ħ^{w}ənap a-k'əlħara jə-k'əla-wp'

art-mouse art-hole 3s.nh.abs-in.a.narrow.opening-pres.stat

The mouse is in its hole.

a-xəlpa Ø-s-xa-wp'

art-hat 3s.abs-1s.dat-on.a.head-pres.stat

I'm wearing my hat.

a-sark^{j}'a a-tdzamts a-tʂ'ə jə-k'ədə-s-ts'a-wajt'

art-mirror art-wall it-at 3s.nh.abs-on.vertically.without.visible.attachment-1s.erg- put-pres.dyn

I place the mirror onto the wall.

Ø-ajɥə-s-ts^{w}'a-wajt'

3s.abs-through.a.long.object.at.a.right.angle.to.its.length-1s.erg-cut-pres.dyn

I cut through it.

Preverbs can also encode **deixis**, or relative reference point.

jə-sə-z-aː-b-ga-jt'

3s.nh.abs-1s.dat-ben-pv-2s.erg-bring-aor

You brought it to me here.

jəsəz-na-bgajt'

You brought it to me there.

Kabardian and Adyghe have a very peculiar affix, sometimes called the HORIZON OF INTEREST preverb, whose exact mechanics are not completely understood. It serves not only to provide deixis (a), but also to establish a change in state (b), highlight something of interest such as a relationship (c), or give idiosyncratic semantic nuance (d).

Kabardian

(a) Ø-q’a-aw-kʷ’a

3s.abs-hor-pres-move.intr

He is coming here.

(b) tjadʒap’a-r Ø-q’a-jə-wəxʲə-ʁa-ɕ

school-abs 3s.abs-hor-3s.erg-finish-past-aff

He graduated school.

tjadʒap’a-r Ø-jəwəxʲəʁaɕ

He finished school (for the year).

(c) ɬ’ə-r Ø-q’a-w-wətʃ’əʒə-ʁa-ɕ

man-abs 3s.abs-hor-2s.erg-kill-past-aff

You killed the man (my own kinsman).

ɬ’ər w-Ø-wətʃ’əʒəʁaɕ

You killed the man (a stranger to me).

(d) Ø-q’-wa-s-t-ʁa-ɕ

3s.abs-hor-2s.dat-1s.erg-give-past-aff

I loaned it to you (and expect it back).

Ø-wastʁaɕ

I gave it to you (to keep).

Other Features

The Northwest Caucasian verb has no shortage of remarkable features. Below are a few constructions that do not fit in one of the above sections.

In a few verb stems, a consonant may be doubled to express intensity of meaning.

a-ħʷa-ra → a-ħʷħʷa-ra

art-say-masd / art-yell-masd

saying → yelling

axra → axxra

chopping → chopping into many pieces

Adyghe verbs may exhibit forms to emphasize change in state (with an INTROVERT suffix) or the place where this change took place (EXTROVERT).

kʷə-m Ø-Ø-ʃə-maxʲə-ʁ

car-obl(dat) 3s.abs-3s.dat-there-faint-past

He fainted in the car.

→ kʷəm Ø-Ø-jə-maxʲ-əħaː-ʁ

– 3s.abs-3s.dat-in-faint-introvert-past

He fainted in the car.

→ kʷəm Ø-Ø-jə-maxʲ-aħə-ʁ

– 3s.abs-3s.dat-in-faint-extrovert-past

He fainted in the car.

Further reading

The examples are taken from the following sources:

John **Colarusso**, *Kabardian (East Circassian)* (2006)
B.G. **Hewitt**, *Abkhaz* (1989)
B.G. **Hewitt**, ed. *The Indigenous Languages of the Caucasus, Vol. 2: North West Caucasus* (1989)
Ranko **Matasović**, *A Short Grammar of East Circassian (Kabardian)* (2010)
Henricus Joannes **Smeets**, *Studies in West Circassian Phonology and Morphology* (1984)

Sign language

Sign languages are true languages, with vocabularies of thousands of words, and grammars as complex and sophisticated as those of any other language, though with fascinating differences from speech. If you think they are merely pantomime, try watching a mathematics lecture, a poetry reading, or a religious service conducted in Sign, and see how much you understand.

For linguists— and conlinguists— Sign is a constant source of exceptions to universals. Linguistic signals and their meanings are arbitrary? All languages have at least two stops? Languages all derive from Proto-World? Not in Sign!

The linguist William Stokoe, who was professor of English at Gallaudet University starting in 1955, became fascinated with Sign and is credited with introducing the subject to linguistics.

Sign families

Sign languages have their own classifications, unrelated to families of spoken languages— though the study of Sign families is relatively new and full of open questions.

- One of the largest families is that based on **French Sign Language** (*Langue de signes française,* LSF), which includes varieties used in Russia, the Netherlands, Italy, Spain, Mexico, Brazil, and the US.

  LSF emerged from the French Deaf community, which was discovered by accident by the Abbé de l'Épée in the mid-1700s. Fascinated by the signs he saw, he started the first free school for the Deaf in 1760.

  Thomas Gallaudet started the first US school for the Deaf in 1817; his co-founder was Laurent Clerc, a graduate of the French school. As a result American Sign Language is a clear derivative of LSF. Gallaudet's son Edward founded what is now Gallaudet University in 1864.

- Another family derives from Danish Sign Language; varieties are used in Norway, Sweden, Finland, Iceland, and Portugal.

- British Sign Language (which is *not* mutually intelligible with ASL) is related to the languages of Australia and New Zealand.
- Japanese Sign Language is apparently related to the sign languages of Taiwan and South Korea.

ASL is not to be confused with Signed English, which is a word-for-word signed equivalent of English. Deaf people tend to find it tiring, because its grammar, like that of spoken languages, is linear, while that of ASL is primarily spatial.

New sign languages

Sign is the only area where we can watch a natural language appearing from nowhere. In 1977 the first Nicaraguan school for Deaf children was established in Managua. The teachers focused on lipreading and finger-spelling— but the students, among themselves, created their own form of Sign.

The first signs were limited, and the grammar seemed not to be fixed. But by the mid-1980s the children's signs were more stylized and fluid as well as more conventionalized; they had developed into a language, the *Idioma de Señas de Nicaragua* (ISN). The process has an obvious resemblance to the development of pidgins and creoles (p. 74), but the children did not need a source language.

Individual Deaf children sometimes develop signs for use within their family (HOME SIGNS), but these are useless outside the home and are not full languages. It seems to require a community to develop a language, as in the school in Managua.

Deaf children learn Sign as readily as hearing children learn spoken language, while adult learners struggle. Derek Bickerton and Steven Pinker argue that children's facility with Sign, and the invention of ISN, are evidence for a LANGUAGE ORGAN that allows humans to quickly master language. This conclusion goes beyond the evidence, however; as conlangers know, inventing a language takes a good deal of effort, and adults are rarely in a position where they need to make one.

We don't have an equivalent of a spoken language being invented from scratch. Hearing people will attempt to get ideas across by miming, and indeed, among Native Americans of the Great Plains, a gestural pidgin developed, Plains Indian Sign Language. Perhaps signs are just easier to develop; indeed, there are theories that human language first appeared in the form of Sign.

Characteristics

Sign languages, like spoken languages, have morphology, semantics, syntax, and pragmatics.

As words can be broken down into phonemes, signs can be broken down into components, which Stokoe called CHEREMES. It's now more common however to simply use the term PHONEME.

However, there are also some features that are characteristic of sign languages or unique to them.

Iconicity

One of the most striking properties of Sign is ICONICITY: most signs have some sort of visual link to what they represent. Some examples from ASL:

Baby loves beards

BABY— cradle and rock hands as if holding a baby

LOVE— cross hands in front of heart

BEARD— pull down from the chin as if stroking a goatee

BOOK— hold hands in shape of a book

LETTER— move thumb from mouth to other fist, as if licking and applying a stamp

BICYCLE— fists circle like a bike's pedals

ROOM— hands face each other, closing off a space

MILK— pull down on an imaginary cow's udder

THINK— point to forehead, rotating wrist

I— point to yourself

Many more signs are not visual metaphors, but they are motivated— often based on finger-spelling. E.g. shaking the hand-shape B is the sign for BLUE. The sign for DAY involves moving the whole arm like the sun moving through the sky, but it's reinforced by making the hand-shape D.

This observation is apparently controversial, because it conflicts with Saussure's statement that the relationship between a linguistic form and its referent is arbitrary. Well, Saussure was wrong; he was leaving out Sign! Still, it should be emphasized that signs are not miming or improvised gestures; they are fixed forms, vary between sign languages, and may not be transparent to non-signers.

Simultaneity

In general, speech consists of phonemes in linear sequence. Sign makes much more use of multiple simultaneous actions. A sign may incorporate or be inflected by facial expression, eye contact, bodily posture, or mouth movements, and the hands can be doing more than one thing at a time.

Non-manual gestures may be part of the lexical meaning of a sign, may be an inflection, or may even communicate pragmatic information (e.g. avoiding eye contact can be a way of keeping the floor).

ASL is sometimes roughly glossed with the English equivalents of the main words— e.g. one textbook glosses a line from a dialog as LOOK.AROUND MAYBE WANT BLUE, with the free translation *Let's see what they have; maybe she'll want a blue one.* But as inflections, deictics, and adverbials are not represented, this is only recording part of the actual ASL utterance!

ASL

This section describes some of the features of American Sign Language (ASL) in particular. I've focused not on how to use the language— you're not going to learn to sign here— but on its underlying structure and interesting features.

ASL doesn't have articles, which to English speakers will make the glosses look like Headlinese. Try to get past this reaction— plenty of languages, including highly inflected ones like Latin and Russian, don't have articles.

The finger alphabet

The ASL finger alphabet is shown below. The signs are all made with the palm facing outward— the table shows what the addressee sees.

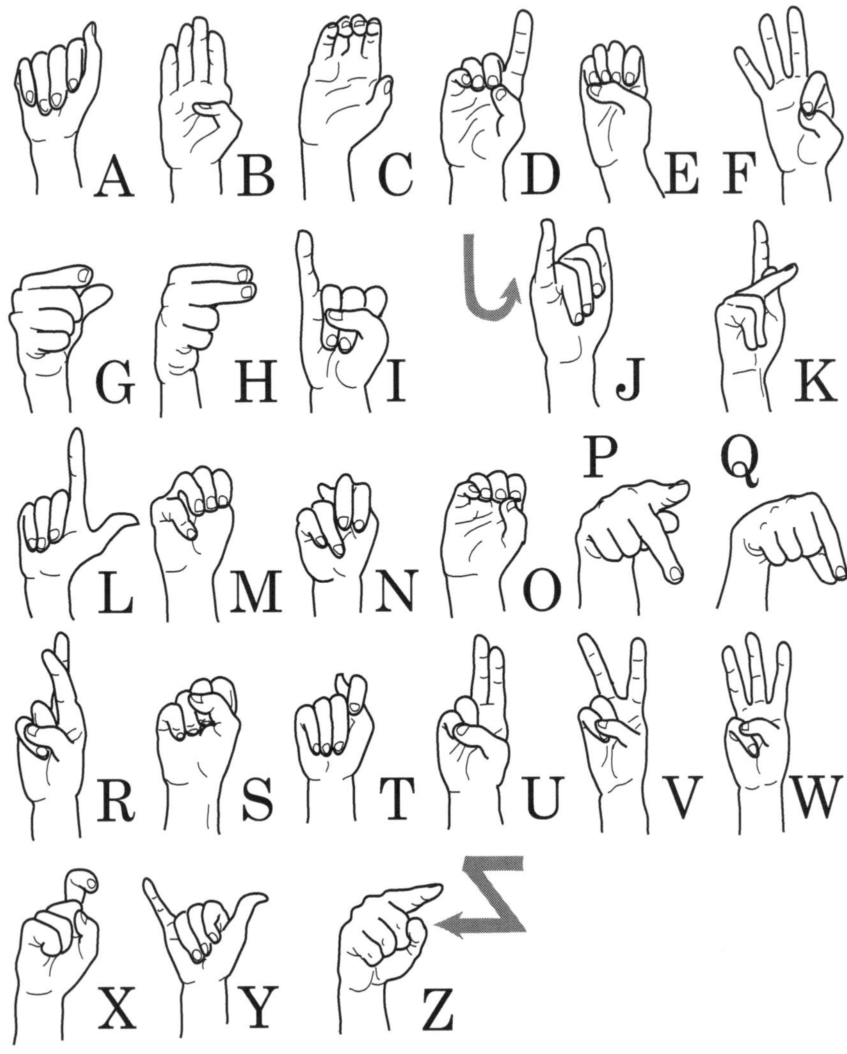

It's used for proper names and technical terms, but also provides a repertoire of basic HANDSHAPES to form other signs. The letter handshapes may be

- a reference to an English word— e.g. FAMILY is signed with both hands in F position, hands raised and making a little circle

- iconic— e.g. CHICKEN uses handshape G, opening and closing the thumb and index finger, which mimics a beak
- arbitrary— e.g. APPLE is signed with handshape X, held near the cheek and twisted several times

Pronouns

Pronouns are iconic in ASL— you point to yourself, to the person you're talking to, to a third party.

Rather neatly, you can build a sort of conceptual space in front of you, and pointing to locations within it functions as a deictic. You can introduce a topic by making a sign or series of signs to identify them (the equivalent of *the house,* or *my brother's girlfriend*), then point to a spot (a LOCUS). To refer to them again, you point to the same locus— or even just glance at it. You can establish several topics, each with their own location to point to.

I borrowed this idea for a spoken language, Elkarîl: it has no pronouns, only variables. You give a reference (e.g. *chnqêt* 'mother') and add a morpheme— e.g. *chnqêtqebut* which assigns the anaphoric variable *-u-*. Now the suffix *-ut* can be applied to verbs to refer to *mother*; all participants in the conversation will use the same suffix.

Nonmanual markers

Yes-no questions are not marked by a manual sign, but by moving the body and face forward and lifting the brows.

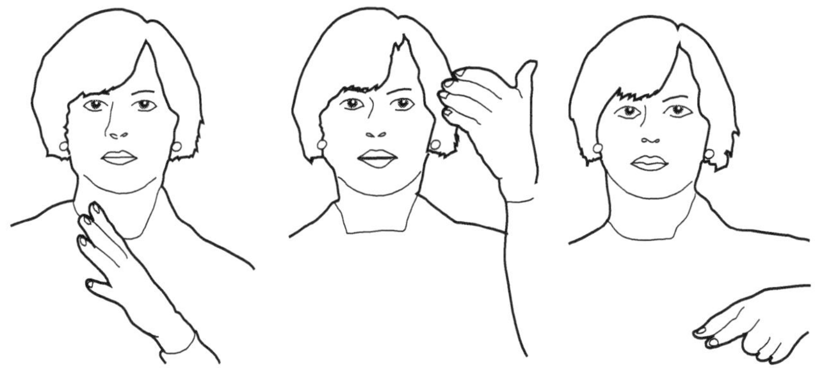

Statement: *The woman forgot her purse.*

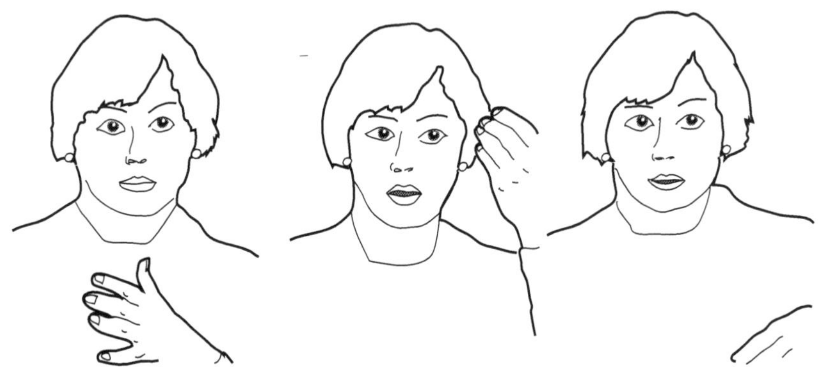

Question: *Did the woman forget her purse?*

Scott Liddell transcribes this as

______________________q

WOMAN FORGET PURSE

Did the woman forget her purse?

to emphasize that the signal is maintained throughout the question. Similarly, one way of **negating** a sentence is with a frown and a shake of the head:

______________________n

WOMAN FORGET PURSE

The woman didn't forget her purse.

The idea is similar to using intonation to mark a question in speech, though I'm not aware of any spoken language where negation is marked solely by intonation.

A neat feature: both these signals indicate their scope. E.g.:

_______t ____________n

WOMAN FORGET PURSE

As for the woman, she didn't forget her purse.

The negation marker *n* is maintained only while signing FORGET PURSE, so it's clear that only the VP is negated. (The other marker *t* is a topicalizer and will be discussed below.)

There is also a lexical NOT (form the 'hitchhiking sign', poke chin with thumb); adding *n* reinforces the negation.

Other examples, with Liddell's abbreviations:

- *rn*– A rapid nod can emphasize that an action did take place
- *mm*– Pursed lips, with the head turned back and to the side is an adverbial indicating *normal functioning* or *relaxation and enjoyment*
- *th*– A tilted head, and the tongue pushed through the teeth, expresses lack of control, inattention, or clumsiness
- Wide eyes and a dropped jaw express the speaker's surprise at an event or condition
- Bared teeth, lowered brow, and tensed eyes express anger

For the latter two signals, the emotion is that of the speaker, not the subject: if you sign BILL LIKE JOHN with the surprise marker, the idea is that you're surprised, not Bill. (However, it's possible to role-play in ASL, temporarily taking someone's perspective, just as in speech, and in this case the surprise would be that of the person role-played.)

These signals can be combined:

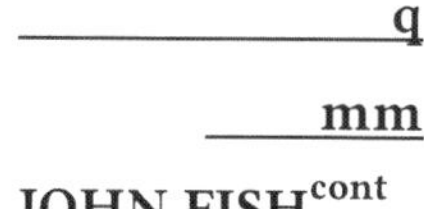

JOHN FISH^{cont}

Is John fishing with relaxed enjoyment?

The question applies to the sentence-with-adverbial: if the man is fishing, but not with relaxed enjoyment, the answer is *no*.

At least one combination has an idiomatic meaning: if the same signs are made, but with *mm* and head-nodding throughout, from the meaning of the two markers we'd expect the meaning *It's true that John enjoys fishing*. But the actual interpretation is *It's a characteristic of John's that he enjoys fishing.*

Nonmanual cheremes can also be **lexical**: e.g. BITE is accompanied by a biting motion, RELIEVED by rapid exhalation, BEG with a pleading expression. For some signs there is evidence that a nonmanual component used to occur but is now omitted– signs seem to be simplified and stylized over time.

Word order and topicalization

The default, unmarked word order of ASL sentences is SVO. (There are references from the 19th century suggesting that ASL was then normally

SOV. French sign language still seems to prefer signing the verb last—both SOV and OSV order are used.)

A topic can be explicitly marked by a nonmanual signal *t*: raising the brows and tilting the head back. (Compare *q*, where the head tilts *forward.*) In addition the topicalized sign is held a fraction of a second longer than usual. A subject can be topicalized without being moved:

> ____t
>
> **DOG CHASE CAT**
>
> *As for the dog, it chased the cat.*

The object can be moved to initial position, but only if it's topicalized:

> ____t
>
> **CAT DOG CHASE**
>
> *As for the cat, the dog chased it.*

The entire VP can be topicalized as well:

> ___________t ___rn
>
> **CHASE CAT DOG**
>
> *As for chasing the cat, the dog did it.*
>
> ___________t ___n
>
> **CHASE CAT DOG**
>
> *As for chasing the cat, the dog didn't do it.*

The topic need not be a constituent of the sentence; e.g. you can sign the equivalent of *As for meat, I prefer lamb.* This should be reminiscent of Mandarin (p. 157).

Other word orders: adjectives and numerals usually follow the noun; modal verbs like CAN follow the main verb. Adverbs precede the verb; most are the same sign as the corresponding adjective.

Classifiers as locatives

ASL has a set of CLASSIFIERS, signs representing a class of objects of a particular type or shape— compare the MEASURE WORDS of Mandarin (p. 160). These can be used in an enormously expressive construction, which can be schematized as *<topic> <predicate-with-classifiers>*.

4CL ________________

FENCE CAT BENT.V.CL

A cat is on the fence.

There is no verb in this example; rather, the signer indicates the two referents, then indicates the relationship between them *using their classifiers.* (The topic marker *t* is not used; this is an alternative mechanism for topicalization.)

The classifier 4CL is just the handshape 4, four outstretched fingers; it can be used for any platelike object— walls, hedges, etc. Note that it's made right after its referent, FENCE, and held for the remainder of the utterance. Similarly the sign for CAT is made, then its classifier, composed of the bent V handshape (think V-for-victory with bent fingers), which is used for humans or animals with their legs bent.

Now the neat bit: the signer puts the two classifiers together indicating their spatial relationship. BENT.V can be placed on top of 4CL, or next to it; the cat's exact posture may be suggested by rotating BENT.V; you can even indicate movement by arcing it over the other classifier (*the cat jumped over the fence*).

Finally, an explicit verb may be added— e.g.

4CL ______________________

FENCE CAT SLEEP BENT.V.CL

A cat is sleeping on the fence.

A variant involves just one classifier, and an action indicated relative to it:

B.CL ____________

TABLE MAN PAINT

The man painted the bottom of the table.

Here MAN PAINT is signed *underneath* the classifier B.CL, indicating that what's being painted is the bottom of the table.

Directional verbs

Some verbs are DIRECTIONAL: the sign is performed with a movement, using the locations established for the conversation (see *Pronouns*, p. 208). For instance, GIVE is signed in the direction of the recipient, or to the locus that represents them.

In the following example, BUY is signed in the direction of Lr, a locus on the speaker's right.

MAN BUY[Lr]

The man bought it.

The subject can be indicated as part of the movement too— e.g. BUY[Ll:Lr] where Ll (a locus on the left) has been established as referring to the man.

Either subject or object, of course, can be I (pointing to oneself) or YOU (pointing to the watcher). E.g. *I see you* would involve signing SEE with the hand moving away from myself, toward you.

Aspect inflections

ASL verbs don't indicate tense, but they can be modified to indicate a wide range of ASPECTS. Some examples, using the verb BE.SICK:

INCEPTIVE	*get sick*
FREQUENTATIVE	*to be sick often*
ITERATIVE	*to get sick over and over*
INTENSIVE	*to be very sick*
RESULTATIVE	*to become fully sick [completed change of state]*
APPROXIMATIVE	*to be sort of sick*
INCREASING	*to get more and more sick*
DURATIVE	*to be sick for a long time*

Most of these are formed with variations of reduplication— e.g. the durative is formed by repeating the sign's inherent motion about three times, slowly. The approximative involves many quick but lax iterations.

Curiously, inflected verbs can't take an object. The object can be stated first, however:

TOMATO GIRL EAT[durative]

The girl ate tomatoes for a long time.

Other inflections

Many nouns are distinguished for **gender** in a systematic way: the sign starts in the upper part of the face for a male, the lower part for a female.

E.g. *brother* has the signing hand making an L handshape, touching the forehead, then changing to a 1 as it moves down to strike the other hand (also with handshape 1). The sign for *sister* is the same, but the initial contact is at the jaw.

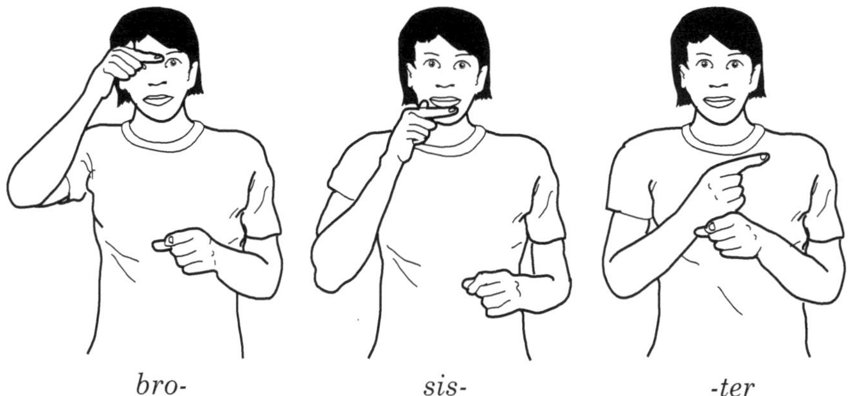

Some verbs are modified to make the **type of action** more specific. E.g. CLOSE involves holding both hands flat and palm down and moving them together, but the sign is modified based on what's closed— referring to closing a window, curtains, a book, the sign resembles the actual hand actions for those activities.

Relative clauses

A relative clause is marked by a nonmanual signal *r*, consisting of raising the eyebrows, tilting the head back, and tensing the upper lip. (This is intriguingly close to the topic marker *t*, which lacks the mouth component. However, the tilt of *r* is more pronounced.)

> **______________r**
>
> **ONE CAN'T SIGN KNOW POSS.1 MOTHER**
>
> *The one who can't sign knows my mother.*

Some spoken languages mark relative clauses with a rising intonation; for instance, Amele:

> **______________rising**
>
> **[Mel mala heje on] mel heu busali nu-i-a.**
>
> [boy chicken illicit take.3s.subj-remote.past] [boy that run.away go-3s.subj-today's.past]
>
> *The boy that stole the chicken ran away.*

This can be done in colloquial English: *The girl I told you about? She's doing a gig at Avalon tonight.* (But this just re-uses question intonation; ASL's *q* is quite different from *r*.)

The *r* signal alone can leave a transitive sentence ambiguous:

______________________r

DOG CHASE CAT RUN.AWAY

The dog who chased the cat ran away.
OR The cat who was chased by the dog ran away.

There are several strategies for disambiguation. One is to insert the demonstrative THAT$_a$:

_____________________________r

THAT$_a$ DOG BITE CAT COME HOME

The dog that bit the cat came home.

_____________________________r

DOG BITE THAT$_a$ CAT COME HOME

The cat the dog bit came home.

(There are at least four similar signs glossed THAT, all starting the same way, with a raised Y handshape. THAT$_a$ simply flips the hand forward.)

Another method uses spatial indexing:

_________________________r

DOG^{l} BITE$^{l\ to\ r}$ CAT^{r} COME^{r} HOME

The cat the dog bit came home.

DOG is signed on the left side of the body, CAT on the right. BITE incorporates a left to right movement. COME is signed starting on the right, signaling that it's the cat rather than the dog which came home.

A third method is to intensify the *r* marker— the eyebrows are raised more, the lip contracted more tensely, and a head nod may be added. This is marked *i* below:

_____i

____________________r

DOG BITE CAT COME HOME

The cat the dog bit came home.

And if that weren't enough, the word order can be changed:

______________ r

CAT DOG BITE COME HOME

The cat the dog bit came home.

Normally we'd expect cat to be marked with the topic signal *t*, but *t* and *r* don't co-occur.

The examples so far all have the relative clause at the beginning of the sentence, but it can occur later:

r ________________________

PRO.1 FORCE BOY THATa EAT POSS.1

______________ r

HAMBURGER GIVE[X:pro.1] ONE-DOLLAR

I forced the boy who ate my hamburger to give me a dollar.

Here we see THAT_a again, but after the noun instead of before it. In that role it functions as an additional marker of subordination.

Another construction uses the SELF.3 sign 'himself/herself/itself' to create nonrestrictive, appositive clauses:

______________ ap

JOHN SELF.3 EAT[habit] ADD.ON 20 POUND

John, who eats a lot, put on 20 pounds.

This type of clause gets its own signal *ap*: the brows knit, the head tilts forward and to one side, and the lower lip is tightened and lowered.

The clause must be seen as descriptive (rather than, say, referring to an event), and seems to be restricted to the third person.

Further reading

Harlan **Lane**, *When The Mind Hears* (1984)

Scott **Liddell**, *American Sign Language Syntax* (1980)

Oliver **Sacks**, *Seeing Voices* (1989)

There are any number of ASL primers and dictionaries available, of variable quality. They're better for getting ideas about possible signs than about the structure of the language.

Putting it all together

Now that you've learned all this stuff, how do you use it? How do you create a bunch of languages with varied interactions, so they create an interesting world?

I'll try to indicate how it's done in this chapter, with reference to my own conworld Almea. (I'll also use terrestrial examples to reinforce the linguistic concepts.)

The *LCK* includes an entire reference grammar, for Kebreni. Rather than do the same here, I've included extracts from several languages.

Setting

Let's start with the context. Here's the eastern portion of the continent of Ereláe:

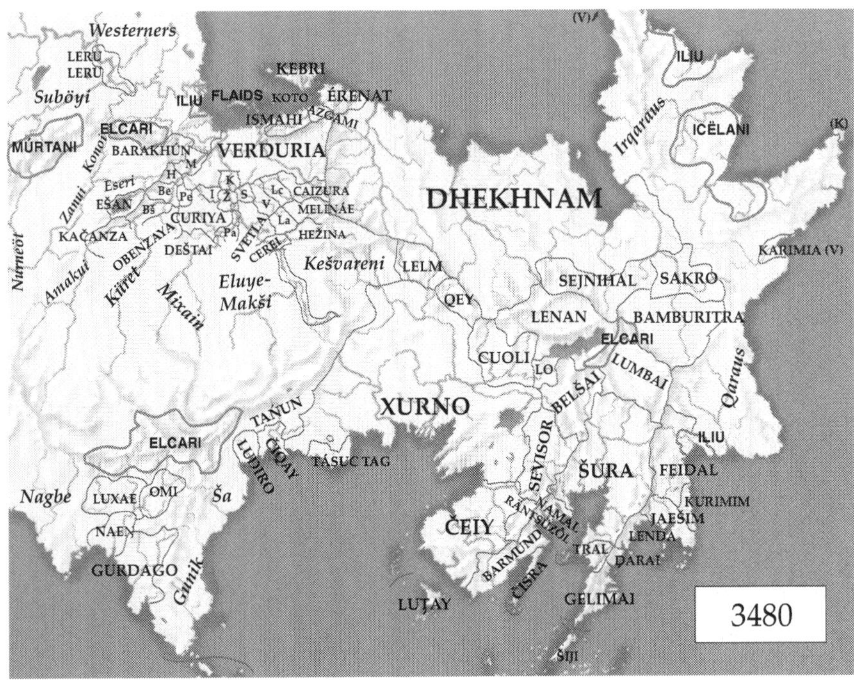

There are three large plains, each the focus of a major civilization:

- Eretald (northwest), dominated by Verduria
- Dhekhnam (north)
- Xengiman (south), most of it occupied by Xurno

We're in the southern hemisphere of Almea, so Eretald and Dhekhnam are warmer than Xengiman. The southern fringe of the map is tundra.

Worldbuilding

How do you put a continent together and determine its climate? How do you create cultures and histories? These are all covered in my *Planet Construction Kit* (*PCK*).

For the history of Almea, start at Virtual Verduria on zompist.com.

Overall plan

Almea has developed over over thirty years; I simply worked on whatever appealed to me at the time.

If you want to work out a world, or a continent, in less time than that, here's what I advise:

- Start with a world map, or at least a whole continent. Work out climates using the *PCK* (p. 49).
- Create an expanded map of the area you want to work on—ideally something Europe-sized. (If you work with just a couple of countries, they'll end up unnaturally isolated from the rest of the world.)
- Create **protolanguages**— at least two of them. They don't have to go much further than a phonological inventory and a word-list. You can use **gen** (p. 254) to save time.
- Use the SCA (p. 260) to develop **naming languages** from these. That means phonemes and lexicon, plus a derivational morphology.

  I advise starting with protolanguages for two reasons: your first conlang is likely to be of poorer quality, and the SCA leads to more interesting, more naturalistic results than inventing a language from scratch.
- Work on the history and culture of several regions.

- Iterate! As you work on the history you'll need names; that's a chance to work on lexicons for awhile. As you work on the grammars, you'll run into words that could be borrowed; that's a chance to think about what cultures would supply that item.
- For extra credit: use this process for the *ancient world.* Then advance things a millennium or two, deriving a whole new set of languages, one of which is for your main culture.

The main idea here is to have some idea of a much larger area than just the setting of your story or game. Nations don't exist in a vacuum; they are influenced by their neighbors, and you'll tend to ignore cultures that don't exist on your map.

If you only have a map of your main country— that's OK, you have to start somewhere. But make a rough world map so you have an idea of what else is in your world.

But I need a major Evil Empire for the sequel!

Fine... that's what C.S. Lewis did when he invented Calormen in *book 5.* But it does raise some questions, like why have we never heard about the place before and if it's a threat now, why was it never a threat before? At least come up with a few names and words— e.g. I knew early on that Verduria would have a southern rival in Xurno before I knew anything else about it.

So, is that how I did it? Er, well, for the continent of Arcél, yes! But for Ereláe I started with Verduria and Verdurian, and worked outwards and backwards. You can still make this work, if you're willing to revise things. I thoroughly revised Verdurian once I learned how sound change works; I completely redid the historical atlas five times; and I even reworked the climate zones when doing research for the *PCK.*

Verdurian is still not the way I'd do it if I started from scratch, but you also need to know when to set the work down and stop tinkering.

You may find that the country you started with doesn't turn out to be the setting for your blockbuster novel anyway. I'm working on two Almean novels; one is set in Xurno and the other in ancient Cuzei.

Borrowings

Having a bunch of languages not only makes your map more interesting, it gives you many sources for borrowing. Whenever I need a word, I think about whether it could be borrowed, and when, and from whom.

Interacting cultures

Your history should be complicated enough to let you answer these questions:

- Over the centuries, which were the most advanced nations? Were some peoples particularly advanced in government, law, mining, shipbuilding, accounting, commerce, art?
- Which cultures feel an affinity to each other, through culture, religion, or shared government?
- What features of your cultures are striking enough that they would be reflected in language? Examples:
    - Dhekhnam is ruled by another species, and even its human languages reflect the ktuvoks' contempt for humans.
    - The elcari are miners and craftsmen, and their language, Elkarîl, allows very specific locatives, useful for giving precise directions.
    - For a client, I created a language for dragons, whose lexicon reflects the *size* of its speakers— e.g. there are no separate words for animals smaller than a cat— they're all just vermin, things too small to eat. And terms relating to two-dimensional barriers (*wall, bridge*) mean little to a creature that can fly.

Interesting worlds are not only diverse, their diversity is **fractal**. For instance, we can zoom in on Almea:

- The other intelligent **species** are very different from humans: the sea-dwelling iliu, inducers of visions and religious teachings; the ktuvoks who coldly create empires over humans; the ancient but plodding elcari...
- Each **continent** has its own character— e.g. Ereláe is the most advanced, Lebiscuri the least; Arcél is a playground for less terrestrial ideas (the female-dominated Bé, the magic-oriented Uytainese, the strange Rifters who are only sentient in pairs...)
- Ereláe is divided into several major **civilizations**: the steam age of Eretald, the artist-run nation of Xurno, the threatening ktuvok empire of Dhekhnam, the nomads...
- The **nation** of Verduria has its rivals within Eretald: the seafaring Kebreni, the warriors of Barakhún, the resentful ex-

imperials of Žésifo (Ž on the map), the sleepy flaids (yet another humanoid species)...

- Each **province** of the kingdom has its own history and character— Verduria province is urbanized and commercial; Šerian is sleepy and dominated by the pagans; Zelm is a military frontier...
- **Neighborhoods** within Verduria city range from the university district to the rich Išira to the crime-ridden Docks to the poor slums where the factories are built...

You don't need to divide every city on the planet into neighborhoods! You can focus your attention on your main conlang, and you can always add more details later. But a world with varied and conflicting regions, factions, and religions is one whose languages will also come alive with borrowings, dialects, registers, slang, and substrata.

How do you decide on these characteristics? You can be random to some extent, but some key factors are these:

- **Ease of access**. Verduria is located on the delta of the main river system of Eretald, and thus is a natural intermediary between the plain and the littoral. By contrast nations like Curiya, Caizura, and Sevisor are remote and backward. The Xurnese cities of Inex and Curau are both populous and rich, but Inex is on the coast and thus more cosmopolitan, while Curau's sense of pride is enhanced by being the traditional capital, in the center of the country.
- **Neighbors**. Barakhún borders the nomadic area, thus its focus on war. Érenat borders the ktuvok empire of Dhekhnam, which gives it a precariousness and a set of hard diplomatic choices that Verduria doesn't face.
- **Terrain**. Obviously, terms for ships and sea creatures will come from countries on the sea. More subtly, gems and minerals are easiest to find in the mountains and so may be named there. Horsey terms may derive from the people of the steppe.
- **Historical change**. In the *PCK* I suggest the formula "(*Place*) used to be –, but is now –", which helps give your history a sense of change. E.g. we can guess a lot about the politics and culture of Žésifo knowing that it was once the capital of the mighty Cad̂inorian Empire and is now a third-tier statelet.
- **Variety**. Don't always make the same choices. Not every medieval state is a kingdom. Not every religion has a pantheon of

twelve gods with simple metaphorical duties. Not every region was calmly absorbed into the ancient empire. Whatever's common in your world, let a few regions be exceptions.

The Verdurian lexicon

To show what can be done with a very developed world, let's look at my most developed language, Verdurian, in some detail.

We'll start with ancient times, when words were borrowed not into Verdurian but into its ancestor, Cad̂inor. (To save space I'll cite only the Verdurian terms, but each word has a history: e.g. *risunen* 'draw' is inherited from Cad̂inor *risunden*, borrowed from Cuêzi *risonda* 'drawing', itself a derivation from *risi* 'reed'.)

Let's look at the geographical context for ancient borrowings. This map is from Z.E. 287, over three thousand years before the map on p. 218.

In ancient times **Cuzei** was far more advanced than the Cad̂inorians. Verdurian terms originating in their language, Cuêzi, include—

- philosophical or cultural terms: *avisar* 'scholarly community', *dunalál* 'planet', *hecu* 'character', *laun* 'circle', *lihse* 'soprano', *risunen* 'draw', *sežlór* 'insect', *zobát* 'sorcery'
- early products: *gerišu* 'ointment', *hend* 'tunic', *lambra* 'linen sheet', *lëšu* 'straightedge', *alcalë* 'treasure'
- minerals accessible to early metallurgy: *azurda* 'sapphire', *erüza* 'cinnabar', *porute* 'marble', *murca* 'magnet'

The Cad̂inorians and Cuzeians both were originally invaders from the south. The **Met̂aiun** languages of the original inhabitants (on the map, these still occupy Ažimbea and points north) are therefore a SUBSTRATE language, providing words of various types:

- items produced in Eretald: *heta* 'bran, rind'; *hasifa* 'sulfur', *peda* 'hops', *seta* 'silk', *vidra* 'iris', *vin* 'wine', *suf* 'cork', *henia* 'toga'

- maritime flora and fauna, as the invaders had never seen the ocean: *akula* 'shark', *bolašo* 'starfish', *sišu* 'jellyfish', *däri* 'seagull', *heto* 'shrimp', *rak* 'crab'
- naval technology: *baita* 'barrel', *penda* 'stern (of a ship)', *cora* 'riverboat', *činžeda* 'anchor', *teba* 'bow (of a ship)'
- dozens of place names: the sea (*Mišicama*), the eastern mountains (*Ctelm*), major rivers, particular cities and regions

There are even more possibilities in modern times:

- The island nation of **Kebri** is small, but advanced out of medievalism earlier than Verduria, leading to many borrowings:
    - financial and accounting terms: *andedau* 'profit', *demedau* 'loss', *düri* 'credit', *pória* 'liability', *porui* 'debit', *gëméša* 'mortgage', *lagu* 'income', *žüngu* 'expenditures'

      The Kebreni words for profit/loss are borrowings from Caďinor. This sort of circularity isn't uncommon; cf. French *la nurse*, from the English word, which derives from Old French *norice*.
    - commercial words: *susaré* 'shop', *tuyo* 'pipe'
    - nautical terms: *culisa* 'fleet', *culso* 'admiral', *nabro* 'ship captain', *navira* 'ship', *čirnu* 'deck', *sefo* 'boy', *vučemu* 'flounder'
    - general words like *bakt* 'terrible', *lür* 'woe', *řulo* 'clown', *zevu* 'pal'
- The mountain nation of **Barakhún** provides words of several types:
    - Minerals and local products: *činzik* 'gooseberry', *meilad* 'cobaltite', *moštol* 'feldspar'
    - terms relating to nomadism or desert living: *čayma* 'tent', *céšuaš* 'tribe', *sezu* 'jerky', *ďarim* 'wild, untamed'
    - miscellaneous cultural terms: *adonic* 'cottage', *kanheu* 'outlander', *ktuvóc* 'ktuvok', *usuku* 'jester'
- The neighboring nation of **Ismahi** provides terms for clothing, music, and food: *čište* 'mandolin', *dedoše* 'scallop', *nilne* 'skirt', *penil* 'preserves', *režučia* 'ballad', *seslina* 'turquoise', *süpa* 'cap', *šaune* 'broth', *velašir* 'elope', *žicse* 'cushion'
- Terms relating to government, law, religion, grammar, and medicine are often REBORROWED from **Caďinor**: *aluatas*

'grammar', *belgo* 'war', *demeric* 'present tense', *huepe* 'equal'. There are many DOUBLETS, where one word is inherited and distorted by sound change, the other taken from Cad̂inor:

božan 'fare'	*bocteica* 'diplomacy'
bome 'old'	*bosme* 'elderly'
brašo 'flour'	*brasco* 'pollen'
ser 'male'	*cer* 'masculine gender'
daš 'pocket'	*dasc* 'bladder'
eucar 'miner'	*elcar* 'elcar'
fron 'a type of mushroom'	*frond* 'penis'
glöma 'snot'	*gleuma* 'mucus'
žonë 'female'	*ionile* 'feminine gender'
žorta 'flower (n.)'	*iortan* 'flower (v.)'
kazë 'pointer'	*kansile* 'deictic'
kašir 'hide'	*kascir* 'eclipse'
metta 'table'	*medeta* 'pedestal'
mišu 'sack'	*miscu* 'scrotum'
pilke 'ball'	*pula* 'sphere'
royi 'spin'	*roheica* 'sprain'
šalea 'air'	*scaleia* 'gas'
šëno 'hinge'	*scerno* 'axis'
čivi 'pain'	*tibri* 'anguish, sorrow'
tošeo 'satisfaction'	*tosceio* 'orgasm'
čuca 'spot'	*tucet* 'pox'

The Romance languages are full of reborrowings, and doublets; cf. French *père* 'father' / *paternel*; *chanson* 'song' / *cantatrice* 'singer'; *parler* 'talk' / *parabole* 'parabola'; *chef* 'leader' / *capital.*

You need an alphabet for such reborrowings. If Uyse? borrows an ancient word, the glyph hasn't changed, so it will have its modern pronunciation. The effect will be that a word will have various antiquated senses.

- The Verdurians can also borrow scholarly words directly from Cuêzi (as opposed to inheriting their ancestors' borrowings): *aguma* 'problem', *bidracon* 'atom, molecule', *caturo* 'rhythm', *celäu* 'swordsmanship', *eléaku* 'material', *lüssë* 'insane', *onemu* 'treatise', *sesy* 'acute (angled)', *uverë* 'clothing'.
- Like English, Verdurian has borrowed terms from all over the world, mostly for flora and fauna and associated products— e.g. *čai* 'tea' from Uyse?, *šual* 'horse' from the southern barbarians, *ruzbideš* 'cider' from Xurnese, *tsesi* 'sugar' from Nanese, *šekšek* 'cacao' from Téllinor.

- Verdurian can borrow from its own dialects:

  boce 'plenty' from Viminian
  bogaty 'rich' from Southern
  čehen 'sculpt' from Ctesifoni
  gdeon 'giant' from Southern
  nuotan 'swim' from Viminian
  pyerir 'regret' from Southern

  English examples include *one* (the original pronunciation is preserved in *only*) and *vixen,* both from southwestern dialects.

A source of terms that's easily neglected: names of **places and people** in your history. Examples from Verdurian include *porute* 'marble', from the ancient town of Poron, and *deníe* 'homosexual', after the artist Miluran Dení. English is full of such terms; many are obvious (*Platonic relationship, Hawking radiation, Ponzi scheme, hamburger, Pyrrhic victory, volt, chinaware, germanium*), others more obscure (*sideburns, calico, ammonia, turkey, cashmere, fuchsia, dollar, cravat, bogeyman, bloomers*).

And really, a word can come from anywhere. *Barbecue, canoe, hammock, hurricane, jerky, petunia, shack, shark, woodchuck* all come from Native American languages; *chow, ketchup, silk, tea, tycoon, typhoon, yen [desire]* from Chinese; *amber, artichoke, candy, chess, elixir, jar, lemon, macramé, sash, sherbet, spinach, zero* from Arabic; *bangle, bungalow, cummerbund, lacquer, loot, orange, pajamas, pal, shampoo, sugar, thug* from languages of India. (My site, zompist.com, has extended lists of these borrowings.)

Semantic change

Don't forget to **twist your meanings**! It's very easy to borrow or inherit a word with exactly the original meaning— but to do this all the time is not naturalistic. Browse the etymologies in a good dictionary and you'll find all sorts of amazing jumps.

E.g. English *mercy* is from Old French *merci,* then having the sense 'compassion, forbearance'; this derived from Christian Latin *mercēs* for the reward in Heaven gifted by God to unworthy men, which was a metaphorical extension of its Classical Latin meaning 'wages, salary, reward'— also the root of *mercenary,* a profession not noted for *mercy* in the modern sense. Note the separate path taken in modern French, where it's used for 'thanks'.

Here's a few unlikely-seeming terrestrial derivations and their etymological origin— check a dictionary for the full story.

dungeon	Lat. *dominus* 'lord'
nice	Lat. *nescius* 'ignorant'
ketchup	Amoy Chinese *kētsiap* 'fish brine'
parlor	Greek παραβολή 'juxtaposition'
chivalry	Lat. *caballus* 'nag, pony'
idiot	Greek ἴδιος 'private'
peculiar	Lat. *pecu* 'cattle'
muscle	Lat. *mūs* 'mouse'
cosmos	Greek κόσμος 'adornment'
bank	Old Germanic **bankiz* 'bench'
simple	Lat. *simplus* 'folded once'
with	OE *wið* 'against'
Fr. *pas* 'not'	Lat. *passus* 'step'

Multiple steps

Borrowings can involve multiple languages. E.g. Verdurian *rinde* 'emerald' is from Cad̂inor *rimide*, which is from Cuêzi *rimidê*, which in turn comes from Elkarîl *rîmiddên* 'great beryl'.

Some of our words have very torturous etymologies, especially if they ultimately derive from eastern languages:

azure, from Old French *azur*, from Italian *azzurro*, from medieval Latin *azura / azzurum*, from Arabic *al-lazward*, from Persian *lājward* 'lapis lazuli'.

orange, from Old French *orenge*, from Old Italian *narancia* or Spanish *naranja*, from Arabic *nāranj*, from Persian *nārang*, from Sanskrit *nāraṅga*.

sugar, from Old French *çucre*, from medieval Latin *zuccarum*, from Arabic *sukkar*, from Greek σάκχαρον, from Persian *šakar*, from Sanskrit *śarkarā* 'gravel, sugar'.

silk, Old English *sioloc*, akin to Old Slavonic *šelkŭ*, from Greek σηρικός 'silken', from Σῆρες 'people who made silk', which itself may derive from some Altaic language, ultimately from Old Chinese **sə* (now Mandarin *sī*).

Prestige

People often borrow based on PRESTIGE. As Richard Hudson puts it in *Sociolinguistics*, a speaker's linguistic choices signal "the kind of person he is (or would like to be) and his position in society." For the conlanger, the question is, who do the speakers look up to, and what words would they borrow?

A good analogy is fashion choices: what you wear identifies you socially, and you can manipulate the message you convey.

As with sound change (p. 100), don't assume that prestige is always a matter of imitating the upper class. People are more likely to imitate their cooler friend than their rulers. We saw above (p. 77) that Jamaican boys move *away* from the acrolect. Much French slang developed in the underworld.

The net effect of a whole society of people borrowing words from each other is likely to be a certain eclecticism, as seen in the Verdurian vocabulary. Good words may come from foreigners, from ancient languages, from minorities, from religion, from other regions. Each borrowing can be seen as someone's attribution of prestige, which other speakers found cool or useful as well.

I should mention that some languages resist borrowing— e.g. Icelandic, rather than adopting the international word 'telephone', re-used *simi* 'wire'. But it's probably not coincidental that Iceland is a remote area. If your conlang's speakers don't borrow much, they'd better have a good reason.

Religion

Religion deserves special consideration, because it will affect languages in several ways.

First, it creates cultural affinities— especially once universal proselytizing religions appear. Consider how Christianity has given English a stock of words from Hebrew and Greek that would be unlikely on mere geographical grounds.

We've seen with *mercy* how religion can redefine a term, which then acquires nonreligious uses. Words like *crusade, gospel, evangelize, propaganda, zealot, idol, cherubic, diabolic, sect, schism, orthodox, canonical, laity, pilgrim, profanity, guru* all have secular uses.

Second, it creates **metaphors** and cultural references. Endajué, the religion of Xurno, relies heavily on metaphors like the Dance (or other types of art) and the Path:

THE COSMOS IS A DANCE

cauč dance → cosmos
caučirc dancer → creature, spirit
bodeusis walk lamely → be foolish

reatudo movement → flux, fortune
rináric grace → acceptance of one's fortune

WRITING IS DANCE

reátuc step, motion → action
reatudo motion → plot
brešísuc gesture → trope

MORALITY IS A PATH

ende path → morality
tegendi pathless → damned, depraved
jivirc walker → believer
pope drive (animals) → morally guide (people)
misustri muddy → morally difficult
bem ga like a road → morally clear

WAR IS A PAINTING

nelima frame → context, casus belli
rímex sketch → strategy
šonasudo brushwork → tactics
ravom canvas → battlefield
šuke paint → blood

SEX IS A PAINTING

šónex brush → penis
ravom canvas → vagina
šukeac paint → have sex
šuke paint → semen

Cosmologies can associate values with substances. E.g. in Verdurian there are seven elements, each implying a temperament:

ur clay → *urise* mortal, fallible; *urete* down to earth, practical
mey water → *mese* benevolent, wise; happy, playful
d̂umë stone → *d̂umise* strong, determined, patient
endi wood → *enil* quiet, shy, timid
gent metal → *geteme* strong, powerful, like a leader
tšur fire → *mëril* fiery, bold, energetic[29]
šalea air → *šaleme* intellectual, unworldly, ivory-tower

---

[29] *Mëril* derives from 'flame' rather than from *tšur* 'fire'.

In ancient Xengiman, femininity was associated with water, masculinity with earth, leading to Xurnese words like these:

myun watery → effeminate
kagas dry → chaste (of males), impotent
rinari like a river → graceful

sustri earthy → macho
saumes earth-lady → lesbian

Religions are also a great source of **invective**; indeed, in a religious society the most shocking terms are not those related to sex and bodily functions, but to religion. Some Xurnese expletives are listed below:

expletive	***gloss***	***English equivalent***
tegendi	*pathless*	*damned (very strong)*
tebengi	*pathless*[30]	*darned, frigging*
nanač	*ungodly*	*damned (less strong)*
berirri	*deluded*	*godforsaken*
bodugri	*lame*	*ignorant, irreligious*
end' eš	*against path*	*dammit!*
cuš eš	*against dance*	*dammit!*
dzunan	*pagan*	*infidel, bastard*
šwečirc	*striver*	*fool*
nansu	*god-man*	*pagan, priest-ridden*
i puide	*spit me*	*damn me!*

Other sorts of **belief systems** can have the same effects. Communism, for instance, has a whole vocabulary providing values and vivid metaphors, many of which were found useful outside the movement: *agit-prop, comrade, reactionary, bourgeois, proletarian, imperialist, paper tiger, fellow traveler, wage slave, politically correct.*

Almost any aspect of **culture** can affect language. In Tolkien's Bree, where men lived with hobbits, we learn that reports of an event require separate counts for each **species**. That's at least partial grammaticalization; I wonder to what extent species was a grammatical category in Bree Westron. In Flaidish I made **age** a separate category in the pronoun system— e.g. 'I' is *ʔok* for adults, *fu* for children.

---

30 An example of TABOO-DEFORMATION: a very strong word is softened by disguising it slightly. Cf. English *darn, frigging, shoot.*

Slang

For Verdurian and Munkhâshi (ancestor of Dhekhnami) I created a fair amount of slang, from the cheerfully colloquial to the obscene. You don't have to do the same, but your conpeople will appreciate it. Slang is popular!

A few choice epithets can help give flavor to a conworld even in an English narrative— you probably recall *hraka* from *Watership Down, smeg* from *Red Dwarf, fracking* from *Battlestar Galactica.*

Most slang words are alterations of existing words, so it's easiest to create them once you already have a good vocabulary. But of course you can also create the source word when you need it.

To come up with alternative words, try to get into the right jocular mindset. Like most humor, it sounds strained or stupid when analyzed, but analysis allows imitation.

Here's some sources of slang, with Almean and earthly examples:

Animals. Premodern peoples lived in close contact with animals, which naturally provided vivid metaphors and insults for referring to people: *kid, vixen, chick, old goat, pig, snake.*

> Ver. *boua* cow → mark, victim
> *koška* female cat → girl
> *leful* little wolf → pimp
> Mun. *pudagno* pigeon → Cad̂inorian
> *katsukil* mammal → human
> *siblaghine* bird on a horse → nomad

Similarly, an animal-related term can be applied to humans:

> Ver. *šaute* hide, skin → hair
> *bruřo* animal's stomach → gut
> Fr. *gueule* animal's muzzle → mouth, face
> Ger. *fressen* eat (of animals) → eat (of humans)
> Eng. *(piece of) tail* → girl
> *beak* → nose

People like **vivid exaggerations**:

> Ver. *hipřanec* bathe → get drunk
> *suian* squeak → speak up, say something
> *raconter* tell epics → tell stories
> *clačir* burst → spill the beans, break (during questioning)

Mun. *nampashin* piss-head → southerner (i.e. blonds)
Latin *muttum* muttering → Fr. *mot* word
Fr. *blairer* smell → tolerate, bear
fauché reaped → broke
poireauter take root → wait
Eng. *dead* → tired

A subclass, especially popular for body parts, is the vaguely insulting physical metaphor:

Ver. *puyok* button → clitoris
urk log → penis
Caď. *uembos* lump → Ver. *uem* heart
Caď. *tuanima* small pot → Ver. *čunima* shield
Mun. *kthe* hole → mouth
tsak bone → leg
Eng. *bubble* → fool, sucker
Fr. *cornichon* pickle → telephone
éponges sponges → lungs
brème bream, a long flat fish → playing card

Curiously, **minimization** is also amusing:

Ver. *sosir* whisper → gossip, squeal (on someone)
pasetir visit → sleep with
pav little → child
Mun. *tujno* paddler → iliu
Fr. *vieille* old (f.) → mother
Eng. *waste, whack, hit* → kill

Synecdoche is using the part, or an associated item, for the whole:

Ver. *nilne* skirt → girl
cilu copper regalia → policeman

People with **special knowledge** like to show it off or allude to it. Students of Greek introduced *kudos* into English as a slang term; hacker slang applies computer technology to everyday situations (e.g. *pop the stack* for ending a digression). Verdurian students reintroduced Caďinor *spurir* 'give up' and *caumen* 'not work, be idle'.

Sometimes people just like a **neat foreign word**. English is more often on the giving than the receiving end of this— note how *OK* has spread worldwide. French has borrowed many terms from Arabic: *toubib* 'doctor', *kiff* 'love', *bled* 'town', *clebs* 'dog', *un chouïa* 'a little', *zob* 'penis'. Some examples from Verdurian:

> Flaidish *ʔaull* → *alir* get along
> Nanese *ufaya* → *ufëa* face
> Kebreni *zeveu* 'friend' → *zevu* 'dude'

Many slang terms are formed by **abbreviation**: *bus, taxi, nuke, Coke, prof,* French *beauf* 'brother-in-law', *sympa* 'nice', *dico* 'dictionary'. I didn't use this overmuch in Verdurian as it seems more characteristic of modern times:

> *acceoren* admonish → *accen* scold
> *sam cistilan* without a crown (a mark of service)
> → *sanci* recruit
> *aržentei* silver coin → *žente*
> Old. Ver. *deriye* supporter + dim. *-ok* → *druk* friend

Babytalk can be used by adults too: Caď̂. *lemma* 'milk' → Ver. *leme*; *goodbye* → *bye-bye*; Fr. *dormir* 'sleep' → *dodo, lait* 'milk' → *lolo.*

Wordplay: I mentioned *verlan* (reversing syllables in French: *poule* 'cop' → *lépou, femme* 'woman' → *meuf*) and rhyming slang in the *LCK* (p. 122). Munkhâshi has a few methods:

- Voice the initial (this also forms the lowest rank of verbs): *tlar* 'city' → *dlar, tsak* 'bone' → *dzak*
- Reduplication of the last syllable: *peksho* 'wife' → *pekshosho.* Compare English *lovey-dovey,* French *chouchou* 'teacher's pet'
- Saying a word backwards (a practice originating in occult rites): *chotno* 'short person' → *ontoch*

Its descendant Dhekhnami has added more possibilities:

- Infixing an obscenity like *blawth* 'shit': *char* 'city' → *chablaw-thar.* Compare Eng. *fanfuckingtastic*
- Punning substitutions:

> *gonavno* foreigner + *gom* noisy → *gomavno*
> *pêkso* wife + *pekin* open → *pêkinso*
> *shivno* companion + *shikh* thin → *shikhno*

Some words are entirely **made up**: *quiz, nerd, dweeb,* Fr. *pif 'nose'.* There are a few of these in Verdurian— *guya* 'prostitute', *šida* 'dude'— but again I've held back here, because such words seem to be rare in natlangs.

Slang can **normalize** over the centuries— e.g. jocular Vulgar Latin terms often became the normal Romance word:

> Lat. *bucca* cheek → Fr. *bouche* mouth
> *testa* pot → *tête* head
> *caballus* nag → *cheval* horse
> *sinus* curve → *sein* breast
> *casa* hut → Sp. *casa* house

Some Caďinor to Verdurian examples are given above.

Diminutives and **augmentatives** are good slang generators, and some languages even have despective affixes— Munkhâshi has one, *wum-*. These forms too can displace the normal word— e.g. French *abeille, oreille, lentille, oncle, aïeul, soleil* 'bee, ear, lentil/lens, uncle, elder, sun' all have the telltale *l* that's a remnant of the Latin diminutive *-ul-*.

Sexual slang is like other slang, only more so. Sometimes it's just randy and earthy, like *screw;* sometimes vividly humorous, like French *services trois pièces* 'three-piece place setting' or *cigare à moustaches* 'cigar with a moustache', both meaning the penis. All too often it's extremely sexist and homophobic; the lesson for the conlanger, perhaps, is that in slang a culture will reveal its innermost desires, values, and prejudices, as ugly as they may be.

For the female-dominated Lé of Arcél, I created a range of terms for unsatisfactory males, e.g.

bǎrtɛ	a man too attached to his mother
bíbi	puppy; a weak or cringing man
čɛ̌hǎs	an amusing but useless fellow; boy toy
hàbɔr	a man with a nice body but an ugly face
hónplè	male prostitute
inbandrás	groper, a man who touches too much
intùn	a man who always seems to be fighting other men
krútle	irrational, emotional, masculine
màeŋor	bossy boy; a boy who acts like a girl
mɔ́ŋtlùs	a man who tries to help but only makes things worse

as well as terms that view men as sex objects:

hór	dick, cock; general slang for a male
ìsuje	having the delicate beauty and hesitant manner associated with early (male) youth
kér	well-formed male ass; cute guy
lamítɛ	hottie, a man who makes you swoon
líŋrɔ̌ŋ	lusty lad, nice piece of ass

prɛ́ŋprɛ́ŋ	a well-built man, an Adonis
sodlàɔ	good-looking (esp. facially)
tǐkɔ̀	a man highly skilled at foreplay
tláejɔs	with long and beautiful hair (associated with aristocratic men)

(This isn't to imply that there aren't despective terms for females— if anything, they're stronger, as Lé women are held to be more moral, thus more to be condemned when they fail.)

Nonhumans

If you've chafed at the implied restrictions in the descriptions of how human languages work, alien languages are your chance to cut loose. Choose the option that *isn't* listed in the descriptions in the *LCK* or this book! Think about some near universal of human speech— division into phonemes, the use of word order, the idea of subclauses, the rigidity of lexical forms— and throw it out entirely, or think of another way to do it.

If that's too hard, you can of course use non-English features to snow readers who don't know linguistics. Klingon, for instance, is OVS, agglutinative, and aspect-based, and has polypersonal agreement and evidentials. These are all exotic for English speakers, but perfectly ordinary in many human language families— it immediately reminded me of Quechua.

Species

Almea has half a dozen intelligent species, most of them limited to certain ecological niches:

- The **elcari** and **múrtani** are dwarflike species that live in the mountains.
- The **icëlani** are primitive hominids living in forests (where they haven't been crowded out by humans).
- The **iliu** mostly live in the sea, and occupy almost the entire continental shelf, plus a few enclaves on land.
- The **ktuvoks** are marine predators, but also live in wetlands; they are the real rulers of Dhekhnam.
- **Humans** occupy the rest of the map, except for the deserts (such as the large one south of Eretald).

The **icëlani** are something like australopithecines— hominids without the brainpower of modern humans. Their language— a mixture of sounds and signs— is thus a chance to create Primitivese (p. 85).

The **iliu** by contrast are more advanced than humans, and also live mostly underwater, on the continental shelf. Their language can be expressed in writing, by gestures, or though sounds. Spoken, it relies heavily on pitch and tempo, which work better underwater than details of place and manner of articulation.

The iliu can communicate visions— complete sensory images— which means that language doesn't really need to get across visual details. Instead it's devoted to emotion, relational signals, play, and style.

(For a glimpse of iliu language, see p. 155 in the *LCK*.)

Elkarîl

The language of the **elcari** in the northwest of the map is **Elkarîl**. As they're not humans, I took the opportunity to violate some human universals:

- The language makes semantic use of the infinite space between sounds. E.g. *rim* is green and *rum* is dark green; vowels in between *i* and *u* give the precise amount of darkness. Similar story with *rim* vs. *rêm* 'light green'.
- This applies to locatives, with the additional parameter of voicing to mean 'leftward' and palatalizing for 'rightward'; the end result is that (say) *tîl* 'on' can be modified to indicate placement anywhere on a two-dimensional surface.
- Augmentatives of various degrees can be made by prolonging a sound: *inth* 'stay', *inththth* 'stay a long, long time'.
- There are no personal pronouns; instead, there are affixes where the vowel is used as a variable to refer to various persons present. Everyone uses the same assignments, so (say) *-at* refers to you and is used that way both by yourself and the people you're talking to. (This is an adaptation from ASL.)
- Verbs don't morphologically indicate tense *or* aspect.
- The writing system is featural, and is based on drawing or carving faces, which takes advantage of the hominid skill at quickly parsing facial expressions.

Rather than choose an unusual **morphosyntactic alignment** (p. 115), I decided to come up with an entirely different way to analyze actions. I'll go into this in some detail as an example of how to question and reinvent a near-universal of human language.

The verb/agent/patient trichotomy can be seen as asking three questions:

- What happened? (verb)
- Who did it? (agent)
- To whom? (patient)

Elkarîl asks a different set of questions:

- What happened, at a physical level? (action)
- What did it happen to? (experiencer)
- What was the immediate cause? (causer)
- What was this for? (purpose)
- Who desired it? (intender)

These are distinguished only by linear order (there is no case marking).

As an aid to understanding, the purpose is underlined in the examples.

> **Têm miphuq xib phishd nduggsh.**
>
> broke window hand escape prisoner
>
> *The prisoner, intending to escape, broke the window with his hand.*
>
> **Lyît kun ndem lyat Tarkhum.**
>
> faceted jewel hammer gift Stormcloud
>
> *Stormcloud used a hammer to facet a jewel as a gift.*

Thus there isn't a single class of verbs in Elkarîl; the action and purpose are disjoint, and are seen as operating at different levels of reality: the action in the physical world, the purpose in the mental realm.

I could have stopped here, but a new alignment is a major change, and I wanted to work out the details. I'll go over some of them here; for even more see the Elkarîl grammar on my site.

First, some reductive cases. An action can be purely physical, in which case it has only action, experiencer, causer:

> **Phiphth lush shikh.**
>
> ruffled water wind
>
> *The wind ruffled the water.*

Or it can be purely mental, in which case it becomes a description of intention or mental state:

Qhôk ktuphuq.

murder ktuvok

The ktuvok intends to murder someone.

The causer (normally the third element) is optional:

Têm miphuq phishd nduggsh.

broke window escape prisoner

The prisoner, intending to escape, broke the window.

The experiencer can't be omitted; if it's unknown, the anaphor *phim* 'something' must be supplied:

Têm (phim/*Ø) xib phishd nduggsh.

broke (something/Ø) hand escape prisoner

The prisoner, intending to escape, broke something with his hand.

(Note the syntactic shorthand, which tells us that the sentence is OK with *phim* in the indicated position and bad with nothing there.)

If the experiencer and intender are the same, the suffix *-ît* can be added to either the action or the purpose, omitting the argument:

Ggaqhît murd gnrêl.

laugh-same cooperate maiden

The maiden laughed out of a sense of solidarity.

A bodily action on oneself can be expressed as a physical event only, but if you act on someone else, a purpose and intender must be specified:

Tird Tarkhum.

washed Stormcloud

Stormcloud washed himself.

Tird nrêl lush xad Thulbelidd.

washed child water care Moonlight

The child washed with water under Moonlight's care.

Or just: Moonlight washed the child.

With verbs of sense perception, the experiencer is the perceiver; the cause is the object perceived:

Miph p-bbôth Thulbelidd chnmum.

saw and-heard Moonlight cow

Moonlight saw and heard the cow.

The semantic analysis is the opposite of ours. We shoehorn perception into the agent/patient framework, treating *I see the cow* as an action of mine on the cow; for the elcari, the cow causes perception in me.

Speaking is an instance of perception: the words spoken are a causer. This can be extended to quoted speech:

Bbôth Shikhpêt bbê qum npêth lyôru êbb shobad Tarkhum.

hear Nightwind lparen suffer neighbor sickness rparen inform Storm-cloud

Stormcloud said to Nightwind, "The neighbor is sick."

(The subclause is marked by the delimiters *bbê... êbb*— note the use of metathesis as a morphological process.)

In our framework verbs of giving require increasing valence, but Elkarîl has enough slots already. The transfer is taken as a physical action, its type as a purpose:

Mox Tarkhum phan lyat dduch.

receive Stormcloud canoe gift human

Stormcloud received a canoe as a gift from a human.

Or just: A human gave Stormcloud a canoe.

Existentials are physical actions: *on elkar* 'there is an elcar'. Attributions are judgments, using the purpose *qurd* 'classify':

On qichidd qurd qîl-kunmegg-nquj.

exist gold classify among-elements-noble-five

We classify gold among the five noble elements.

Or just: Gold is one of the Five Noble Elements.

Comparisons are a similar construction, with the action expressing the type and direction of difference and the purpose the act of comparison:

Mush elkar rênga b-ggaltha lemêj tîn-dduch

more elcar strength and-endurance compare to-human

An elcar is stronger and more durable than a human.

Triliteral roots

Morphology by vowel change was only briefly mentioned in the *LCK*, and it's worth a closer look. I could discuss Arabic or Hebrew, but instead I'll use Old Skourene (OS) as an example. (This is an ancient language, spoken in what is now Šura.)

I should emphasize that OS is not a close imitation of the Semitic languages. That's all right! Though I encourage studying natural models, I think some conlangers get too hung up on them. I compare it to drawing: when you invent a character, you have to give them a nose, but it doesn't have to belong to an existing person.

Most OS verb roots are **triconsonantal**, e.g. **b-k-ş** 'break'. Different verb forms (as well as derived nouns) are created by placing vowels before, between, or after these consonants, or by adding affixes. For instance, **ṭ-l-p-** 'write' has forms such as these:

ṭelp	it was written
ṭelpu	I wrote
ṭuloup	we will write
ṭalpu	I want to write
ṭoulup	I'm afraid I'll start writing
aiṭlope	they made me write
ṭeilop	he was always writing
inṭulup	I may try to write
ṭlepa	document
aṭelop	writer
ṭilap	pen
uṭalpas	the art of writing
aṭalpi	written
gauṭulip	you write clumsily
nilṭulrap	she can write

Though these look and sound very different to us, they are all standard derivations, easily recognized by an OS speaker as belonging to a single root, and in fact they are all written using the same glyph, with diacritics that tell where the vowels go:

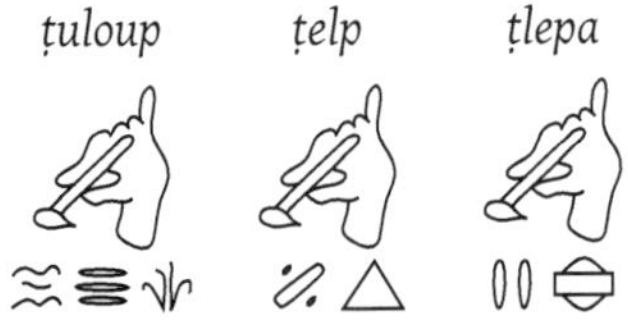

The diacritics (*triuṭittar*) form a syllabary that doesn't distinguish consonants— e.g. (under *ṭlepa*) stands for any syllable *CCe*, and stands for any syllable *Ca*. The combination *CCeCa* thus gives the vowel structure. (It's written right to left.)

For ease in discussion, it's convenient to name the positions within the root; I will refer to the three consonants as **C1, C2, C3**, and the positions adjacent to them as **P0, P12, P23, P4**. Thus instead of saying "an -**a**- inserted between the second and third consonants signals a noun" we can say "an -**a**- in P23 signals a noun".

P0	*C1*	*P12*	*C2*	*P23*	*C3*	*P4*
	ṭ	e	**l**		**p**	u
ai	**ṭ**		**l**	o	**p**	e
	ṭ	i	**l**	a	**p**	
	ṭ		**l**	e	**p**	a
u	**ṭ**	a	**l**		**p**	as

The OS stress rule is that stress occurs at P12 (*ṭélpu, ṭílap*) unless there's nothing there, in which case it moves to P23 (*aiṭlópe, ṭlépa*).

There is a stem vowel in P12 (unpredictable, but always one of *i e a*) associated with each root, so the citation form of 'write' is *ṭelp-*.

Verbal morphology

OS is ergative-absolutive, with polypersonal agreement. Ergative infixes apply in P23, while absolutive suffixes apply in P4. There are special suffixes for reflexives, also in P4.

	erg	*abs*	*refl*
1sm	**-u**	**-e**	**-ei**
1sf	**-ru**	**-et**	**-eṭ**
2sm	**-i**	**-a**	**-ai**
2sf	**-ri**	**-at**	**-aṭ**
3sm	-	**-u**	**-ui**
3sf	**-ra**	**-ut**	**-uṭ**
3sin	**-ḷa**	**-um**	**-uim**
1px	**-obu**	**-ep**	**-eip**
1pi	**-ou**	**-eg**	**-eḍ**
2du		**-as**	**-aş**
2p	**-oi**	**-ag**	**-ad**
3pm	**-o**	**-i**	**-iri**
3pf	**-o**	**-it**	**-irit**
3pin	**-ḷo**	**-im**	**-irim**

Compare *kisne* 'I was heard', *kisran* 'she listened', *kisrane* 'she listened to me', *kisnaş* 'you two listened to yourselves.' These all have a perfective meaning.

There are four **moods**, formed by changing the stem vowel in P12:

- intentive: to *u*
- desiderative: to *a* (but existing *a* → *au*)
- metutive (fear or negative consequence): to *o*
- negative: delete stem vowel[31]

The imperative is formed with *u-* in P0 and nothing in P12.

There are three **aspects**, formed by inserting a vowel before C2 (thus, after the stem or mood vowel in P12):

- durative: *-a*
- inceptive: *-u*
- cyclical: *-i*

Nonpast actions must be referred to with one of the modal or aspect infixes. A general rule is that if someone's taking care of the action now, use the intentive; if not, but we'd like it done, use the desiderative, otherwise the metutive. The aspects can be used for actions that started in the past and are still going on, e.g. *kiurkeḍ* 'we began to fight each other' can be used if we're still fighting.

There are also a number of prefixes indicating manner, associated actions, and even common objects, allowing nuances like these:

mekisun	I pretended to listen
kpanulin	he spoke wrongly, he was mistaken
kussemritu	she outran him
tiuḍeḍugu	I cut it in half
unatisipe	he tore my clothes
umboŋke	I have a headache

This sort of morphology isn't restricted to three-consonant roots, of course— OS has some biliteral roots too, and you could certainly create a system with more consonants, or where the template isn't consonantal at all.

31 Negative forms are thus shorter than affirmative forms, which is enough of a rarity on Earth that universals have been proposed against it.

Derivational morphology

There's a set of nominalizations made by applying a pattern of vowels to the root:

process	eCuCeCa	*ekusena* listening, hearing *emulena* nurture, mothering
instance	CCiuCCa	*ksiunna* an act of listening *ŋiulla* utterance
art	uCaCCas	*ukasnas* listening skills *uṭalpas* writing
artifact	CCeCa	*ṭlepa* document, essay *gdira* pot, vessel
patient	CoCCim	*molnim* child *korkim* opponent
actor	aCeCoC	*amelon* mother *akerok* fighter
device	CeCCeC	*ṭellep* a writing device *getter* mold
tool	CiCaC	*kisan* ear *milan* breast
place	CCaCali	*ṭlapali* scriptorium *mlanali* foster home, orphanage

Thinking in verbs

OS is also notable for being highly verb-oriented. Names and even ordinary nouns often derive from complete sentences:

ḍadnim	they are inside	intestines
guşouri	we rule them	hinterland
nuilmim	they will cyclically shine	moons[32]
mianum	it is always below	floor
muḍureg	we will be whole	federation
raḍḍoug	we have finished harvesting	harvest festival

You can check the morphology description to see exactly how these were derived. E.g. *nuilmim* is the root *nalm-* 'shine' with intentive mood, cyclical aspect, 3p inanimate absolutive.

English also heavily uses nouns and adjectives, while the equivalent sentences in OS would be more verbal. Here's an attempt to capture the stylistic difference using English alone:

---

32 Almea has three moons.

English style	OS style
This is amusing	*This amuses me*
He's rich	*He has become rich*
My house is here	*I live here*
He is the ruler	*He rules*
I'm happy	*I rejoice*
That's a lie!	*You're lying!*
He's dead, Jim	*He just died, Jim*
We are at war	*We have begun to fight*
My son is worthy	*I praise my son*
She's ready for marriage	*She has matured*
I'm a storyteller	*I habitually tell stories*
I have orders	*They ordered me*
I am a parent	*I'm raising children*
He's the Lord's advisor	*He advises the Lord*
He is naked	*He undressed*
She's a hottie	*She attracts me*
This is my father	*Meet my father*
I am 24 years old	*I lived 24 years*
That's a great idea	*I admire your idea*
This is a 'saddle'	*We call this a 'saddle'*
You are a wonder	*I marvel at you*
This is my answer	*I reply thusly*

Using advanced linguistics

Here's a whirlwind tour of how some linguistic features are used in Almea.

Sprachbunds: Dhekhnam is an example: the national language, Dhekhnami, has greatly influenced Sarroc, a descendant of Caȃinor, and Carhinnian, a Qarau language. There are huge numbers of borrowings, the phonology approximates Dhekhnami, and Sarroc has even switched to VSO and changed its person-based verbal morphology to one based on rank.

The classic SPRACHBUND is that of the Balkans, affecting Greek, Romanian, Albanian, Bulgarian and Macedonian— all Indo-European, but their common features don't go back to I-E:

- an analytic rather than inflected future
- loss of the infinitive, generally in favor of the subjunctive
- added clitic object pronouns

- postposed articles (not in Greek however)

Kupwar (p. 82) can be seen as a sprachbund of a single village.

For the conlanger, a sprachbund is a rare chance to be lazy without guilt, as you can re-use large chunks of grammar in several languages. But to have one you need a fairly full world, like Almea: you need several languages as participants, plus the surrounding non-member languages which they contrast with.

Typology: I've tried to mix up overall language type, not only for naturalism but to make the language creation process more fun. The Eastern family that includes Verdurian and Xurnese is fusional, while Wede:i and Kebreni are agglutinative. Dhekhnami relies heavily on reduplication, initial consonant mutation, and infixing. Lenani-Littoral relies mostly on vowel change within triliteral roots, much as in the Semitic languages. Uyseʔ and Lé, over on Arcél, are both isolating.

Writing systems: The northern countries all use alphabets; Xurno uses a combination of logographs and syllabic signs. Elkarîl uses a featural system. Uyseʔ has a logographic system which was also adapted to Lé.

Bilingualism: Mastery of both Sarroc and Dhekhnami is common in western Dhekhnam. Verdurian is widely spoken across Eretald; in earlier centuries Caďinor was used as the language of scholarship. Belšai, which lies in the mountains at a crossroads of several civilizations, is noted for having no dominant language; it's common to learn several languages. Southern Čeiy is a meeting ground between Xurnese and Skourene civilization, and both Čeiyu and Uṭandal are spoken there. In the southern fringe of Eretald there's a pattern of farmers speaking dialects of Verdurian and pastoralists speaking Naviu languages.

Ethnic enclaves: The Kebreni have neighborhoods in many northern ports. Verdurians comprise the commercial sector in less advanced nations such as Barakhún and Caizura. In ancient times, the Caďinorian empire conquered Cuzei, and this created a diaspora of Cuzeians across Eretald; there were patches of them in remote rural areas for centuries.

Dying languages: Jeori, a Wede:i language, has been slowly replaced by a variant of Xurnese in Tásuc Tag; but rather like Gaelic in Ireland, it's still an official language that's important for distinguishing the country from its powerful neighbor. A distinctive version of Kebreni is dying out on the island of Koto.

Pidgins: A Verdurian-based pidgin is used in the colony of Karimia, in the east. A Gurdagor-based pidgin is still common in the peninsula of

Luduyn, once ruled by Gurdago. The Tžuro colonized part of Arcél, and many natives now speak a creolized version of the original pidgin.

Mixed languages: the town of Emet, near Flora, is noted for universal bilingualism in Verdurian and Kebreni; the local forms of the language are almost identical in syntax, rather like Marathi / Urdu / Kannada in Kupwar.

Sign: There are schools for the Deaf in Verduria and Xurno, and sign languages have developed there, such as *Manačel verdury*. The icëlani have a simple language which mixes sound and signs. The language of the iliu can be spoken, signed, or written.

How do you decide where to put these things?

For typological elements, anywhere you like! It's hard to have too much variety... look at all the variation in Europe. It's all right if features cluster somewhat— indeed, it's to be expected, as nearby families do influence each other.

Things like writing systems, numeric bases (10, 20, ...), and learned vocabulary tend to correlate with civilizations (and their offshoot, religions), and these of course can cross language families.

For things like bilingualism, refer to your history. Widespread languages get that way by conquest or by trade. Religions can spread a scholarly language. Pidgins develop when traders or settlers come by intermittently or are outnumbered by natives.

Any border could be a site for language contact, but think about *who* will cross over and why.

Using pragmatics

Some readers have suggested that the Pragmatics section in the *LCK* (p. 129ff.) doesn't offer enough practical advice— what do you *do* with this information?

Nothing, if your language and culture aren't unusual in these areas. If your turn-taking strategies (*LCK* p. 136) or conversational maxims (*LCK* p. 131) are just the same as in English, there's no need to say so.

But each area is an opportunity to think *What if it didn't work like that?* In Xurnese, for instance, the **maxim of quantity** is violated: speakers feel under no obligation to give accurate quantities or correct mistakes;

they feel it's none of the interrogator's business. This is seen in the response of a Xurnese diplomat to an indiscreet query from a Verdurian:

> **V: Oyes ros cu treše nowsuc na seješi ma?**
>
> your country that black.powder burn-3p sub machine-pl have-3s
>
> *Does your country have machines that burn black powder [i.e., cannons]?*
>
> **X: Am.**
>
> one
>
> *We have one.*

A very hierarchical society is likely to have complicated **request strategies**. E.g. in the ancient ktuvok empire Munkhâsh, there were four ways to form imperatives, all direct in form but very clearly marking relative rank:

- For clear inferiors, use the future: **gzhudôth!**, literally 'you will come!'
- For fellow students, siblings, workers, or soldiers— prefix **po**- to the bare verb. The verb is still inflected by rank. Thus **Po-kshuth!** 'come (D form, to a superior)', **Po-gzhuth!** 'come (E form, to an inferior)'.
- For clear superiors, you add -**in**, thus **kshuthin**! 'please come (D form, to a superior)', **kthuthin**! 'please come (B form, to a far superior)'.
- In a set of written instructions, where one is addressing unknown persons, use the bare D form without a subject: **kshuth** 'come'.

By contrast, the egalitarian flaids of Flora prefer indirect requests, as we do in English:

> **Jaaʔ ʔok maukse ʔozen ʔy porrt chaiʔys?**
>
> q I can-dur get-and one cup-acc tea-gen
>
> *Could I get a cup of tea?*
>
> **ʔok garse jimpo lin soochiot chezmom.**
>
> I if-dur have-partit two teaspoon-acc sugar-gen
>
> *If I could have two spoons of sugar?*

ʔok dordejno ʔy pridmot kaanys, ʔejme.

I enjoy-irr one slice-acc bread-gen too

I might enjoy a slice of bread, too.

Xurnese keeps its imperatives direct, but softens them using diminutives:

Déruis, bic i de.

Deru-dim grape 1s.acc give-inf

Deru darling, pass me a grape.

Politeness affects languages in other ways. Kebreni (as shown in the LCK) has verbal inflections for politeness, as well as a set of deferential pronouns. Verdurian, like many European languages, has a polite 2s pronoun (actually it re-uses the indefinite pronoun). Lé speakers are noted for never saying 'thank you'; on the other hand they find it very rude not to say *Bŏ ís re* 'my condolences' on hearing any bad news.

Pragmatic particles

A set of pragmatic particles is very useful for conversation. The *LCK* section on conversation (p. 136) will help you think of these.

Here's the set I came up with for Lé:

Marker	*Usage*
mɛ̆	Marks DISPREFERREDS (less desirable responses, such as disagreements and refusals). **Mɛ̆ déŋ Kúŋsàɔ prɛ̀n drê tràŋ na.** well / neg Uytai seem have queen acc *Well... Uytai doesn't really have a queen.*
ɔ̆	Expresses acknowledgement, agreement, or simply that one is listening. **Ɔ bàr tlúr na.** OK six tlúr acc *Mm hmm, (you want) six bananas.*
trɛ́s	Excuses jostling or interruptions. **Trɛ́s— àr nonnèn ɬɔ̆ krɛn má?** excuse / q customs there.is here q

Excuse me, is this the customs office?

kisbo mɛ Marks a sudden change of topic.

Kisbo mɛ júŋlɔ tân brù ŋɛs drûr na má?

another-thing topic someone know kill this monster acc q

So... anyone know how to kill this monster?

hibo łɔ̆ Ends a digression (of one's own).

Hibo łɔ̆... łɛ̆n mɛ.

that.thing there.is / dinner topic

Anyway, what about dinner?

ŋé "Yes but..."— acknowledges or simply dismisses a point, but insists that it's really irrelevant.

Éŋ tlɛ̀ ŋan plɔ̀r ŋé.

3sf damn hab lie yeah

Yeah, sure, but she's still a damn liar.

ɛ Prolongs a turn or marks dispreferreds; can occur anywhere in the sentence.

Trăɔ ŋɛ̀ čaelu na ɛ... bluŋ bu rɔ̆r čaelu na.

1s want tea acc um bluŋ com warm tea acc

I'd like tea um... warm tea with bluŋ [a spice].

dɔ̀n "So..."— acknowledges a point, but presses on to insist on something or demand action.

Dɔ̀n bɛ́bo na jàɔ jăɔ trun má?

therefore what-thing acc 1p.two do fut q

So what do we do now?

jì Expresses surprise or appreciation.

Jì his tɛr pă prépré!

wow that guy be sexy

Wow, what a sexy guy!

è As a clitic, expresses commiseration or self-pity; as an interjection it's the word for "ouch!"

His tras rɛ̀ ŋan plɛ̀ŋ bún na è.

that my girl hab tread.on foot acc ow

Oy, that child of mine is a handful.

In Barakhinei, the pragmatic particles differ by sex, one of several differences between male and female speech— underlining that Barakhún is a sexist traditional society dominated by warriors. I borrowed this particular idea from Japanese.

In a novel

As it happens I'm writing a novel set in Xurno, called *A Diary of the Prose Wars*, and I have a fairly full grammar of Xurnese.

So, where am I using the language? Or from a conlanger's perspective, what can I show off / get away with forcing on the reader?

- The characters' names (*Deru, Itep, Gašnue, Reusune...*)
- Names of cities and other geographical features (*Inex, Corau, Čeiy, Rašageor...*)
- Allusions to historical peoples or figures (*Wede:i, the iliu, ne-Duox, Timaï*), religions and movements (*Revaudo, Endajuê*), astronomical bodies (e.g. the planet *Aušimex*)
- Measures (e.g. *jiveč* for distance) and coins
- Cultural titles and practices for which there's no English equivalent— e.g. *dzusnar* for an Endajué structure which isn't quite a temple, a monastery, or a meeting hall; *dzusey* for the leader of a *dzusnar*
- The epithet *end' eš* (which we saw above, p. 230; it means 'against the Path' but the English doesn't convey its brevity and ferocity)
- Words cited in Axunašin or Verdurian, languages which are foreign to the characters

Just as importantly, here's some of the things I translate— that is, leave in English:

- Greetings, *yes* and *no*, other polite formulas
- Titles, as far as possible (I write *Emperor, Member, Student, Academician, Walker*, instead of *Nyei, Raysu, Xairc, Bicikesiy, Jivirc*)

- The seasons (which mark the calendar and thus head each diary entry)
- Artistic terms, such as Prose in the title; names of other aspects of the artist-run society, such as Academies, Salons, and Ateliers
- Names of neighborhoods within Inex

The thing is, it's not nice to bury the reader with terms they don't understand. They're fun for you, but a burden for the reader. Mostly I use Xurnese only when there's no English equivalent. Anyone who wants more Xurnese can read more on my website!

If you're trying to give the flavor of your society, translated terms are more suggestive anyway. For instance:

- *Unillusioned* doesn't sound like a title in English, but suggests something about the concerns of Endajué, while *beylusu* would be opaque.
- The Xurnese week is nine days long; using *nineday* reinforces the difference while *week* or *nedim* would obscure it.
- Some terms are calqued: using *Verdurian glass* for *berduru nozau* 'telescope' helps communicate that the device is a foreign novelty in Xurno.
- Similarly, allusions like *the adversarial method* give hints on what they are, as opposed to using a native term like *ešikävu.*

Here's a passage from the novel, showing about the maximum use of the language:

> Dzusey Councillor Gašnue • 51st of Fall 682
>
> Academician Wéneš's presentation yesterday was serviceable though uninspired; she did her best to anticipate Councillor Aulic's arguments, and naturally he was unable to adapt to this nor to respond to her rebuttals. He simply rang the changes on his overall contention, that the Academy is for the traditional arts, that scholarship is not an art and does not require a Salon of its own. The *Šivines* of Čeiy, so often held up as a model for a Salon of Prose, or the Universities of Verduria and Érenat, are not part of the governments of those countries. Nothing prevents investigations into natural philosophy, or even the establishment of a Xurnese *Šivines.*

Here's an alternative version of the passage, using Xurnese wherever possible:

> Dzusey Joraumirc Gašnue • kuludo o 51 dis, Xurno o 682 sus
>
> *Bicikesiy* Wéneš's *šwedudo* yesterday was serviceable though uninspired; she did her best to anticipate *Joraumirc* Aulic's *šwedudo,* and naturally he was unable to adapt to this nor to respond to her *ešinseš.* He simply rang the changes on his overall *šwedu,* that the *Bicikes* is for the traditional *wemoxaú,* that *gejupudo* is not a *wemoxau* and does not require a *xamunaur* of its own. The *Šivines* of Čeiy, so often held up as a model for a *Gejupudo o Xamunaur,* or the *Šriftanâî* of Verduria and Érenat, are not part of the governments of those countries. Nothing prevents investigations into *jam nao gejupudo,* or even the establishment of a Xurnese *Šivines.*

Though this would be fun for the two or three people who really like Xurnese, I hope it's clear that for most readers it would be absurd.[33]

It's a balance, of course, and you may draw the line in different ways than I did. (You may feel in fact that the first passage has too much Xurnese! But it's from the middle of the book, when the reader has already become familiar with many of the names.)

But Tolkien used Elvish all over! Well, no, he really didn't. He uses his linguistic inventions quite sparingly in *Lord of the Rings,* mostly for names, plus scraps of poetry. In fact he goes much farther than I do in avoiding his own linguistic work! The book is supposedly written in Westron, the language of men, but he scrupulously replaces Westron with English even in names (Frodo was really *Maura*), and goes so far as replacing archaisms with Old English-based archaisms— e.g. *Samwise* for *Banazîr.*

When do I get to show off a full sentence? Good opportunities are proverbs ("As the Caďinorians said, *aldel aiďos kascul es*"), ancient inscriptions, spells and rites (great chances to show off the parent language), songs, and encounters with foreigners. Just use some tact: your reader doesn't know your conlang and isn't going to learn it from your novel.

You have more options in other media— e.g. Enya's album *Amarantine* contains several tracks in a conlang, and movies and video games can show off quite a bit of a language. A video game can use a conlang as a

---

33 The second passage does show that the single word *gejupudo* is translated *prose, scholarship,* or *(natural) philosophy.* None of the English terms precisely express the Xurnese concept. But this is something that has to be explained anyway, as the reader doesn't know Xurnese!

puzzle, though (say) a highly fusional, erg/abs language might not be a good choice.

Of course, you can write all the sentences you like in a reference grammar!

Tools

Gen

I've long advocated either hand-crafting every word, or using the SCA to derive families. But inspiration does flag, and sometimes you want to use a vocabulary generator.

The usual problem with these is that they make all the possibilities equiprobable, which is highly unnaturalistic. So I've created a generator called **gen** which applies a cheap power law, so the first choice is chosen most often, and so on down, smoothly, to the last choice which get chosen the least.

Overview

Open up gen at my site:

http://www.zompist.com/gen.html

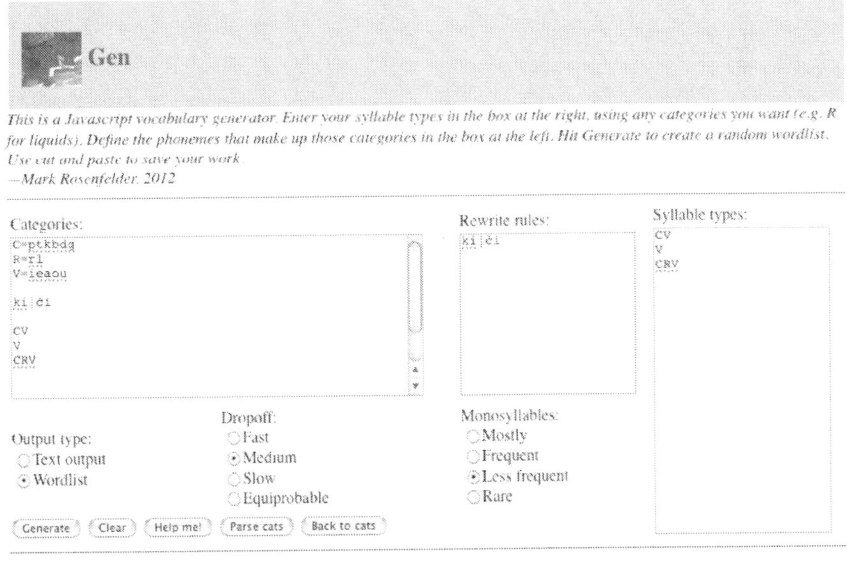

Gen randomly creates a number of words following the **syllable types** you define on this page. The syllable types are themselves defined by

categories, like C for consonant + V for vowel. These inputs define the PHONOTACTICS of your language (*LCK* p. 47).

If you load the page and hit **Generate**, you'll get a pseudo-text, something like this:

> Keo iu eu pipi tete o. Peke obetikei te pipibe dreti ke! Prupra a datri aapači čipui eii? Opi dri ipleeplapli a droe pra. Pie pio igii epa ioe pae! Atoi iatudi čitrata drepii tri tretotlopli. čia pepapiko tličite kupa itipi. Toči ti iplapri tobituu. Gope tradri i draete tree pio? Pube pubreke apla ičiio predi pi. Boatepipi ipriplipapi keplopu tuu plibeeti pačiipa. čidiee bropipriu bripra krikreku ko. Bi krigate pleku pipa ee aa i dute bogluete bidapi ota. Ibii buu e ago popepi idao! Tike eo trotako tee pekupe apa kro trepe. U ublipi pee aa pečiči. Tupitrake čipre utu preupo tritikubiti. čitrupeboo i čikri piepo iti upo!

Hit **Generate** again for an entirely different text. This output format is designed to simulate what your language might look like.

With these categories and syllable types

C=tdgpkb	CV
N=nŋm	VN
S=sś	NV
V=aioɔɛeu	SCV
J=iu	CVJ
	CVN
	SNV
	SVJ
	NVJ

we get pseudo-text like this:

> Ko de na goaŋ iŋŋaim steinin. Nabo kitaŋo tiiniŋpa tandi. Ɔŋaŋ taibi śgastɛtidɛ nɔon gamingɔom dɛgasdo dispi. Nɔan on ta da tote ŋaśdi? Taudɛ sdaŋibośta ganin nasdadi mu. Teto anta ɔnomkɔśdu tɔutɛśpɔ ta aŋpa. Nitu dɔ ŋipaɔn du dɔtispisŋa om! Nada tɔ gotɛkɛdɔnɛ ŋɛstain datii amŋo? Timɛ daaŋ anŋosto kustitɔ dɔge. Padiko on omga ta be pingaŋ. Nadɔi antoonśtɛke ɛm diaŋ sdɔanske taiŋbidɔ gɛnɔanna tiam aŋiŋdɔgii taingapa dauśdain napɔgɔga ɔnaŋŋita!

The controls

Here's what the various controls on the page do.[34]

[34] By the time you read this more features may be available. But everything here will still work.

Output type tells whether you want pseudo-text, a table, or a word list. Pseudo-text is better for seeing what your language looks like, given the phonology and syllable types you've defined. Once you're happy with the look and feel of the language, the word list is better for actually generating vocabulary.

Dropoff determines how fast the power law declines. If you have `C=ptkbdg`, then when outputting a C, normally **p** will come up the most, **t** a little less often, and so on, with **g** the least frequent. If you select **Fast** dropoff, the probabilities will stack even more in favor of **p** (i.e. the first choice). If you select **Slow**, the probabilities will distribute more evenly.

To turn off the power law entirely select **Equiprobable**; then **gen** will select the choices with equal frequency. (Again, this is a bad choice for a naturalistic language. But maybe you're doing an auxlang or something.)

Monosyllables tells **gen** how much of the output should be monosyllabic. You could set this to **Mostly** for an isolating language, for instance. (Longer words will still be generated— even isolating languages have compounds.)

Generate generates a new text.

Clear erases the output. (This isn't necessary but it's provided for neatness' sake.)

Help me! brings up a help file in a new tab.

Parse cats and **Back to cats** are aids to saving your definitions in a text file; see p. 259.

Categories

These are your phonological classes, defined by enumeration. The format is exactly the same as used by the SCA (p. 260).

For instance, I might define my fricatives like this:

```
F=fvszšž
```

That means that any time **gen** wants to output an F from the syllables list, it will randomly pick one of **f, v, s, z, š, ž.**

As you can see, you can use **Unicode**. The phonemes in a category have to be single characters, but we'll see how to output digraphs below.

The key thing to grasp is that **the order determines the probability.** The program runs through the phonemes in a category, with a 30%

chance of stopping at each one.[35] So the `F` definition above says that we want **f** to occur a lot and **ž** not that much.

The main corollary: **Put the sounds you like first!** Don't list them in place of articulation order unless you really like labials. Try varying the order and hitting **Generate** to see how changing the order changes the output.

Don't overdo the classes— **gen** doesn't know any phonology, and will be perfectly happy with a single class C for all consonants. You define a class for two reasons:

- To control probabilities. E.g. we usually want stops to occur more than fricatives.
- To enforce phonotactics. E.g. if the only initial clusters you allow are stop + liquid, then you need classes for stops and liquids.

Syllable types

The **Syllable types** field defines the allowed syllable types. E.g. the first sample above is defined with these syllables:

```
CV
V
CRV
```

The syllable types also follow a power law, so **put the ones you like first**. Or to be precise, if you want a particular type to be more common, move it up in the list.

Put just one syllable per line; otherwise **gen** will just treat whatever you put on one line as a syllable type.

In general, more complex types should occur further on. However, I find that pure vowel syllables (like V in the example) should be less frequent than ones that begin with a consonant.

The process **doesn't handle parentheses.** So if you have a syllable type like `(C(R))V(V)(N)`, you must list the possibilities— in this case, `V, VV, VN, VVN, CV, CVV, CVN, CVVN, CRV, CRVV, CRVN, CRVVN`. *This is a good thing,* because it allows you to set the relative probabilities of each syllable type.

---

[35] That is, 30% for the recommended **Medium** dropoff. It's 45% for **Fast** and 15% for **Slow**. Also, for computation speed, if it gets to the end of the choices it starts over.

(How do you decide on the order? Trial and error works fine. Change the order and hit Generate again. Repeat till it looks good.)

The symbols you use here (in the last example `C V R N`) should be **defined in the categories box**— they are your phonological classes.

So when **gen** needs to generate a syllable, it selects randomly from the syllable type— lets say it picks `CRV`. Now it looks up `C` in the Categories box. Suppose it finds the definition `C=ptkbdg`. It randomly picks one of those choices. Then it moves on to `R`, then `V`. And so on.

If there are any **undefined symbols**, they will be passed through to the output. E.g. you could add a syllable `khV` and **gen** will cheerfully generate `khe, khi`, etc.

Rewrite rules

These are entirely optional, but they allow you to apply global substitutions to the output; the chief purpose is to support **digraphs**. The simplest form is to replace a single character:

```
θ|th
```

That tells **gen** to replace every occurrence of θ in the output with `th`.

Or you can handle combinations. E.g. maybe `ti` always changes to `či`. You'd write that as `ti|či`. The facility is actually even more powerful than that, because the left-hand side is a **regular expression**. So for instance you could change both `br` and `bl` to `bj` with the formula `b[rl]|bj`.

Rules are applied **in order**; make sure they don't unexpectedly feed into one another. For instance, I had some rules for generating pseudo-Japanese, and I had rewrite rules

```
ty|ch
hu|fu
```

The intention was to rewrite (e.g.) *huji* as *fuji* and *tyatyo* as *chacho*. But I was getting weird output like *cfu*. Finally I realized that the first rule changed *tyu* to *chu*, and the second changed *chu* to *cfu*. The solution was to change the order:

```
hu|fu
ty|ch
```

For fancier changes (such as those that are sensitive to the following phonemes), use the SCA.

Saving your work

Gen is implemented in Javascript to make it immediately available to anyone with a browser. The disadvantage is that Javascript is restricted from reading and writing files. (If web pages could write files, they could mess up your computer.)

- To **save** your work, hit **Back to cats**, which will copy the contents of all three input boxes into the Categories box. Then copy the contents of this box into a text file.
- To **restore** your work, copy the contents of a text file into the Categories box. Then hit **Parse cats**, which will move the syllable types and rewrite rules to the correct boxes.

If you want to work **offline**, save the web page to your computer.

Don't be cheap!

To avoid the pitfalls of cheap vocabulary generation:

- Follow the usual rule of recording new words in the lexicon, so you don't re-use words.
- Don't just copy the output and use every word in your lexicon. Pick the words you like; you can hit **Generate** to get a new set.
- Multisyllabic words are output to simulate what text would look like. However, avoid very long words as roots.
- Always use derivational morphology or compounding when you can, rather than just grabbing words from **gen**! E.g. for *religion, divinity, theology, sacrilege, priesthood,* don't just create each of these as roots, create etymologies.
- If you're getting ugly words— well, you probably have ugly phonotactics! Move the sounds you like up within your classes, and put simpler CV syllable types earlier in the file.
- If the output words seem too similar, add more syllable types. Or change the consonant order and regenerate.

SCA²

SCA² is an update to the Sound Change Applier, which was discussed extensively in the *LCK* (p. 170ff.). The most important change is support for **Unicode**.

Open up SCA² at my site:

http://www.zompist.com/sca2.html

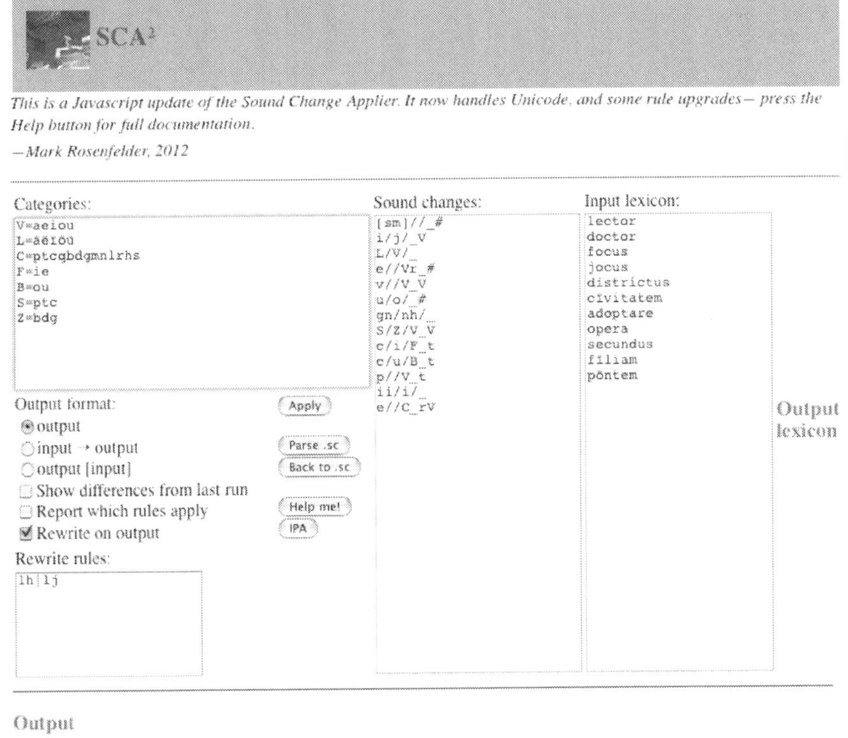

If you're familiar with the old SCA, this should look quite familiar, and you can skip right to the new features (p. 264).

Example

Try it out! With the default inputs, hit **Apply**. You should get output like this:

```
leitor
doutor
fogo
```

```
jogo
distrito
cidade
adotar
obra
segundo
ponte
```

As if by magic, a selection of Latin words has turned into Portuguese.

The controls

Here's what the controls do.

Output format tells how you want each line of the output to look. Here's a comparison of how an output line looks in each format:

```
fogo
fire → fogo
fogo [focus]
```

The first option prints output words only; this is good for generating a new list of words (e.g. as input for the next round of changes). The second includes the input word too. The third is suitable for use in a dictionary with the etymology in brackets (see p. 265 on how to add glosses).

Show differences from last run, if checked, will **boldface** any changes from the last run when you hit Apply. This can be very useful to see what the effect of a changed rule is. (Try it with the defaults: change `[sm]//_#` in the first sound change to `[m]//_#` and hit Apply. You should see several of the words change, now retaining their final s.)

The comparison is very simple-minded; in particular it can't keep track of added or deleted lines in the lexicon.

If you hit Apply without making any changes, all the bolding is removed (since in fact nothing changed between runs).

Report which rules apply prints a report in the Output section listing every time a rule applies, like this:

```
u/o/_# applies to districtu at 8
```

This is useful for understanding why a rule applies (or doesn't) when you expected the opposite.

Rewrite on output controls whether the rewrite rules (p. 266) should be reversed when writing the output lexicon.

Apply applies the sound changes to the input lexicon, generating the output lexicon.

To protect your computer, Javascript cannot read or write **files**. Instead:

- To **save a file**, hit **Back to .sc**, copy the text in the Sound Changes box, and save it yourself in a text file.
- To **read in a file**, grab the text from your file and paste it into the Sound Changes box. Then hit **Parse .sc** to move the lines into the appropriate boxes. (Comments, meaning anything the program can't recognize, stay in the Sound Changes box.)

Help me! brings up a help file.

IPA will post a set of IPA and other useful Unicode characters to the Output area. You can then copy and paste a character into any of the input boxes.

On Safari and Firefox, **Undo** will work as it should: you can make a change, hit Apply, and if you don't like the results, click on the text box you changed and select Undo. This doesn't work on IE.

Defining sound changes

The Sound Changes box contains rules for modifying the input lexicon. The format of the rules should be familiar to any linguist. For instance, here's one sound change:

```
c/g/V_V
```

This rule says to change `c` to `g` between vowels. You can use → in place of the first slash, so this rule can also be written

```
c→g/V_V
```

More generally, a sound change looks like this:

`target/replacement/environment`

that is, the target string is changed to the replacement string within the given environment.

The environment must always contain an underline _, representing the part that changes. That can be all there is, as in

```
gn/nh/_
```

which tells the program to replace `gn` with `nh` unconditionally.

The character # represents the **beginning or end** of the word. So

```
u/o/_#
```

means to replace u with o, but only at the end of the word.

The replacement string can be **blank**, as in

```
s//_#
```

This means that s is **deleted** when it ends a word.

Categories

The environment can contain **variables**, like V above. These are defined in the Categories box, in the same format as for **gen**.

I use capital letters for this, though this is not a requirement. Variables can only be one character long (unless you use rewrite rules). You can define any variables needed to state your sound changes— e.g. S for any stop, or K for any coronal.

So the category definition and rule

```
F=ie
c/i/F_t
```

means that c changes to i after a front vowel and before a t.

You can use variables in the target and replacement strings as well. For instance:

```
S=ptc
Z=bdg
S/Z/V_V
```

This means that the stops ptc change to their voiced equivalents bdg between vowels. Each character in the replacement string (here Z) gives the transformed value of each character in the target (here S). If the replacement category is shorter than the target category, the matching input will be deleted.

A variable can also be set to a fixed value, or deleted. E.g.

```
Z//V_V
```

says to delete voiced stops between vowels.

Rule order

Rules apply in the **order** they're listed. Now, between vowels, Portuguese normally voices unvoiced stops (*opera* → *obra*) and deletes voiced ones (*ego* → *eu*).

So with these rules

```
o/u/_#
S=ptc
Z=bdg
S/Z/V_V
Z//V_V
```

we get `ego` → `eu`, but `opera` → `oera`. Oops! The first rule changed `opera` to `obera`, and the second changed `obera` to `oera`. We need to reverse the order of the last two rules:

```
Z//V_V
S/Z/V_V
```

Now we correctly get `ego` → `eu` and `opera` → `obera`. (The rule `e//C_rV` will delete the `e` to get `obra`.)

Optional elements in the environment

One or more elements in the environment can be marked as **optional** with parentheses. E.g.

```
u/ü/_C(C)F
```

says to change `u` to `ü` when it's followed by one or two consonants and then a front vowel.

New features

SCA² treats **spaces as word boundaries**. So if you have a rule

```
k/s/#_
```

then it will not only turn `kima` to `sima`, but `kima kimaka` to `sima simaka`.

Epenthesis (inserting new material) is supported by leaving the target part of the rule blank. The replacement string must not be blank, and the environment must contain at least one symbol besides _. For instance

```
/j/_kt
```

will insert `j` before every instance of `kt`.

Simple **metathesis** is supported by the special replacement string \\. For instance

```
nt/\\/_V
```

will turn all instances of `nt` before a vowel to `tn`. (To be precise, the input string is reversed; it can be of any length.)

Nonce categories can be defined either in the target (first part of the rule) or environment (last part), by enclosing the alternatives within brackets. Examples:

`k/s/_[ie]`	Change `k` to `s` before either `i` or `e`.
`[ao]u/o/_`	Either `au` or `ou` is changed to `o`.
`m/n/_[dt#]`	Change `m` to `n` before dentals and word-finally.

With the old SCA I found myself writing a lot of similar rules (e.g. `au/o/_` and `ou/o/_`), and nonce categories let them be combined.

Nonce categories in the environment can include the word boundary #.

Degemination (reducing double phonemes) uses the special character ². (This is the first character in the IPA display.)

`m//_²`	Change `mm` to `m`.
`M=mn` `M//_²`	Change `mm` to `m` and `nn` to `n`, but leave `mn` and `nm` alone.

Extended category substitution is now supported. The target must still begin with a category; however, other material may occur after it. And the replacement string may contain any number of characters, with a category string given at any point. Examples:

`Bi/Dj/_`	Instances of `B` plus `i` are changed to the corresponding member of `D` plus `j`.
`Nd/bM/_V`	Instances of `N` plus `d` before a vowel are changed to `b` plus the corresponding member of `M`; note that this is a more complicated metathesis.

You can do **gemination** (doubling of phonemes) on category substitution, like this:

```
M/M²/_
```

This will geminate all members of category `M`.

Including a gloss

It can be convenient to include a gloss in your lexicon which isn't affected by the sound changes. This is done by separating the gloss with a space plus the special character ‣ (this is the second character in the text shown by the IPA button). For instance:

```
focus ‣ fire
```

Here's the output you'll get from that (with the default sound changes), in each of the output formats:

```
fogo ▸ fire
focus → fogo ▸ fire
fogo ▸ fire [focus]
```

No sound changes will apply to anything after ▸, but rewrite rules do apply, so if you use this option I recommend using non-English characters for the rewrite rules (e.g. use χ rather than `x` for `kh`).

Rule exceptions

Sometimes you'd like to say that a rule applies in environment *e*, **except for** environment *x*. You can generally handle this by writing more rules, but SCA² also allows you to state this directly by adding *x* after another slash, e.g.

`k/s/_F/#s_`	`k` changes to `s` before a front vowel, but *not* after word-initial `s`.
`M/N/#_/_CF`	Category `M` changes to category `N` word initially, but *not* before another consonant followed by a front vowel.

Because of the difficulty of lining up the _ in both environments, the exception environment can't include optional characters (those in parentheses) before the underline. (They can occur after it.)

Rewrite rules

These allow you to apply global substitutions to the input and output. The most important use is to allow **digraphs**.

If you use digraphs, you must follow the rules in this section. SCA² won't handle digraphs properly on its own.

Rules with diagraphs will work so long as they can be treated as sequences of characters. For instance, these all work fine:

```
c/ch/_a
sh/zh/V_V
u/o/_ng
```

But you can't define categories with digraphs. E.g. the following was probably intended to define three fricatives `kh sh zh`—

```
F=khshzh
```

but in fact it defines F as `k h s h z h`, which won't at all do what you expect.

The old SCA required that you use single characters instead. E.g. you might write

```
F=xßΩ
```

That still works, but you can use rewrite rules instead. E.g. define some rules like this:

```
kh|x
zh|ž
sh|š
ng|ŋ
```

Now you can use kh zh sh ng in any of the other input boxes— categories, sound changes, input lexicon. The SCA will apply the rewrite rules to provide single characters it can work with, and then apply them again backwards to provide output using digraphs.

You can also use rewrite rules to allow longer or mnemonic names for your categories. E.g.

```
<front>|F
```

Now you could write sound changes like

```
i/ü/_<front>
```

(The category names still have to be unique— you can't use F to define both front vowels and fricatives. But recall that you can use any Unicode character now for category names.)

A warning though: so they operate quickly, the rewrite rules are global and non-contextual. The results may surprise you if you didn't realize your transcription system was ambiguous. E.g. don't use kh both for IPA /x/ and for the cluster /k h/.

If you need contextual rewrite rules... just use SCA^2! For instance, to have some rules that apply only word-initially, add

```
zh/ž/#_
sh/š/#_
```

at the top of the sound changes, and these at the bottom:

```
ž/zh/#_
š/sh/#_
```

Sometimes you want the rewrite rules to apply only to the input. (For instance, the orthography with digraphs may apply only to the parent language.) In that case, make sure **Rewrite on output** is unchecked.

Index

THE INTERNATIONAL PHONETIC ALPHABET (revised to 2005)

CONSONANTS (PULMONIC)

	Bilabial	Labiodental	Dental	Alveolar	Post alveolar	Retroflex	Palatal	Velar	Uvular	Pharyngeal	Glottal
Plosive	p b			t d		ʈ ɖ	c ɟ	k ɡ	q ɢ		ʔ
Nasal	m	ɱ		n		ɳ	ɲ	ŋ	ɴ		
Trill	ʙ			r					ʀ		
Tap or Flap		ⱱ		ɾ		ɽ					
Fricative	ɸ β	f v	θ ð	s z	ʃ ʒ	ʂ ʐ	ç ʝ	x ɣ	χ ʁ	ħ ʕ	h ɦ
Lateral fricative				ɬ ɮ							
Approximant		ʋ		ɹ		ɻ	j	ɰ			
Lateral approximant				l		ɭ	ʎ	ʟ			

Where symbols appear in pairs, the one to the right represents a voiced consonant. Shaded areas denote articulations judged impossible.

CONSONANTS (NON-PULMONIC)

Clicks		Voiced implosives		Ejectives	
ʘ	Bilabial	ɓ	Bilabial	ʼ	Examples:
ǀ	Dental	ɗ	Dental alveolar	pʼ	Bilabial
ǃ	(Post)alveolar	ʄ	Palatal	tʼ	Dental/alveolar
ǂ	Palatoalveolar	ɠ	Velar	kʼ	Velar
ǁ	Alveolar lateral	ʛ	Uvular	sʼ	Alveolar fricative

VOWELS

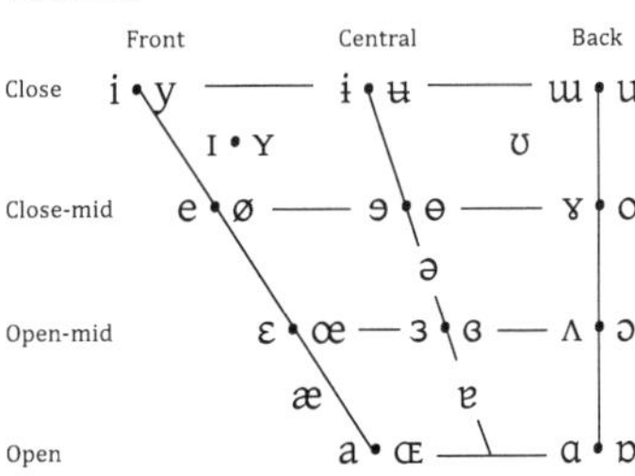

Where symbols appear in pairs, the one to the right represents a rounded vowel.

OTHER SYMBOLS

ʍ Voiceless labial-velar fricative

w Voiced labial-velar approximant

ɥ Voiced labial-palatal approximant

ʜ Voiceless epiglottal fricative

ʢ Voiced epiglottal fricative

ʡ Epiglottal plosive

ɕ ʑ Alveolo-palatal fricatives

ɺ Voiced alveeolar lateral flap

ɧ Simultaneous ʃ and χ

Affricates and double articulations can be represented by two symbols joined by a tie bar if necessary. k͡p t͜s

DIACRITICS

Dicacritics may be placed above a symbol with a descender, e.g. ŋ̊

̥ Voiceless	n̥ d̥	̤ Breathy voiced	b̤ a̤	̪ Dental	t̪ d̪
̬ Voiced	s̬ t̬	̰ Creaky voiced	b̰ a̰	̺ Apical	t̺ d̺
ʰ Aspirated	tʰ dʰ	̼ Linguolabial	t̼ d̼	̻ Laminal	t̻ d̻
̹ More rounded	ɔ̹	ʷ Labialized	tʷ dʷ	̃ Nasalized	ẽ
̜ Less rounded	ɔ̜	ʲ Palatalized	tʲ dʲ	ⁿ Nasal release	dⁿ
̟ Advanced	u̟	ˠ Velarized	tˠ dˠ	ˡ Lateral release	dˡ
̠ Retracted	e̠	ˤ Pharyngealized	tˤ dˤ	̚ No audible release	d̚
̈ Centralized	ë	̴ Velarized or pharyngealized	ɫ		
̽ Mid-centralized	e̽	̝ Raised	e̝	ɹ̝ = voicedalveolar fricative	
̩ Syllabic	n̩	̞ Lowered	e̞	β̞ = voiced bilabial approximant	
̯ Non-syllabic	e̯	̘ Advanced Tongue Root	e̘		
˞ Rhoticity	ɚ	̙ Retracted Tongue Root	e̙		

SUPRASEGMENTALS

ˈ Primary stress

ˌ Secondary stress

ː Long eː

ˑ Half-long eˑ

̆ Extra-short ĕ

| Minor(foot) group

‖ Major (intonation) group

. Syllable break

‿ Linking (absence of a break)

TONES AND WORD ACCENTS

LEVEL			CONTOUR		
e̋ or	˥	Extra high	ě or	˩˥	Rising
é	˦	High	ê	˥˩	Falling
ē	˧	Mid	e᷄	˦˥	High rising
è	˨	Low	e᷅	˩˨	Low rising
ȅ	˩	Extra low	e᷈	˧˦˧	Rising-falling
↓		Downstep	↗		Global rise
↑		Upstep	↘		Global fall

Made in the USA
Lexington, KY
21 May 2014